"As I lay nearly lifeless on a gurney in early April 2005 in Balad, Iraq, God used Dr. Warren's expertise, tenderness, encouragement, grace, and love to save my life. And now, in this book, Dr. Warren's words are not only encouraging but also thought provoking as he helps us all understand our individual purpose on this amazing journey of life. I urge you to read *I've Seen the End of You* because your life will be forever changed."

—SCOTTY SMILEY, author of *Hope Unseen* and CEO of Bellator
Asset Management

"Dr. Lee Warren's book is so well written that it is hard to put down. It will challenge you and encourage you to live life to the fullest, never doubting that we have a great Creator who has a remarkable purpose for us all. A must-read!"

—TIFFANY SMILEY, president of Hope Unseen, founder of More
Than Me, and advocate for veterans and caregivers

I've
Seen
the
End
of
You

I've Seen the End of You

A Neurosurgeon's Look
at Faith, Doubt, and the Things
We Think We Know

W. Lee Warren, MD

WATERBROOK

I'VE SEEN THE END OF YOU

All Scripture quotations, unless otherwise indicated, are taken from the Holy Bible, New International Version®, NIV®. Copyright © 1973, 1978, 1984, 2011 by Biblica Inc.® Used by permission. All rights reserved worldwide. Scripture quotations marked (ESV) are taken from the Holy Bible, English Standard Version, ESV® Text Edition® (2016), copyright © 2001 by Crossway Bibles, a publishing ministry of Good News Publishers. All rights reserved. Scripture quotations marked (KJV) are taken from the King James Version. Scripture quotations marked (MSG) are taken from The Message. Copyright © by Eugene H. Peterson 1993, 1994, 1995, 1996, 2000, 2001, 2002. Used by permission of NavPress. All rights reserved. Represented by Tyndale House Publishers Inc. Scripture quotations marked (NCV) are taken from the New Century Version®. Copyright © 2005 by Thomas Nelson Inc. Used by permission. All rights reserved. Scripture quotations marked (NLT) are taken from the Holy Bible, New Living Translation, copyright © 1996, 2004, 2007, 2013, 2015 by Tyndale House Foundation. Used by permission of Tyndale House Publishers Inc., Carol Stream, Illinois 60188. All rights reserved. Scripture quotations marked (Voice) are taken from The Voice™. Copyright © 2008 by Ecclesia Bible Society. Used by permission. All rights reserved.

Hardcover ISBN 978-0-525-65321-9
eBook ISBN 978-0-525-65322-6

Copyright © 2020 by W. Lee Warren, MD

Cover design by Kelly L. Howard

Published in the United States by WaterBrook, an imprint of Random House, a division of Penguin Random House LLC.

WATERBROOK® and its deer colophon are registered trademarks of Penguin Random House LLC.

Library of Congress Cataloging-in-Publication Data
Names: Warren, W. Lee, 1969—author.
Title: I've seen the end of you : a neurosurgeon's look at faith, doubt, and the things we think we know /
    W. Lee Warren, MD.
Description: First Edition. | Colorado Springs : WaterBrook, 2020.
Identifiers: LCCN 2019010274 | ISBN 9780525653219 (hardcover) | ISBN 9780525653226 (electronic)
Subjects: LCSH: Christian life. | Life—Religious aspects—Christianity. | Neurosurgeons—Religious life.
Classification: LCC BV4501.3 .W37115 2020 | DDC 277.3/083092 [B]—dc23
LC record available at https://lccn.loc.gov/2019010274

Printed in the United States of America
2020—First Edition

10 9 8 7 6 5 4 3 2 1

SPECIAL SALES
Most WaterBrook books are available at special quantity discounts when purchased in bulk by corporations, organizations, and special-interest groups. Custom imprinting or excerpting can also be done to fit special needs. For information, please email specialmarketscms@penguinrandomhouse.com.

Dedicated to

Elmer, the first friend to become my patient
Mike, the first patient to become my friend
Mitch, for teaching me how to grieve and still laugh
Philip, for encouraging me to write this
Patty, for a life well lived
Lisa, for showing me the way forward,
no matter how dark the path sometimes is

Contents

Part Two: During

Part Three: After

Author's Note

The stories in this book are true. I've changed the names and some details of all the patients and most of the physicians I discuss. In addition, some of the patients are composites of several real people in order to illustrate aspects of their care without risk of identifying them. Conversations are reproduced from my memory, and the dialogue is true to the spirit of the conversations, even if the actual words I use have been changed. Pastor Jon is an amalgam of numerous hospital chaplains, and Drs. Stinson, Grossman, Grimes, and Jackson are wholly fictitious representatives of colleagues.

Prologue

Life Gets Messy

After all they had endured, they remembered that God,
the Most High,
was their Rock, their Redeemer.

—PSALM 78:35, Voice

The most difficult and dangerous surgery I've ever performed, I wasn't trained for. I had to do something no surgeon would ever do in the operating room.

I had to learn on the job.

In the story that follows, you will learn that the title of this book refers to a kind of brain tumor—glioblastoma multiforme—that is almost 100 percent fatal. My experience with this tumor made me ask questions about how I could honestly pray for my patients or give them news with any credibility or integrity when I already knew they would die. This moral dilemma put me in touch with my spiritual mentor, Philip Yancey, who encouraged me to write about it.

I did, but I wrote a different book.

I thought when I wrote my story of being a combat surgeon at Balad Air Base in Iraq, operating on soldiers, civilians, and terrorists alike while coming to terms with the end of one life and the beginning of another, *that* was the story. But often the things we think we know are just that—things we only *think* we know.

I have been a person of faith for all my life. But I learned early on, in the trenches of a crumbling first marriage and the bunkers of the Iraq War, that dog-matic belief is not life sustaining. Only grace is worth believing in. Then, with my patients and in my own story, I thought I saw grace disappear under the onslaught of brutal reality, a reality that could never be changed and that time would never heal.

I used to look at my patients' brain scans, see the glioblastoma I knew would ravage their minds and destroy their lives in the coming months, and say to myself, *I've seen the end of you.* But in the aftermath of war, divorce, rebuilding, and then unimaginable loss in my personal life, I realized I was standing at the deathbed of my shattered faith.

I'd seen the end of me too.

So I faced the greatest surgical challenge of my life: stitching together fatal cancers, dying children, and Christian clichés to heal the faith I'd lost and hoped to resurrect in some unforeseen new form.

What happens when our messy lives mess with what we think we believe?

PART ONE

Before

Hope, in its stronger forms, is a great deal more powerful *stimulans* to life than any sort of realized joy can ever be.

—FRIEDRICH NIETZSCHE, *The Antichrist*

1

Riptide

If you have questions, ask away. Just be prepared
when God answers.

—CRAIG GROESCHEL, *Hope in the Dark*

Rosemary Beach, Florida
Summer 2007

Don't get so far out!" I yelled over the wind and the crashing surf. The kids were playing in the waves, laughing and grinning and dunking one another, their heads popping out of the water and going back under like fishermen's bobbers.

The day had been almost magical. For a blended family like ours, getting everyone together in the same place at the same time was something of a miracle in itself. Lisa and I sat on the beach, soaking in the sun and the love and the togetherness we so needed.

Our older son, Josh, was twenty-two and about to move from Alabama back to San Antonio to work for his dad. Caity was eighteen and head over heels for my scrub tech and Iraq War colleague, Nate, who had come to work for us after the war and had tried for years to resist falling for his employers' daughter, to no avail.

Kimber was fifteen and lived in a nearby town with her mother, along with thirteen-year-old Mitch and our youngest daughter, Kalyn, who was ten.

Our family was a beautiful blended mess, but it was *our family,* and having everyone at the beach together meant the world to us.

When God brought Lisa into my life, "her" kids (Josh and Caity) and "my" kids (Kimber, Mitch, and Kalyn) instantly became "our" kids—they even said vows to one another at our wedding. But as the years went by and everyone got older, we knew schedules and jobs and weddings would make days like these even rarer and more special.

An hour earlier Lisa's dad, Dennis, had baptized Nate in the ocean. All of us stood in the waist-deep water and held hands while Dennis led us in prayer and thanked God for the day and the sun and the love swirling in the waves around us. Nate had never been baptized, and he'd asked Dennis, whom the kids have all called Tata since Josh's first attempt as a baby to say "Grandpa," whether he would do it.

Nate confessed his belief in Jesus, Tata dunked him under the water, and we sang hymns in the Gulf of Mexico.

A few miles offshore a storm was pushing bigger and bigger waves to the beach. It made the bodysurfing a lot of fun, but at the same time the rough water brought seaweed and countless jellyfish with it. Josh and Mitch were the first to realize this, and they both came screaming out of the water with jellies in their shorts. We all laughed and cringed simultaneously.

And now, as the sun began its brilliant dive into the western sky and our memory-filled day was drawing to a close, I noticed that Mitch was getting farther and farther from where the other kids still splashed.

"Come back in!" I called as loudly as I could. Mitch didn't seem to hear. He just waved and dove back under the surf.

I stepped out into the water and felt the undercurrent picking up with each departing surge.

Mitch wasn't a strong swimmer, and I knew he was too far out to be safe. I waded into the surf to get him, but when Josh heard me call, he noticed his little brother and swam out and brought Mitch in.

Josh and Mitch came bounding out of the ocean together, laughing and smiling with their arms around each other. Lisa snapped a couple of pictures of them, which are still in a frame on Josh's desk to this day.

I can see that scene in my mind's eye now, a decade later. That's what our family does: we swim out to help one another. From the moment Lisa and I decided to blend our two families into one, it's been all in for all of us. The kids never called one another "step" siblings. It's been a beautiful, healing experience to see God turn two hurting groups into one whole tribe.

The rest of the family went back up the hill to the house we were renting, and Lisa and I stayed on the beach for a while to enjoy the sunset. We held hands and talked about how faith and family and days like this were so important.

As darkness sneaked over the horizon, marking the end of a day I was thankful for even as I mourned its conclusion, we walked back to the house together.

In my mind that night, I replayed the pictures of our five kids in the same frame. I could see their smiles, hear their voices, and feel the love and emotion during Nate's baptism and our special time together. The next morning we would be returning to Auburn, Alabama, and I knew that within a few days our vacation would slip into memory as we got back to work. Lisa ran our practice, and the business of solo-practice neurosurgery gave both of us more work to do than we'd ever imagined.

My last thoughts before I slept that night took me back to the kids in the surf. I could see them playing, see the waves getting rougher and the hidden dangers like jellyfish and riptides lurking around them, see Mitch getting pulled away by the tide and Josh going to help him. Lisa and I talked about how hard it was to not have all of them with us every day and how much we wished it could be different.

When they were younger, I could wrap my arms around all of them, pull them out of trouble, keep them safe. Now they were moving and growing and spreading out all over the place: Josh heading to San Antonio, Caity going back home with us, and Kimber, Mitch, and Kalyn leaving for their mom's house an hour from Auburn. It would be a while before we were all together again.

How was I supposed to keep them all safe from the riptides of time, growth, and change?

While I was growing up, my parents gave me a simple faith. They taught me to trust that God would take care of us and make everything work out all right. We weren't naive to the troubles of the world, but we believed that they were all part of a plan and that we could trust in God's provision in the future because he'd never failed us in the past. I'd applied that same philosophy to raising my own kids, trying to give each of them the peace of mind that comes when faith becomes real in your life.

But teaching your kids something is one thing. When you turn off the lights at night and it's just you and your thoughts, how real is it?

We were about to spread across the country, go back to our daily lives, be distant from one another. Josh wouldn't be close by to swim out for Mitch anymore, Caity and Kimber would no longer share a room, and Kalyn wouldn't be right down the hall every night as she'd been all week in the beach house.

But God had always been there before, no matter how stormy life had been through times of war, divorce, and stress.

In the darkness I reached over and took Lisa's hand. "Everything's gonna be okay."

"Yes, it will," she said.

I believed it—then.

2

Not-So-Happy Birthday

To ask people to be brave is to expect them to think of their lives in a new way.

—Gordon Livingston, *Too Soon Old, Too Late Smart*

East Alabama Medical Center
Opelika, Alabama, 2008

I'd just finished my first operation of the day when my cell phone buzzed. I looked at the screen.

Call Dr. Stinson in ED. 35 yo male, S/P MVA, probable brain tumor.

A thirty-five-year-old man, status: post a motor-vehicle accident, probable brain tumor? That got my attention. So instead of calling Dr. Stinson, I decided to walk down to the emergency department (ED) and check it out.

"Morning, Doc," Claudette said when I entered. She's been the unit secretary of our hospital's ED for at least three hundred years, and I've never seen her out of the chair she was sitting in.

"Good morning. What's the story?" I said.

"Guy had a seizure or something. Wrecked his car on the way to work. Scan shows something wrong. Dr. Stinson's got his chart."

I turned toward the doctors' workstation to find Stinson. "Oh, and Doc?" Claudette called. "Today's his birthday."

I shook my head and shoved my hands into my lab coat pockets. If Stinson's text message was correct, the patient was not going to have a very happy birthday.

I found Stinson sitting in front of a computer, a pile of charts next to it. He was looking at a chest X-ray on the monitor; half a doughnut sat on the keyboard. This guy has been eating every waking moment since 1988, but he seems to be thinner every time I see him. He travels to developing countries with Doctors Without Borders, and I sometimes wonder whether he's got a tapeworm or something. He's almost a foot taller than me and razor thin; if you ran into the side of him, it might cut you in half. He wears a yarmulke over wavy black hair, and he has a sloped forehead that leads your eye right down to an extreme nose. You can't look away the first time you meet him because he looks like a Jewish Abraham Lincoln.

"Hey, Stinson," I said. "Emancipated many patients today?"

He sniffed and wiped a little powdered sugar off the corner of his keyboard. "About fourscore and seven. It's been crazy down here."

At least he has a sense of humor. You'd lose your mind working the ED if you didn't.

Stinson was a sight with all six foot six of him stuffed into his office chair, his knees above his thighs. He handed me a patient's chart. "Sad situation, if it's what it appears to be."

"Yeah," I said. "Pull up the scan."

He clicked his mouse a few times and brought up an MRI scan of the patient's brain. I leaned over and assumed control of the computer to work my way through the scan.

The label read "Martin, Samuel. Thirty-five." Three years younger than me. It was his birthday, just as Claudette had said.

I started at the skull base, and as the images flipped by, I saw the organ that made Samuel who he was. Inside that skull sat the six hundred billion or so cells that somehow harbored *him*—his mind, memory, personality, beliefs, intellect, everything. When I got up to the temporal lobes, the problem jumped right off the screen.

"Nasty," I said.

Stinson squinted at the screen. "What do you think it is?"

I adjusted my glasses. "Can't know for sure without a biopsy, but I'd bet it's a GBM."

Glioblastoma multiforme. Grade IV astrocytoma, malignant glioma. This tumor goes by a lot of names, but they're just aliases, a.k.a.'s for what ought to be called the brain assassin. A stone-cold killer. Takes your mind long before it takes you. GBM is pretty much the most malignant, mutated, destructive form of human cancer.

Stinson's long nose flared, and he looked a little nauseated. "Man, I hate those. My sister-in-law had one, died in thirteen months. Left my brother with three little kids. That thing's a nightmare."

"I'm sorry," I said.

I watched as the memory crossed his mind: the subtle softening of his eyes, the momentary slump of his shoulders. Her life in toto, the loss, the pain.

Then he doctored up. Back to work. He waved a hand. "Circle of life, brother. See similar stories in here every day. Have they made any progress with that disease? When my sister-in-law was sick, the doctors said it was almost always fatal."

I shook my head. "No real advances in forty years. Most everybody dies. I hope for his sake it's something else. I'll go see him and biopsy it later today."

"Thanks." Stinson straightened himself and sighed. "Good luck," he said, looking more rabbinical than presidential, "and God bless."

———

On October 7, 1939, my father was born in Idabel, Oklahoma. As if unwilling to be blamed for a population explosion, Harvey Williams Cushing died on the same day in New Haven, Connecticut, to balance things out. Harvey Cushing was not related to my family, but he is the intellectual father, or at least grandfather, of neurosurgeons everywhere.

Cushing's impact on neurosurgery and all of medicine cannot be overstated. He was world famous for his contributions to the basic science and clinical practice of neurosurgery, anesthesia, neurology, physiology, endocrinology, and other fields. He was a decorated World War I combat surgeon and even won a Pulitzer for his biography of Sir William Osler.

Thirteen years before his death, Cushing and his protégé, the young polymath

Dr. Percival Bailey, published a book with the exhaustive title *A Classification of the Tumors of the Glioma Group on a Histogenetic Basis with a Correlated Study of Prognosis.* This book presented the world with the first coherent understanding of tumors of the glioma family and their cellular structure and behavior; it formed the foundation of the modern discipline of neuro-oncology. They delineated the tumor we now call glioblastoma multiforme and set it apart from all other brain tumors as its own entity.

While Cushing and Bailey gave us seminal knowledge of what these tumors are and the cells from which they arise, by the time Cushing died, this understanding had left no meaningful impact on the survival or quality of life of the people afflicted by them. In Cushing's era surgical treatment was likely to kill the patients, and radiation treatment was in its infancy. Chemotherapy was still a fantasy in chemists' minds, and even years later when it became available, gliomas would scoff at it, hide behind the blood-brain barrier, and continue their death march through people's brains.

Cushing died, my father grew up, and thirty years later I was born. I've dealt with dozens of patients with GBM, and although I understand their disease more completely because of Cushing's work, my patients' long-term outcome is not significantly better than the outcome of his. Our diagnostic technologies and treatment strategies are superior, and our surgeries are safer and much better tolerated. Yet for the eighteen thousand or so people diagnosed with it in the United States every year, GBM still carries a ten-year survival rate of basically 0 percent.

It's a family legacy, common to all neurosurgeons, of becoming better and better technically with each passing generation—yet with each generation equally frustrated by the seeming futility of treating this disease. Eighty years after Harvey Cushing's death, sometimes it feels as if the best thing we can do for our GBM patients is pray the diagnosis is incorrect.

You know that old question about what happens when an unstoppable force hits an immovable object?

That's close to how this situation feels to me.

I'm a brain surgeon. I'm a Christian. A man of science and a man of faith.

Years of training and experience have filled me with knowledge, facts, things that are always true. Things I *know.*

And I'm a firm believer in God's desire and ability to heal, to repair, to make things right when all the doctors believe there's no hope. I've seen far too many inexplicable turnarounds, impossible saves, people who beat the odds and defied the textbooks.

There are some cases in which my knowledge as a surgeon doesn't determine the outcome because God's out there doing his thing.

I *believe.*

So what happens when the things you know and the things you believe smash into one another like the object and force in the question above?

I was about to find out.

———

I pulled back the curtain in slot 11 after walking past the guy in the adjacent bed who had just vomited all over the place. EDs are always an amalgam of sounds and smells. Moans, tears, urine, sweat, and desperation hang in the air, competing like pheromones, trying to lure the doctor and win the battle of who gets seen first.

Samuel was lying on the bed, his wife, Christy, sitting next to him on a plastic chair. He had an IV in his arm, an oxygen tube in his nose, and a wary look I've seen a thousand times, as if thinking, *Are you here to help me or tell me something awful?*

He was solidly built, square jawed, with crew-cut brown hair. He had a University of Alabama Crimson Tide tattoo on his left bicep. In any other context I would have teased him about the fact that Auburn had beaten them in football that year. But on that day—really any day in the ED—scores and rivalries didn't seem as important. Because if he had a GBM, the only score that would matter to him would be GBM 1, Samuel 0.

"I'm Dr. Warren," I said. Every time I meet a patient like this, I have a decision to make: Do I go with *distant, emotionally detached surgeon* or with *compassionate, approachable guy who happens to be a surgeon*? It has to happen instantly because you really can't change it later. How will I play it?

"Hey, Doc," he said, "is the man next to me okay? He seems like he's really sick."

His gentleness disarmed me. Here he was, lying in an ED bed in a gown, sur-rounded by the smells and sounds of misery and fear, and having just crashed his car after having a seizure, but he was concerned about another patient.

"I don't know. I'm sure Dr. Stinson will take good care of him."

Samuel smiled. "Has anyone ever told Doc Stinson he looks just like Abraham Lincoln?"

I laughed. This guy was something else.

"What happened to you today?" I logged on to the computer next to his bed and loaded his MRI scan while he replied.

"I was driving to work, going in two hours early because we're having a get-together tonight for my birthday." He pinched the bridge of his nose. "I'm so glad it wasn't later in the morning. If there had been other cars on the road . . ."

Christy reached over and took his hand. Samuel let out a long breath. "I've had a weird headache behind my right eye for a couple of months now, but today it was worse."

"You never told me you've been having headaches!" Christy stood and cupped his face in her hands. "You have to tell me these things," she said. Her green eyes pooled with tears, but there were other emotions too: Anger at not knowing some-thing that might have made a difference. Fear of the unknown medical bogeymen hiding in a headache.

He looked at her and nodded. "I know. I didn't think it was a big deal. Any-way, the last thing I remember is seeing flashing lights. Then I woke up in the ambulance."

The next part was identical to a thousand other conversations I've had with patients: "Here's your scan. This looks like a tumor, but we can't know for sure what it is until we do a biopsy. Don't worry; we're going to find out what you're dealing with and then make the best plan for getting you better."

I suspect patients don't hear a word after I say "tumor."

Samuel looked up at me, grabbed my arm, and said, "Let's do this, Doc. I trust you. I'm gonna be okay."

I nodded slowly. "All right. We'll go to surgery this afternoon."

But when I turned to walk away, my eyes crossed the computer screen again, and I saw the white-and-black image of the tumor nestled deep inside his right temporal lobe. Samuel's assertion that he would be okay echoed in my mind, and even as my words were leaving my mouth, I had a very different thought. Thousands of patients the world over, including Stinson's sister-in-law, had met the tumor Cushing and Bailey called glioblastoma multiforme. All of them, except perhaps a few whose diagnoses were inaccurate, had succumbed to its power.

In a few hours I would know, but I already *knew*. I kept the thought to myself and left the ED. As much as I wanted to smile and agree with Samuel—"Of course you'll be okay!"—I instead said to myself, *I've seen the end of you.*

3

The Devil, Magnified

With that, the future I had imagined, the one just about to be
realized, the culmination of decades of striving, evaporated.

—PAUL KALANITHI, *When Breath Becomes Air*

Two hours later I stood in the operating room with Samuel's head in my
hands. There's a moment before every brain surgery in which I hold the
patient's head and apply the Mayfield head holder, a big U-shaped metal device
with three sharp pins. I squeeze it onto the scalp until the pins break the skin and
press into the skull with sixty pounds per square inch of pressure. This clamps the
patient's head to the table so it doesn't move while I'm drilling a hole in it.

Once I've got the head secured, I always place my hands on the scalp for a
second and look down at the patient. It's my moment of silence, of acknowledging
that the thing I'm about to do is bigger than I am. The place I'm going is holy, and
the job I'm doing is sacred and dangerous and beautiful and delicately violent. I
don't want to cross into that world without reminding myself there are things I can't
control in there. I need help.

*God, direct my hands to accomplish this task safely. Let me enter his brain
but not his mind, diagnose and treat his disease but leave no trace of my tres-
pass. Let Samuel wake and still be Samuel. And let the answers be good, the
scans be wrong, the problem be manageable. Above all, let me take care of him
in a way that honors you.*

Fifteen minutes into the surgery, a hand-sized piece of Samuel's skull was sitting in a sterile basin on the back table, and I looked down at his brain. It was ugly, gray instead of pink, and not pulsing with his heartbeat as it should.

Nate, my scrub tech, leaned down and squinted. "That vein's pretty swollen, Doc," he said. Nate and I have been to war together, literally. (In fact, I wrote about him in my first book, *No Place to Hide: A Brain Surgeon's Long Journey Home from the Iraq War*.) We've been in bunkers in Iraq together while mortars landed around us, and we've saved and lost a lot of lives side by side. There's no one I trust more than Nate in the operating room. He came to work for me after the war, and along the way he became my son-in-law and the father of my first two grandchildren.

I've learned over the years to listen to Nate's comments in surgery. He's got this way of seeming to be off in space, thinking about or discussing something irrelevant like fantasy football or who the Red Wings have in the playoffs next, and then he'll drop a Socrates-like bit of wisdom on you.

At the front end of the hole I'd cut in Samuel's head was a vein the size of my little finger—the vein of Labbé. It was blue and bulging, and when I saw it, icy fingers crawled up the back of my neck. The clotted Labbé vein could stop the blood flow out of Samuel's head. If I couldn't fix it, the pressure would rise until he died of a massive intracranial hemorrhage when the blood vessels finally ruptured.

Nate and I looked at each other for a second and passed the thought between us without words: *Samuel's in trouble.* We'd lost a sergeant in Iraq from a thrombosed Labbé vein, and I wasn't ready to watch another young man die from the same problem. If I could relieve some pressure, the blood flow in his vein of Labbé might not clot off and he might not have a stroke.

That's when I remembered another patient.

———

Wilford Hall Air Force Medical Center
San Antonio, Texas, 2001

The colonel stared straight ahead, blinking every few seconds. I flashed my penlight into his eyes and watched his pupils constrict. He smelled like death. His skin was pasty, green, and cold. He wore a stocking cap because his wife worried about his head being cold. He'd lost all his hair after the fifth radiation treatment, his appetite after the twelfth, and his mind after the thirtieth.

But his tumor kept growing.

I sat down next to his bed that day, held his wife's hand, and looked at the skeleton in development who used to command warriors and shoot down MiGs. Now he looked as if he'd spent five years in a POW camp. But he kept blinking. And breathing.

I remembered the last time I'd heard his voice—the last words he ever spoke. It had been a couple of weeks before, when the MRI showed that his GBM had doubled in size despite surgery, chemotherapy, and radiation. I gave him the news, and he cleared his throat. He set his jaw, no doubt choking down his fears and ordering his thoughts as he must have in war, and looked directly into my eyes.

"If you knew this was going to happen, you should have let me die in surgery. Why'd you do this to me?"

———

As that memory flashed through my mind, I looked into Nate's eyes, and he nodded as if he knew what I was thinking.

From the head of the bed, the anesthetist, Gary, leaned over the drapes. "Doc, his pressure's up a bit. Heart rate's slowing too."

The enlarged Labbé vein, increased blood pressure, and slow heart rate could mean only one thing: Samuel's brain was swelling. Left unchecked, it would cause the brain to bulge into the opening I'd made in his skull and eventually kill him. All I had to do was nothing, and Samuel would be spared what I knew was coming for him if his tumor turned out to be a GBM.

I thought of the colonel's accusing eyes, his desperate and angry final words, and wondered what Samuel might choose if he were given the choice.

Glioblastoma kills everybody.

One hundred percent fatal. The old adage in neurosurgery is that if you've got a ten-year survivor of GBM, you made the wrong diagnosis.[1]

And it's an ugly death.

You see, brain tumors don't just steal your life. They let you know they're eating up bits of who you are, taking away your ability to engage in the few and precious remaining moments you have on this planet. They hurt you, maim you, wipe out your command and control centers like enemy missiles before the ground invasion. Shock and awe on your nervous system. And in the early months, you're fully aware of their attack.

Brain tumors steal pieces of your mind—and your peace of mind.

"Doc," Nate said. His eyes met mine and then looked down at Samuel.

I had to act.

I wasn't here to discern what Samuel would want. I was here to take out this tumor, identify the enemy, and form a treatment plan. Glioblastoma would eventually kill him, I was sure.

But not today.

"Fukushima suction, bipolar," I said. Nate handed me the instruments, and I quickly removed most of Samuel's right temporal lobe, the one with the tumor buried inside it. Years ago Dr. Jack Wilberger in Pittsburgh taught me epilepsy surgery. The most frequent procedure we performed together was a temporal lobectomy because that area of the brain is a common culprit in seizure development. Dr. Wilberger's skill and speed prepared me well for days like this one, in which a clean temporal lobe resection not only removes the tumor but also quickly relieves brain pressure and saves the patient's life.

I put the tumor-filled, fist-sized portion of Samuel's brain into a plastic jar and sent it off to the pathology lab with an orderly, who handled it as if it were a vial of Ebola or anthrax. She held it away from her body, a sickly look on her face. The OR staff has seen enough of these cases to know when they're in the presence of death.

Samuel's Labbé vein relaxed; his pressure normalized; his heart rate returned to normal.

I'd saved him.

But had I helped him?

———

Once Samuel was in the recovery room, I walked down the hall to the pathology lab. Dr. Grossman was working frozen sections that day, so I stepped into his office and found him sitting at his microscope.

"Hey, Grossman," I said.

He looked up, a surgical glove on his right hand and a turkey sandwich in his left. "Suppose you're here to see the tumor," he said after swallowing. He had a dab of mustard in the right corner of his mouth and a pink stain on his shirt, presumably from the bottle of solution sitting on his desk next to the microscope. Pathology is the only medical specialty in which a practitioner can have lunch and treat a patient at the same time without anyone protesting.

"Yeah, tough case. The patient had a seizure and crashed his car. Turned out he had a brain tumor."

"A nasty one at that." Grossman motioned with his sandwich for me to sit across the scope from him.

I moved a stack of papers from the chair on the observer side of the microscope and sat. I leaned forward and looked into the eyepieces, using my left hand to adjust their width to fit my eyes.

When Grossman moved the slide into position, I saw a cellular nightmare.

"Trifecta of terminality, we call it," he said. "Hypercellularity, highly mitotic, necrosis. Lots of blood vessels too. Everything you need to make the call."

"GBM," I said.

Grossman moved the slide around and showed me all the tumor's features. Too many cells, most of them dividing. When cells divide, it means the organism is growing. But brain cells don't divide in adults.

Cancer cells do.

In the middle of the slide was a lake of deadness. Cells had grown so quickly that this portion of the tumor outpaced its own blood supply. Whole regions of the tumor starving for oxygen and dying off so the edges could continue their invasion of Samuel's brain. This is called necrosis, and it is the sine qua non of glioblastoma.

GBM got its name because of the variety of things going on inside itself. When a pathologist looks at the whole tumor, there are multiple regions that can look stunningly different. *Multiforme* means what it says—there are multiple forms (types of cellular activity) in each one. We always take several biopsy specimens in these cases because if you move the biopsy needle a few millimeters inside a GBM, you can go from a highly malignant, obviously cancerous sample to a region where all the cells look more normal.

But once you find necrosis, you know it's a GBM.

Samuel's tumor was highly necrotic.

Slide after slide showed the malignant freak show happening in Samuel's head. The leading edge of the tumor was composed of cells lined up like Satan's legion, heading out to steal, kill, and destroy. It was the devil, magnified for me to see. Taunting me: "You can't stop me, Doc. I'll take this guy out but on my timeline."

I pushed back from the table and stood. "I hate looking at those things."

He motioned with his sandwich again—*Hang on a second*—swallowed the bite in his mouth, and said, "At least it looks like you've got a clean margin behind the tumor. I think you got it all."

I looked up at Grossman and shook my head. "You know as well as I do that margins don't matter in this disease. He's done for. Thanks, buddy. I have to go talk to his wife."

"Good luck." He gave me a look that said *Glad it's you and not me* and slid his stare back into the microscope.

I'd seen enough.

4

Roll Tide

Their's not to make reply,
Their's not to reason why,
Their's but to do and die:
Into the valley of Death . . .

—ALFRED, LORD TENNYSON,
"The Charge of the Light Brigade"

I went to the surgical waiting area and asked the volunteer to take Samuel's family into the conference room. They shuffled in, too many for the space but none of them willing to miss what I had to say.

Christy's face was a stone mask. Her eyes had dumped all their tears, her lips spent all their trembles, and she seemed resigned to whatever I had to say. People have a notion of how their lives will play out. When we marry, we envision growing old together with our spouses, our children growing up and giving us grandkids, the years filled with these people, our people. We don't let our minds wander down the side alleys of life—tumors, accidents, addictions, untimely deaths. Those are for other people. Christy's life vision had taken a hard turn into one of those alleys back in the ED, when I'd first uttered the words *brain tumor*.

While Samuel was in surgery, Christy had no doubt already traveled to the end of the new mental path my words had directed her toward. Now, hours later, she'd been through all the possible outcomes so many times that her brain, her heart, had settled into numbness. "Let's hear it. I'm ready."

"He came through the surgery fine. I was able to remove the entire tumor, but it is malignant," I said. The family waited for my words as if they were oxygen. Samuel's mom had a tear hanging on her eyelashes. I'm no mind reader, but I knew what she was thinking—*I'm going to lose my son.*

Next came the part where I had to decide how honest to be. I already *knew* how this was going to turn out. Been there, done that with GBM.

I'd been through this enough times to know that Christy would play mental tennis with me when I began to speak again. Every word I would lob at her, she'd return as another thought:

Me: Malignant.

Christy: *He's going to die.*

Me: Chemotherapy.

Christy: *What do I tell the kids?*

Me: Radiation treatments.

Christy: *I'll have to go back to work.*

Me: There are some five-year survivors.

Christy: *I'm going to be a widow at thirty-four.*

At this stage it's easier to cop out. But there are some trust bridges you can burn here if you're not careful because people know when you're being disingenuous.

I chose to stall.

"Of course, it will take the pathologists a couple of days to complete their analysis of the tumor. There are many different types of brain cancers, and how we treat it and how he'll do depend on the final pathology report. For now let's focus on getting him through his surgical recovery so he'll be strong enough for what comes next."

Waiting for the final pathology is a safe fallback position for a surgeon who doesn't want to get too far into it with a family. It's completely legitimate, but it's also a way to let the human work fall to someone else—an oncologist, internist, radiation specialist—so the surgeon can distance himself from the emotional heavy lifting of delivering the news. I can walk out to the waiting room, look the family in the eye, and say with total integrity, "We won't know what this is until we have the final report."

The problem is that in GBM the final diagnosis rarely differs from the preliminary answer we get from the pathologist's frozen-section diagnosis. If Grossman sees necrosis, the terminal trifecta, it's a done deal. Sure, sometimes they find a few genetic markers in the tumor that might predict a longer survival or a better response to chemotherapy. Oncologists, eternal optimists that they are, get excited about these nuances and say things like "20 percent increase in quality-of-life survival!" But in this disease, that plays out to an eighteen-month survival instead of fifteen.

Usually I'm not the type of surgeon to let someone else handle that for me. If I'm a big enough boy to take the patient to surgery and put his life into my own hands, why would I make the family wait three more days and hear the news from a doctor they haven't even met yet?

But for some reason Samuel and Christy got under my skin. Maybe it was how close he was to my age; maybe it was his personality. But that day I just couldn't let myself say, "He's going to die in a year or so."

I wanted it to be different.

I wanted God to heal him.

Of course, I want this for all my patients, but this time I just couldn't swallow the disparity between my faith and the medical facts.

The Bible says to "pray without ceasing."[2] It says that if you pray in faith, God will heal the sick.[3] I believe that to be true. I have seen it with my own eyes.

But at the same time, here's a disease that God almost never heals.

Now I had a patient with a terminal illness, and I wanted him to fight it, to try, to be tough. To have faith. I didn't want him to be depressed and spend the rest of his too-short life wallowing in his impending demise. His wife and kids deserved for him to have the highest possible quality of life despite the coming apocalypse in his cerebrum.

I felt stuck in a cross fire between my faith—*God can heal our disease*—and my knowledge—*This disease is 100 percent fatal.*

How could I navigate this in an ethical way? How could I handle myself as a Christian who's also a scientist? A scientist who believes that medicine doesn't provide all the answers to life?

My upbringing and my basic personality lead me to say, "Everything's gonna be okay," but when GBM is the diagnosis, everything is *not going to be okay.*

Christy was grief stricken, terrified, unanchored.

She looked in my eyes and asked, "When do we tell him?"

Samuel came through his surgery fine, and after three days he was ready to be discharged. He handled the news of his cancer with a squeeze of Christy's hand, a single tear from his right eye, and a promise to eat, sleep, and get stronger before starting radiation in two weeks.

The day I sent him home, I stood at his bedside and went through his instructions, telling him what to watch out for and when he should call me.

When I finished, he looked up and opened his mouth but didn't say anything.

"What is it?" I said.

He looked at Christy, who stood from the chair where she'd been sitting and moved to take his hand. "Tell me the story of one of your patients who beat this disease."

I stared into his eyes for a little too long, and he knew. "Samuel, let's just get you well from the surgery, and then we'll take it one thing at a time."

He squeezed Christy's hand but didn't say anything.

"It's going to be okay," Christy said.

Samuel cleared his throat. "Give it to me straight. How long do people live?"

"When we can remove the tumor, fifteen months or so is average."

Fifteen months. You thought you'd see grandkids, beaches, Europe, your spouse's hair silvering, but now you're hoping to see her next birthday. Your life's timeline, previously open ended, now extremely compact, finite. I see it in the eyes every time. I saw it in Samuel's and Christy's then: *fifteen months.*

"I'm going to give you a story to tell, Doc," Samuel said.

"I'm praying for you," I responded with a guilty conscience.

That night Lisa told me I'd done well, that it was my job to tell the truth but also to pray that God would come through for Samuel. She knew she'd be meeting Samuel and Christy in the office in a couple of weeks, and as always she would get involved with them emotionally. Our practice was like that—Lisa related to the patients and got to know them. It was neurosurgery meets family medicine, and the patients loved it. We were not a distant, cold, superspecialized organization but more like a family. We believed that people did better if they knew we were on their side.

But it came home with us.

Lisa reminded me of a book we'd read together not long before, *Where Is God When It Hurts?* by Philip Yancey. Yancey was like my faith guru. I'd been raised in a fundamentalist tradition that leaned heavily on rules and largely eschewed grace. When I was in my early thirties, my faith hit a wall, where the things I had been taught just didn't seem to work anymore, and two of Yancey's books saved me. *What's So Amazing About Grace?* taught me a better way, and then *The Jesus I Never Knew* introduced me to Jesus as a savior instead of a cosmic assassin waiting to take me out whenever I went astray.

Lisa tenderly suggested that I email Philip Yancey and ask his take on this situation, my faith-versus-facts quandary.

I've learned over the years not to argue with her when she says something like that. She has a Nostradamus-like prescience that results in scary-good things happening when people listen to her insights. So I stifled my questions—*How will I even find out how to reach him, and why would he bother to read an email from someone like me?*—and started googling.

I found an email address for Philip through his publisher and wrote a long query asking him how a doctor who believes in God but also knows facts about certain diseases can honestly tell a terminal patient to have faith and believe and not give up. How can I pray for my patients when I already know how God is going to answer?

Isn't that dishonest? Isn't it mendacious?

I pressed Send and figured I would never hear back. But it felt good to at least write down the questions.

———

Samuel and Christy came to the office two weeks later. I removed his skin staples, and Lisa spent a long time talking with the couple. As I expected, they became fast friends, and the four of us had a good conversation about his disease, their kids, and our mutual faith.

His determination to beat this tumor was inspiring. Christy seemed ready for the fight, and I decided he was healed enough to start radiation therapy.

"We'll get a new MRI to make sure the tumor's all out, and then you'll start radiation," I said. Then I looked into his eyes and leaned closer. "It's going to make you sick. Your hair's going to fall out."

He snorted. "Good." He ran his hand through the half of his hair I hadn't shaved for his surgery. "Because you made me look ridiculous. Who shaves half of someone's head? You're a great surgeon but a terrible barber."

I winced and shook my head. "Touché. Most folks like to comb it over."

"Next time just take it all off."

"Hopefully you won't need any more surgery, but if you do, I'll keep that in mind."

His face darkened, and he suddenly looked like a little boy. "Seriously, though. Will it grow back after the treatment's over?"

I nodded. "Probably. The hair loss can be permanent, though. I just thought I'd warn you about it. Look, this is going to be hard, but you've got to do it. Are you ready to get started?"

He reached out and squeezed my shoulder. His grip was strong, reflecting his underlying spirit. He blinked twice and said, "Roll Tide."

I must pause to say that in Alabama, battle lines are drawn between fans of the University of Alabama Crimson Tide and the Auburn University Tigers.

Bama fans say "Roll Tide" at any opportunity. Someone gets engaged? "Roll Tide." You win the lottery? "Roll Tide." Your friend bought a new truck? "Roll Tide." Faced with adversity? "Roll Tide." It's their universal, unifying motto.

Auburn fans, however, do not say this.

Ever.

Unless they are mocking Bama fans.

It's a Mason-Dixon Line running through the state. You can't be for both teams. People actually ask strangers, "Who do you go for?" which means, "Which team do you follow?" Friendships, marriages, and business partnerships quiver on the brink of the question, for in certain circles the wrong answer eliminates one from consideration.

I held an affiliate faculty position at Auburn University. Our middle daughter, Kimber, was planning to go to school there, and her brother Mitch would follow in her footsteps. My office was on the campus. Thus, as an Auburn man, my phrase is "War Eagle."

But on this day Samuel's "Roll Tide" hung in the air, a call to action, a rallying cry like Tennyson's "Forward, the Light Brigade!"[4]

It was an implied question: "Are you on my side?"

"Roll Tide," I said.

We scheduled another appointment for Samuel in six weeks.

As they left the office, he turned and said, "Hey, Doc, will you pray with us?"

"Of course," I said.

We prayed that he would be healed, that he would win the coming fight and hold up well in it. But the whole time we were praying, I had a double mind.

"God," I prayed out loud, "help Samuel overcome this disease."

But silently, secretly, my inner voice accused me. *How can you say those things? You don't believe them. He's cooked, and you know it.*

On his way out the door, Samuel turned back. "Doc, are you gonna put me in the medical books when I become the first ten-year survivor of this disease?"

Yes, I would, Samuel, if that were to happen.

Except I knew it wouldn't.

———

One morning later that week, Lisa was reading on her iPad when she smiled and looked over at me. "Guess who emailed you?"

"No idea," I said.

"Philip Yancey."

I took the iPad from Lisa and read a very thoughtful and detailed reply from Philip. It was quite surprising to me that such a well-known and successful writer would take the time to reply to an email from a stranger like me.

Philip's response to my question—"How do I handle telling a patient to have faith when I don't?"—was for me to write my way through understanding the issue. He said he would approach it the way he tries to learn the answers to every hard question he faces: research, question, write. He suggested that people would appreciate hearing from a doctor that we don't always know the answers.

As happy as I was to hear from him, I was frustrated at not being handed an easy answer. I didn't want to *work on it.* I wanted it explained to me.

Samuel didn't have years to wait while I tried to figure out my problem so I could help him deal with his. Samuel was at war. I was his reluctant field marshal, leading the charge in a battle I could describe for him but only he could fight. And like a commander leading his troops into a hopeless conflict, I already knew the outcome.

5

Back to the Future

The very word *prayer* comes from the Latin root
precarius—a linguistic cousin to *precarious*.

—PHILIP YANCEY, *Prayer*

Sometimes I drive myself crazy thinking about my prayers to a God who already knows everything. The Bible says that God has known all the days of my life before one of them came to pass.[5] And that he has a plan for me, to prosper and not to harm me.[6] So how can my prayers possibly change God's decisions if he's known for eternity how my life is going to play out or if what I'm asking for isn't in line with the plan he's already made for me?

There's a scene in the movie *Back to the Future* in which Marty, played by a young Michael J. Fox, is up on a hill looking into a mall parking lot below him. He's watching a time-traveling version of himself performing something he's already done. He's afraid to let his current self encounter his past self because he doesn't know what effect that would have on either version of his reality.

The implications are staggering: If you could go back into the past and tinker with how certain things happened, it could change everything about your life in the present. What if your parents never met? What if you could warn yourself not to do a certain thing, marry a certain person, go to a certain place? How would it change your world—the whole world—now? Would you even exist?

Sometimes that's how I feel about prayer.

I sat in my office with Samuel's post-op MRI on my computer screen, predicting where it was going to recur and thinking about all the prayers that must have been uttered on his behalf since the word *tumor* came out of my mouth. I knew the ones Lisa and I had prayed, most of which had been along the lines of "Please, God, cure this nice and faithful man."

But when I pray that type of prayer, I'm Marty on the hill.

If God already knew what was going to happen, then he already knew I was going to pray this prayer and how he'd answer it. Perhaps the ultimate outcome for Samuel would be the result of a prayer that God knew about before any of it happened. Perhaps he changed his mind before he even made Samuel. *Back to the Future,* the prayer version, spun around in my head until I couldn't make sense of it anymore.

It's this type of thing that forms a barrier against believing in God for some people.

My friend Aaron, an ophthalmologist I worked with in Iraq, is one of the smartest people I know. But he calls Christians *afterlife believers,* and he thinks we're nuts. To him the notion that there's someone outside our experience and time who can influence the outcome of our lives via the power of words we utter on our knees is impossible to believe and insane to contemplate. It's far more logical to Aaron to think that somehow nothing became something because of a big explosion a billion years ago, that life sprang forth from all those happy accidents, and that whatever happens in our lives is a combination of luck, nature, and nurture.

Some days I'm inclined to agree with him.

Like when I try to pray for my patients with glioblastoma.

A few years ago I heard that a girl I knew from my hometown of Broken Bow, Oklahoma, had lost her husband to a brain tumor. They were high school sweethearts, prom king and queen, the perfect love story. His death devastated her, and her life fell apart for a while.

But one day while in Broken Bow to visit my family, I happened to bump into her. I met her new husband and saw pictures of their two lovely kids. She'd found happiness and had a nice life.

What about all those prayers for her first husband? The pleading and begging for God to save him while the brain tumor marched through him and put him in the ground? What if any of those prayers had been answered positively?

Two children would not exist.

When I let myself think about these things, I get progressively more Aaron-like. It doesn't make sense to me that God can know everything yet still tell us he wants us to pray and believe that our prayers can make a difference and sometimes change his mind. When I follow this train of thought very far, my faith plummets and I want to throw up my hands and denounce any possibility of God existing at all.

But then, in the quiet of night when I try to sleep—on those frequent occasions when all I see when I close my eyes is the bloodshed and mayhem of a mass casualty in Iraq or the day I was caught outside in a mortar attack alone and unprotected—I remember that in those desperate moments I wasn't shaking my fists at God and renouncing my faith.

No, in the terror and horror of war, I prayed.

I prayed long, hard, and fervently. I prayed even in the moments in which everything I saw implied that the world must have been abandoned by God.

Even when things felt as bad as they could possibly get, I still had a sense that without him it would have been even worse, because despite the horror, unexpected mercies always seemed to arrive to help us through.

The chaplain who showed up just as I was on the brink of emotional collapse after watching another sergeant bleed out.

The concrete wall I found to hide against when the bombs were falling.

The rocket that landed steps away from the ED, which would have killed me and many of my colleagues if it had detonated but didn't because it landed in mud after a heavy rainstorm the night before in that desert country.

Little reasons to believe, to hope, to hang on.

Reasons to keep praying.

So I feel like the guy who came to Jesus and said something like "Heal my son if you can."

Jesus said, *"If I can?"* [7]

I imagine God saying, "Lee, you moron. Don't come to me and half believe I'm able to do the things you need."

If I believed and did not doubt, would my prayers for my patients be more effective? After all, didn't Jesus also say that if we have enough faith, we could move mountains? [8]

So I end up being like the "if you can" guy, and I say two things at once: "I do believe; help me overcome my unbelief!"[9]

So I prayed for Samuel, not sure whether I believed more in the power of the glioblastoma or in the God who allowed it.

I'm sure my friend who lost her first husband sometimes quietly, guiltily struggles with the dilemma: Would she rather have her storybook marriage with her first love or the two children she has now?

Because she can't have both.

I knew that Samuel and Christy were now facing the battle of their lives—*for* Samuel's life—and that no matter what happened, it would change them forever.

Dr. Warren, the neurosurgeon, knew what was going to happen.

Lee Warren, the Christian and "everything's gonna be okay" guy, prayed for Samuel anyway. Somehow it made sense to me to do so.

It would be a while before I saw Samuel again. But I knew a lot about what was happening inside his head.

I prayed for his heart as well.

6

Malevolent

Cancer's life is a recapitulation of the body's life, its existence a pathological mirror of our own. . . . Down to their innate molecular core, cancer cells are hyperactive, survival-endowed, scrappy, fecund, inventive copies of ourselves.

—Siddhartha Mukherjee, *The Emperor of All Maladies*

We have long stood helpless in the presence of brain tumors.

—Dr. Harvey Cushing, Johns Hopkins University, 1907

Mrs. Knopf lived one of her first years of life as a prisoner in the Nazi concentration camp at Dachau, where both her parents died. Raised by relatives, she wound up as a teenager in occupied West Berlin. There she fell in love with an American army sergeant who married her and took her to America.

Over the next sixty years, she never shrank from a challenge: losing her first son to rubella and her second to a landmine in Vietnam, surviving a bout with cervical cancer and the hysterectomy that nearly killed her, and pressing through her husband's death from a stroke the year before I met her.

She was cooking for her great-granddaughter's birthday party when her daughter noticed her clutching her forehead with both hands.

"Mama, what's wrong?"

When Mrs. Knopf replied, the family took her to the emergency department because Mama had never said "Blaf, cake smulp teaking blaf" before.

After her MRI showed a brewing intracranial storm, Stinson gave her a dose of IV steroids. Her speech improved rapidly, and by the time Stinson called me, Mrs. Knopf was speaking clearly again.

"I hope this isn't what I think it is," Stinson said as I walked up to his desk. Today's hoagie and yesterday's *USA Today* sat on his desk along with a cup of coffee. He bent his neck toward his computer and pointed a bony finger at the white-and-gray image on the screen, the enhancing edge of an infiltrative tumor in Mrs. Knopf's brain lining up against the margins of more normal tissue like rebel invaders facing off against the Union troops at Gettysburg.

"The world will little note nor long remember what we think it is, brother," I said. "Tissue is the issue. She'll need a biopsy."

"You can't just remove it?"

I shook my head and touched the screen. "Nope. See how it's crossing the corpus callosum? It's already in both sides of her brain. I can make the diagnosis with a needle biopsy, but if this is a cancer, I can't do much for her."

———

If you're not a medical person, the amount of information doctors can infer from lab work and imaging before we ever meet a patient might surprise you. As I looked at Mrs. Knopf's MRI, I saw a path before her, and I was *certain* how her journey would proceed. I hadn't walked in and examined her yet, didn't have a clue what she looked like or what her personality was, and wasn't even completely sure what her biopsy result would be.

But I had seen this so many times that I already *knew.*

Left untreated, the tumor growing in her frontal lobes would continue its march, preceded by a tidal wave of devastating brain swelling. Her scan showed severe compression of her lateral ventricles, the structures inside the brain where cerebrospinal fluid, or CSF, is made. Once the ventricles are compressed enough to obstruct the flow of CSF, hydrocephalus ensues, with a subsequent rise in intracranial pressure and certain death as the pressure chokes out blood flow to the brain and stroke occurs.

On the other hand, we are good at controlling brain swelling with medications, and I can insert catheters to drain off excess CSF and control intracranial pressure.

Thus, we can usually keep people from dying of these secondary problems created by the tumor. When I envisioned Mrs. Knopf choosing to treat her tumor, I saw myself giving her steroids and mannitol, drilling holes in her skull to relieve pressure, and asking my colleagues to treat her with chemotherapy and radiation to stave off tumor growth and further invasion. This would surely slow the march of the invading cells and prolong her survival.

But I was convinced that as the tumor infiltrated her frontal lobes more completely, her personality would flatten. Her speech would worsen. Her seizures would become more difficult to control.

I saw her moving along a timeline: three weeks to a depressed, robotic affect. Six weeks until she would lose interest in eating and thus require a feeding tube. Eight weeks to right-sided arm and leg paralysis, with the left side following shortly, and death in four months from debilitation and respiratory failure.

———

"You okay, Lee?"

Stinson's question shook me from my thoughts.

"Yeah. Just planning what I'll tell her," I said.

"Good luck, buddy. This one looks bad."

I shook Stinson's hand and went off in search of Mrs. Knopf, past a college kid on a stretcher with a broken arm after a drunken fight, a guy who'd fallen twenty feet after trying to paint a wall while standing on two ladders he'd roped together, and a boyfriend whose lover's home-early husband had thrown him through a second-story window. People whose bad choices of beverage, behavior, or association had led to injuries that threatened their quality and length of life.

But trauma surgeons know that survival against all odds is the frequent fate of the inebriated, the idiotic, and the immoral; these guys would all be fine.

Mrs. Knopf, who by all indicators had led a life worthy of emulation and admiration, lay waiting to see me, destined to hear my proclamation that despite her good choices and strong character, she was under attack by a foe she had not sought out via belligerence, encountered because of dumb decisions, or willingly partnered with through an inappropriate relationship.

She was sitting on the edge of her bed, changed from her hospital gown into a terry cloth bathrobe her family had brought from her home. It was white and had a monogrammed *HK* on the left breast. Helga Knopf, although elderly, had a timeless beauty and quiet strength, revealed in her posture and the way she stretched out her arm to shake my hand before I could say a word. She possessed a poise and a royal quality obtained more from perseverance and determination than genetics and cosmetics.

"Good morning, Doctor," she said. "I am Mrs. Knopf. And what do you have to say for yourself, ordering me stuck with all these needles?"

In my position as white-coat-wearing brain surgeon, people do not often put me on the defensive. I was almost speechless.

"I'm sorry," I said. "But the tests are necessary so we can figure out how to help you."

"*Nein*. It's shameful to make an old woman get undressed like that. Do you know how cold it is in here?"

I fell back on the only option I had. One of the prime rules in medicine is to establish blame and distance yourself from it when a patient is unhappy. I did what I had to do.

"Actually the MRI and the labs were ordered by Dr. Stinson. I'm Dr. Warren, the neurosurgeon." I felt a tiny bit of guilt over throwing Stinson to the wolves. Very tiny.

"Stinson, the tall man who looks like your former president?"

"Yes, ma'am," I said.

"Tell him he's on my list, *ja*?"

Mrs. Knopf went on to tell me her entire story—normally I direct people to skip to the relevant medical history, but her life was so interesting and she was frankly so intimidating I never cut her off. As more of her family arrived, they helped her focus on her recent problems, and the medical picture became clear.

The headaches had started a few months ago, accompanied by a tingling sensation on her right side. A few days ago she had vomited several times, but she decided she had a stomach virus and did not tell her family.

But when she spoke gibberish in front of her family, everyone knew she had a real problem.

After I explained the MRI to Mrs. Knopf and her family, I carefully went through the biopsy procedure and its risks.

Ralph, Mrs. Knopf's only surviving son, held his mother's hand. "What do you think it is?"

"Honestly, I suspect it is a cancerous brain tumor called glioblastoma," I answered.

"Then we shall attack it," Mrs. Knopf said.

———

Three hours later I'd told the family the news: Mrs. Knopf indeed had a GBM. What I didn't know yet was that this disease and this particular patient had a few surprises in store for me that day.

I was standing in the recovery room when Mrs. Knopf opened her eyes after the anesthesia faded. She looked at me and smiled the drunken smile of waning gas and residual narcotics people always have when the anesthetist has done the job perfectly. No nausea, no thrashing or screaming as some people do as they awaken. Just a one-too-many-drinks grin and a few minutes of asking the same questions over and over before the patient remembers why she's here.

I saw it cross her mind: *Am I okay? Is it cancer?*

"Mrs. Knopf, everything went well. Surgery is over," I said.

She grasped my hand. "How bad is it?"

I wouldn't know the full answer to her question until a few minutes later. "It's definitely a cancer. We'll know more in a few days," I said just as my cell phone beeped with Grossman's message.

Come to the path lab. You want to see this.

———

"Unbelievable," I said, squinting as I followed Grossman's pointer around the microscope field. We were looking down on a battle being fought in Mrs. Knopf's brain.

I was watching a war, an invasion by a superior attacker against a hapless foe. And I was powerless to change any of it; it was as if I were watching the battle via the video feed from an unarmed drone. I could see the cancerous attack on her brain, and I could see why Grossman called me.

"This is the most malignant glioma I've ever seen," he said. "Every cell is dividing. They're all mutated and enlarged, and no two look the same. This thing is malevolent."

From the MRI I knew the tumor was already growing in both sides of Mrs. Knopf's brain. And now, with this aggressive tissue type, I knew it wasn't going to go well for her, but there were still things I didn't know.

I thought about the five or six biopsies I'd taken outside the obviously abnormal part, the ones I take to determine how far the tumor has already invaded the more normal-appearing brain. I asked Grossman, "What about the margins?"

He shook his head. "I saw tumor cells in all of them."

The trifecta of terminality, more malignant than Samuel's tumor, already in both hemispheres of the brain, and expanded beyond the MRI's depiction of the tumor's extent.

Bad news for Mrs. Knopf.

I turned to leave the lab and had my hand on the doorknob when Grossman said, "Hey, I know it's been a tough day, but I forgot to tell you." He lowered his eyes, and his voice softened, as if he was sorry to pile more bad news on me. "I got the results back from Emory on your other patient, Samuel Martin."

Grossman had sent Samuel's tissue off to the neuropathology lab at Emory University for genetic testing.

I waved a hand. "It's okay. Let's hear it."

"The MGMT promoters are unmethylated," he said.

I let out a long sigh. MGMT is a DNA repair enzyme that has something to do with a cell's ability to fix things when they go awry as cells divide. Cancer cells appear to rely on this enzyme to maintain their fanatical growth. Glioblastomas, almost half the time and for unknown reasons, attach a methyl group—one carbon and three hydrogen atoms—to the tumor cell's mechanism for producing the MGMT enzyme. When this happens, the genetic machine that tells the cell to make MGMT is switched off, and the cancer cells develop a vulnerability to a chemotherapy drug called temozolomide.

It's not a cure, but people who have methylated MGMT promoters in their glioblastomas live twice as long as those people who do not, and three times more of those people live at least two years.

This might not sound like much in the grand scheme of things, but if you're talking about seeing your little boy's next two birthday parties versus being dead, it matters to you.

If having a GBM was strike one for Samuel, having unmethylated MGMT promoters was strike two.

In Siddhartha Mukherjee's Pulitzer Prize–winning biography of cancer, *The Emperor of All Maladies,* brain tumors receive only a few lines. This is probably because the author had little good news to report on the subject of how far treatment has come as our understanding of these diseases has evolved. While he gives hundreds of pages to breast cancer and the leukemias, brain tumors are largely ignored. It's easy to understand why, when the best news for GBM patients in the last forty years has been the development of temozolomide, which extends life only by a few months in around half the patients who take it.

And Samuel wasn't going to be one of those people.

There's an old joke: "Why do they put nails in coffins?"

The answer: "To keep the oncologists from trying another drug."

Samuel would get temozolomide anyway.

———

Mrs. Knopf handled the news with elegance and class. She had pools of tears in her eyes, a granddaughter on the edge of her bed, a Bible on her bedside table, and her husband's picture on her chest when she said, "I've lived a good life. I will not have my hair fall out and die looking like Mr. Clean. I want to go home, Doctor. Pray for me, please."

I did pray, with her then and for her later. But as they had with Samuel, the words did not ring true for me. How can I pray for God to heal someone of something no one ever survives? How do I ask God for something he never does?

With hospice nurses keeping her comfortable and her family keeping her loved, Mrs. Knopf stayed conscious for about three weeks. During that time the tumor marched through her brain, destroying and laying waste to her faculties and intellect as Hitler's armies had pillaged Europe and crushed her family decades before. The woman who had survived the Holocaust, losing two sons and a husband, and even the attack of a lesser cancer died in twenty-four days at the hands of glioblastoma, proving once again there are some things we always know to be true.

7

The Thing Worse Than Fear

The opposite of faith is not doubt, but fear.

—Philip Yancey, *Reaching for the Invisible God*

Around the time Mrs. Knopf died, Samuel came into my office for his three-month checkup. He'd finished his radiation and his first round of temozolomide, his hair was gone, and his scalp was puffy.

Radiation kills cancer cells by causing fatal mutations in their DNA while they are dividing. During cell division the machinery of tumor growth is in high gear, and those rapidly multiplying cells are particularly vulnerable to injury. This is the entire premise of radiation oncology: attack the dividing cancer cell while its flank is exposed. Mutate the cells and they will die. The more malignant a cancer, the higher the percentage of its cell population that's dividing and the more likely a passing gamma ray or proton beam will cause it to mutate.

The problem is, those radiation beams are not specific in their attack.

Any cell that happens to be dividing and in the path of the beam is equally vulnerable.

This is why hair falls out, skin burns, cataracts form, thyroid glands fail, and Samuel's now-bald head was part purple and part lobster red, with patches of dermatitis and scabbing along his incision line.

But although radiation leaves its marks on a person's skin, it does something else that's harder to describe. People make a remarkable psychological shift when they run the gamma ray gauntlet, and I saw the look on Samuel's face that day.

It's the look of irreversibility.

It's a face people have when they've encountered something that alters them in a permanent way. After your first mortar attack, once the sirens stop and the dust settles, your face changes. You no longer live in a safe world; there are people close by who want to kill you.

It's the look Adam and Eve probably had when they ate of the tree of the knowledge of good and evil.[10] Now they knew. They weren't naive anymore, and they could never be again.

People *after*, such as when people finish radiation for the first time, look different.

Just as Samuel did now.

Now he *really* had cancer.

He'd stuck his head inside a gamma ray machine five days a week, and every time he had to hope the girl running things pushed the right buttons and didn't fry his brain instantly. He'd gone to sleep every night with his wife next to him, the physical distance the same as it had always been but with a growing gap between his former idea of their future and the reality that he was dying, which grew stronger with every fallen clump of hair on his pillow, every gut spasm as his intestinal lining sloughed off, every rash and headache and painful spot of eczema on his scalp.

He was different now. Before, he'd believed he would be cured. He would be the one. Now he doubted it every time he looked in the mirror or hugged the toilet.

He didn't have to say it. His eyes told me.

"How you holding up?" I asked.

"Worse than Bama losing to Auburn," he said.

I laughed. "You look strong."

He pushed his index finger into his scalp. It left an imprint in the swollen tissue thanks to fluid retention from the steroids and radiation. "I look like a bullfrog."

Christy put her arm around him. "You're still gorgeous."

Samuel sniffed. "You forgot your glasses," he said. "Doc, what's the MRI show?"

I pulled up his new scan on the monitor in the exam room. While I reviewed the images, I could feel Samuel's and Christy's eyes watching me. They weren't looking at the screen; they were studying my face for my reaction, hanging on for my opinion. People never really care what the screen shows. They care what I think it means.

"Whatcha see, Doc?" Samuel said when he couldn't wait any longer.

I didn't like what I saw.

"This area of enhancement wasn't there before." I traced the edge of his scan with my finger, outlining a bright area along the inside border where I'd removed his temporal lobe and tumor three months before. The white matter around it was swollen, and there were two bright spots in his frontal lobe that had not been present on the postoperative scan.

Christy put her hand on Samuel's knee. He laid his hand gently on hers.

"What are you saying?" she asked.

I turned on my stool to face them. "The tumor is growing back around where it was before. And there are two new areas." I pointed to them. "These are probably tumor as well."

"Did it spread there? Could it go anywhere else in my body?" Samuel said. His right hand went to his chest slowly.

I shook my head. "No, GBM doesn't usually leave the nervous system. And it doesn't spread around like other cancers. It's more like a genetic switch in your brain cells. Once the DNA is switched the right way, every astrocyte in your head can transform."

Christy leaned her head back a little and blinked at the light as her eyes welled. I handed her a tissue. "So this has happened in only three months, despite the medicine and the radiation therapy," she said. "Tell us what happens next."

"Well, I need to talk to your other doctors," I said, "but we will find you a trial to join, something with a good chance to kill this thing."

Samuel leaned closer. "I'm not dying, Doc," he said, less confidently than he had a few months before.

"No. We have lots of treatment options. Keep fighting, Samuel."

He nodded. "I ain't even started fighting yet."

As they walked out of my office, I heard Samuel say to Christy, "Let's go get the kids out of school. I want to spend some time with them."

That evening at dinner I looked over at my son Mitch. Lisa had made spaghetti and meatballs, one of Mitch's favorites, and he held his fork in attack position as she spooned his serving onto his plate. Although he was fourteen years old, dinnertime somehow transformed Mitch into a little kid every night as he devoured whatever delicious feast Lisa made for us.

Mitch had come to live with us the previous summer after we convinced him that some of the friendships he'd made in the town where he lived with his mother weren't helping him. The change of venue had been good, and navigating the stormy seas of male adolescence seemed easier for him in our close environment.

"How was school today?" I asked.

"Good. I really like jazz band," Mitch said between bites. He'd auditioned for and made the school's jazz ensemble as an electric bass player. Being part of a group was important for him, and the community he'd found among musicians had eased his transition to the new school. "My bass won't stay in tune, though."

Mitch's bass, the first he'd owned, was a starter model, and he'd been after us for a better one since he'd really learned how to play.

"Well, Christmas isn't far away," Lisa said.

"Your spaghetti sauce is like Christmas in my mouth," Mitch said with a laugh as he reached past me to spear another meatball with his fork.

I looked at Mitch's delicate hands and remembered when he'd broken his arm on the playground in third grade. He came home from school the next day, proud of the notoriety he'd achieved by being the first one in his class with a cast. His friends had signed it, and Mitch climbed into my lap to show off his collection of signatures.

I remembered him leaning into my chest, the fresh smell of his hair, and the warmth and power of knowing that my little boy was safe and would always be there, even though I knew he would grow and in time would no longer sit in my lap and view me as his place of strength and safety. I recalled my feeling of powerlessness watching the orthopedist cast Mitch's arm—me a doctor yet unable to take care of him—and the gratitude I felt that his injury was so insignificant in the big picture. He would be okay.

While we ate and talked and laughed, I wondered how Samuel might feel with his children. The sense of futility I had in not being able to prevent or fix Mitch's small problem—a broken bone—had to be miniscule in relation to Samuel's feeling that something was trying to take him away from his family. That he might not be there for any of their struggles, breaks, or issues.

I pushed it away—the transference that was dragging my mind into someone else's life—and tried to be present in my own. I knew that those moments, family dinners and kids willing to sit and talk to their parents, were gifts that would not always be there. I needed to be here now.

But the memory of Mitch's third-grade injury stayed with me. When I turned out the lights that night, belly full of Lisa's pasta, my heart full of time with family and heavy for Samuel's diminishing time with his, my own third grade returned to me.

My third-grade classmate—and my first crush—was a pigtailed beauty named Annie. In my memory she was flawless. The only fistfight I ever had was over her: future-business-tycoon and then-playground-bully Jimmy pulled Annie's hair, and I punched him in his pig nose.

He might have punched me back, might have knocked me flat onto my backside and bloodied my nose, but this is my book, so I'm not saying.

What exactly happened to Annie is fragmented in the disordered memories of my childhood. I clearly remember the last day of third grade, her returning my note with the YES box checked next to my question, "Do you like me?" And I remember her getting on the school bus at the end of that day, my heart in the seat beside her since we rode different routes.

Then I recall my mother sitting me down one day that summer. In her soft voice she said, "Lee, Annie's sick. She might not be at school next year."

Halfway through fourth grade, the teacher announced that Annie would be joining us the next day. I was over the moon.

When she walked into the classroom, though, Annie was a different person. Her face, freckled and flawless before, was puffy; I remember thinking she looked like a chipmunk. Her hair, for which I'd gone to war, was a straw-colored wig. I remember her giggling, her words not making sense. The teacher had to help her to her desk, and she wasn't allowed to go to recess.

Annie died around spring break of that year. The teacher said, "Brain tumor." I didn't think about it until years later, but it is likely that my interest in neurosurgery started then. Knowing what I know now, steroids accounted for her swollen face; chemotherapy and radiation for her hair loss. The 1980s-era surgery on her brain stem was the reason for her wobbliness and inability to play on the playground.

Based on her short survival and her neurologic symptoms as I remember them, I suspect she had a tumor called diffuse intrinsic pontine glioma, the deadliest form of childhood brain cancer.

Losing a friend—my first love!—at such a young age unmoored my youthful sense of the world being a safe place. I struggled to sleep and had bad dreams.

My mom sat on the edge of my bed one night and talked with me about it. I remember bits and pieces of our conversation as she drew from me what I was feeling: If Annie could die, maybe I could too. If her doctors couldn't save her, maybe I could get sick and my doctors couldn't help me either.

The world was suddenly dangerous.

As fuzzy as that memory is, one part of it is clear to me. My mom lay down next to me, prayed with me for Annie's family, and then stroked my face and turned off the light. "Don't be afraid, Lee. God loves you. Never doubt that. Have faith, and everything will be okay."

I know now you can have faith and it doesn't always mean everything will be okay. At the time, however, I think it was enough for me. I managed to be comforted by my mother's encouragement to have faith and not doubt that God would take care of me.

The problem I didn't see then took me years to figure out. But the night after I discovered Samuel's tumor recurrence and new growth and after I watched Mitch devour Lisa's cooking, I stumbled onto it.

Doubt is not the absence of faith.

You can doubt and believe at the same time. I do—every day. In my childhood I thought this meant that I didn't have enough faith and that if I were stronger or more like God (or even more like my parents), I would no longer struggle with doubt. But in my bed that night, I figured out what was bothering me.

That night in the darkness, an icy spider crawl worked its way up from my heart, step by tingly step, into the conscious part of my brain, and I could no longer deny what I was feeling: I did not doubt that God could heal Samuel; I knew he could. I was afraid that he wouldn't.

And the thing worse than fear is discovering that what you're afraid of is actually true.

8

Billy Club Biopsy

She'd asked him if she could donate Paul's body to science.

"Will they pay something for him?" she asked. "There's got to
be a college somewhere that wants to see what the inside of a loser
looks like."

—C. J. Box, *Force of Nature*

Surgical care for patients with brain tumors is segmented. Long periods elapse between appointments because we want people to spend as little time as possible in hospitals and doctors' offices. If you've got a year left, you shouldn't spend most of it talking to me.

So once the immediate postoperative period is past, wounds are healed, and radiation treatment is completed, we spread out the visits.

I'd called Dr. Wilma Grimes, Samuel's medical oncologist, and informed her about the new tumor growth. She found a clinical trial of a drug that held some promise of starving the tumor of blood vessels and causing it to shrink. Samuel met the criteria, and Dr. Grimes enrolled him in the trial.

I was to see him again at the six-month recheck after surgery.

Lisa and I prayed for him and his family frequently, heard from Christy on Facebook occasionally, and went about the business of running a busy neurosurgery practice.

A considerable percentage of my work involves trauma, and the law of trauma is that there are very few true accidents. As callous as it may sound, a high percentage of people who are injured were doing something to invite their troubles. This is why most injuries happen at night to males between eighteen and twenty-two years of age, especially those with elevated blood alcohol levels or positive urine drug screens or both.

These actuarial facts have led me to develop Warren's corollary to the law of trauma: you can't fix stupid, but you often have to operate on it.

The good news is, sometimes injuries can actually lead to something good happening.

When I was in Iraq, I met a surgeon named Dino who in a previous deployment had been hit in the scrotum by shrapnel from an enemy shell. During the surgery to remove his ruptured testicle, the urologist noticed something unusual. Instead of simply discarding the damaged organ, he asked a pathologist to look at it. The diagnosis was early testicular cancer.

The exploding shell saved Dino's life.

And so it was for Joey Wallace, a patient I met in the ICU one night two months after Samuel started his drug trial.

I received the call from an outside hospital and agreed to accept their thirty-year-old patient via ambulance when the CT scan revealed he had a head injury. When I met him three hours later, he had a bloody bandage wrapped around his head, glazed eyes, a homemade swastika tattoo on the back of his right hand, and another tattoo of a naked woman on the left side of his neck.

He also had his left ankle shackled to the rail and a Drug Enforcement Administration (DEA) agent sitting next to his bed. The agent rose when I walked into the room. His right hand rested on his handgun.

"I'm Dr. Warren," I said.

He nodded. "Keaton. DEA. We busted a meth lab tonight." He motioned toward the stretcher with his head. "This moron tried to run from me."

The patient groaned.

"And when I caught up with him, he pulled a knife." Keaton actually smiled while he told me the story. "So I hit him in the head with my billy club, and he dropped like a rock."

Keaton was six four, had (I guessed) 7 percent body fat, and could probably bench-press a Kia. Not the sort of person you want clubbing you in the head.

"He dropped because you fractured his skull," I said. The CT scan showed a depressed skull fracture above Joey's right eye and a hematoma in his right frontal lobe.

"How long till I can process him for jail?" Keaton said.

I shook my head. "He needs surgery. At least a week."

Keaton turned to Joey. "Enjoy your little vacation, meth head. I pulled your record. This will be your third felony drug arrest. Plus pulling a knife on me, you're done running a small business."

Joey turned his body to face the wall, curled up into a ball, and ignored us.

"These guys, these dopeheads," Keaton said, "they're all the same. Total scumbags. I'll leave a guard, and he has to be chained to the bed at all times. You wouldn't believe how often these guys try to run." He turned and walked out.

I gave orders to the nurse to prepare Joey for surgery, and I went out to the waiting room to look for his family. Since it was two in the morning, I had no trouble guessing which family was Joey's. There were only two people in the room, and they were together.

A woman who looked about eighty-five sat with her hands crossed, looking down at the floor, motionless as if asleep. Next to her was a younger woman, probably in her late twenties, so thin I could see the pulse above her collarbone as I approached. She was wearing a tank top and cutoff denim shorts. A faded skull tattoo decorated her left shoulder.

She raised her head as I walked up. Her face was blank, apathetic, the look you see in the lobby of the driver's license place.

"I'm Dr. Warren. Are you with Mr. Wallace?"

Her mouth opened to show off four black teeth angled toward one another like a crosscut saw blade.

"Yeah, his sister, Louise. That's Gramma." The older lady did not stir.

With skeletal, delicate fingers that might have played piano or cello if she'd had a different upbringing, Louise lightly scratched the back of her left hand with her right. Her skin was marked with multiple old scars. Add that to the thinness and bad teeth and it was clear that Joey wasn't the only meth addict I'd met tonight.

Louise caught me looking at her hands. "Joey gave me drugs for my sixteenth birthday," she said. "I spent the next eight years in that life. I got straight after a social worker took my baby away and I went to live with Gramma. She told me about the Lord. I've been sober for three years."

Gramma raised her head. "How's my grandson?"

"He has a skull fracture and some bleeding in his brain," I said. "He needs surgery right away."

I explained the procedure and its risks.

Gramma nodded. "I reckon you better get on with it."

"Does he have any medical problems? Any history I should know, medications he takes every day, or drug allergies?"

Louise shook her head. "Joey never met a drug he couldn't take. He quit school in ninth grade, stole our mom's pain medicine when she had her knee replaced—that was before she died—and has caused so much trouble that nobody in our family except me and Gramma will talk to him. He knocked up a couple girls, got arrested and spent a year in the system, OD'd twice. We figured something like this was coming eventually, no matter how hard we pray for him."

"The surgery should take me an hour or so. I'll be back out to talk with you when I'm done."

I started walking away, but Louise called out, "Hey, Doc?"

I turned back. "Yes?"

She stood and put her bony hand on my arm. "Joey ain't worth killing, but I love him 'cause he's kin. Take good care of him."

———————

When you tap a hard-boiled egg on the counter, the shell fragments into multiple pieces, each of which must be peeled off from the adherent tissue underneath. If you can picture that, you can see what Joey's right frontal bone looked like in the operating room that night. Fifteen or so bone fragments fanned out from the crater that had formed when Keaton's baton cracked into Joey's head. I spent a few minutes

opening his scalp, stopped a few bleeding blood vessels, and peeled the bone fragments off the underlying dura mater, the covering of Joey's brain.

Then I opened the dura to remove the small blood clot and brain contusion.
That's when I noticed something funny.

I used the operating microscope to magnify Joey's brain. In the middle of the
clot was a clump of tissue too firm to be blood or normal brain. I washed away
the blood with sterile saline irrigation, and the area was yellow, slightly harder than
the white matter around it, and obviously not caused by the blow to his head. Deciding I'd better send it to the pathology lab, I removed all the abnormal tissue,
including a rim of what appeared to be swollen white matter around it.

An hour later Grossman called into the operating room. He didn't sound
pleased at having been dragged into the hospital at three in the morning. "I've been
looking at the tissue you sent over. He's got contused brain, blood, and some swollen normal brain on the edges. But the center is abnormal. I see deranged astrocytes,
hypercellularity, and a lot of blood vessels. This is an intermediate-grade glioma."

"What about the margins?" I asked.

"It looks like you got it all. The edges blend into normal white matter."

Joey had a brain tumor directly underneath his head injury. An intermediate-
grade glioma meant it wasn't really benign, but it was not yet malignant either.
Removing the whole thing before it became a GBM gave Joey a chance to survive.

If he hadn't pulled the knife on Keaton, Joey may have never discovered the
tumor until it was too late.

And since low-grade gliomas develop very slowly and influence the function of
the normal brain around them as they grow, it wasn't unreasonable to think that
some of Joey's poor choices and bad behavior might have been related to his frontal
lobe harboring a brain tumor for most of his life.

Later in the intensive care unit, Joey woke up. His face reflected childlike innocence from anesthesia and pain medicine and the lingering effects of concussion.
He opened his eyes, the right one only partially because his scalp was swollen on
that side.

"Joey, I'm Dr. Warren. Surgery went fine. You're going to be okay."

He looked around the room. "I'm hungry."

"We'll get you some breakfast later."

"What happened to me?" he asked.

"You were hit in the head."

"That big cop."

"Right. You were running away, and Agent Keaton says you pulled a knife on him."

Joey shook his head, and his jaw opened a little. Apparently he and Louise had the same dentist.

"I didn't *pull* a knife; I was *carrying* a little knife. I was cutting product before they kicked our doors in." He sniffed and wiped his nose with his forearm. "Pull a knife on a DEA agent. Do I look like an idiot to you?"

Was that a trick question? Swastika tattoo on his hand, three teeth, gauged ears, needle marks all over both arms, his head wrapped from brain surgery . . . I snapped myself out of the list.

"Anyway, he hit you in the head and broke your skull. You had some bleeding into your brain, but when I took it out, I found a brain tumor."

Joey's eyes had begun to glass over again, the carousel of arousal everyone rides when concussed and anesthetized. But when I said "brain tumor," he sat up straighter. Behind every mask we wear—whether one of tattoos and piercings or of vanity and designer-labeled clothing—lies the naked, unprotected little person who's still afraid of something.

And all of us are afraid of brain cancer.

Joey projected rebel, tough guy, rule breaker. But the darkness on his face and the catch in his breath gave him away. "But I haven't even been sick."

I nodded. "It was small, too small to have caused you any obvious symptoms yet. And it's all out. It wasn't malignant, so you may be cured."

He turned his head to the left to look out the ICU window at the gathering dawn. His left hand reached up and touched his bandage.

A monitor beeped, someone down the hall moaned, and Joey assessed his life.

"You're really blessed," I said. "If you hadn't had this injury, the tumor would probably have become a cancer before you knew it was there."

When Joey turned back to me, his eyes were narrower. "Blessed? My entire life has been a constant stream of crap. Dad left when I was three, my mom died, my sister and my gramma constantly feed me this Jesus garbage, some caveman cracked in my skull with a club, and now you're telling me I have a brain tumor? And I'm blessed? Get out of my room."

Joey turned back to the wall. I didn't know what to say, since what I *had* said was one of those Christian platitudes that are never helpful but that we can't seem to avoid saying, such as "He's in a better place now" or "God needed her more than we did." I hoped the morphine and the head injury would make him forget what I'd said, and I decided to let him rest.

I walked to the nurses' station, intending to write some orders and put in a consult for oncology and radiation oncology to see Joey in the morning. I needed sleep, but I had to make rounds, and my regular day of surgery started in two hours. So instead I walked toward the ICU exit, planning on a cup of coffee and whatever breakfast facsimile the doctors' lounge cooks had prepared for the day.

When I got to the door, I heard Joey call out, "I'm still hungry."

It hit me then: Joey had been hungry his whole life. And his appetites, the pursuit of what he thought would satisfy him, and all those bad choices had led him here—skull caved in by a Goliath in DEA clothes, a disaster that ultimately may have saved his life. I thought of Samuel, whose tumor was certain to kill him. Samuel was a "good" guy—churchgoer, family man who had done all the right things. He was going to lose his battle with GBM, yet he seemed to believe that God was taking care of him. And Joey—a "total scumbag," as Keaton had described him—was still blasting God for the troubles of his life despite the gift of early diagnosis and almost certain cure.

They say there are no atheists in foxholes. But I've actually been in today's equivalent of foxholes—bunkers we sought out in Iraq during mortar and rocket attacks—and I'd say the truth is that it's a toss-up. One man finds himself in trouble and is driven to his knees, begging God for help. Another person looks at the problem and decides God has given him the middle finger, so he gives up on God completely.

And then, I thought as the ICU doors closed and muffled Joey's voice behind me, *there are people like Aaron.*

9

Foxhole Atheists

The real question, then, is not whether we will face failure. It is how well we will face it. How we respond to the challenges and trials in our lives . . . makes all the difference in the world.

—Wayne Cordeiro, *Sifted*

332nd Air Force Theater Hospital
Balad Air Base, Iraq, 2005

C heckmate," Aaron said. I'd lost at chess, again, to Major Aaron Chambers, an ophthalmologist from Cleveland. He was an army reservist who had volunteered to go to war and had done heroic work in our tent hospital to save the vision of countless soldiers and even enemy combatants. Aaron had now beaten me something like seventeen games in a row, and this game had lasted only nine moves.

We had had several extremely bloody days, and although we didn't know it, there were several more to come. Aaron had removed irreparably damaged eyes from a group of Iraqis who'd been bombed for having the audacity to vote, and I'd been operating on their brains for seventy-two hours. When you reach a certain point of fatigue, you can't sleep.

So we played chess.

I liked Aaron because he was a great surgeon, steady under pressure, and a calming influence when things, literally, blew up. He once was so overwhelmed with patients—when IEDs explode, eyes are the most frequently injured body part—that he asked whether I could help him in surgery.

I'd never had any ophthalmology training other than learning to remove optic-nerve tumors. When neurosurgeons approach the eye, it is from the inside of the head. But when I scrubbed in with Aaron, he handed me a pair of scissors and taught me how to remove an eyeball that had been punctured by shrapnel. The technique is gruesome, amazingly fast, and, for lack of a less clichéd way to put it, not brain surgery. Suffice it to say, this is why your mother told you not to run with scissors.

Aaron had returned the favor a few days later when he scrubbed in with me to help remove part of an Iraqi woman's temporal lobe after a rocket attack on her village. She and her colleagues had been targeted for daring to open a school to teach girls to read.

Chess took our minds off the war. For a while.

But war always comes back around.

A new game, and I opened with a pawn out two spaces—*f4*.

Just as I lifted my finger from the piece, Aaron chuckled.

"Again, Lee?" he said. "If you weren't a brain surgeon, I'd think you were a moron."

I laughed and remembered a few games before, when he'd beaten me in five moves. That wasn't going to happen again. I had a plan this time.

He moved a pawn—*e6*.

The phone rang, an ICU nurse calling to let me know the medevac crew was leaving with the army private I'd operated on that afternoon. He'd been shot in the head by a sniper, and I'd worked all afternoon to stabilize him.

"Thanks for letting me know. I'll be praying for him," I said. I hung up the phone, then noticed that Aaron was shaking his head.

"What?" I said.

"Prayer? Why do you say things like that? Isn't it disingenuous?"

I tilted my head. "What do you mean?"

He tapped a finger on the board. "I mean you're a scientist. Are you just trying to make the nurse feel better? You can't actually believe that stuff."

"I do believe it," I said.

"You really think there's something after this life? That we're more than a skin sack of nerves and bones and electrical impulses? What scientific evidence do you have to support those ideas?"

I shook my head. "What scientific evidence do you have to support yours? Other than the tautology of 'I believe in science because science says it's true'?"

Aaron sniffed. "Whatever. I'm glad it makes you feel better. I'm surprised though."

Here it was again. I'd faced the "you can't really believe in God if you're a scientist" attitude ever since I worked in an immunology lab before medical school. It usually goes unspoken, but the raised eyebrows, mild smirks, and shaken heads say it loudly enough: faith and science don't play well together for most "real" scientists.

"It doesn't, actually," I said.

His eyes opened wider. "How do you mean?"

"Sometimes believing in God makes it harder for me."

"I've never heard that before," Aaron said.

"All this death, war, the things people do to each other. I don't understand how God allows it." I moved another pawn—*g4*.

Aaron shook his head. "That's the whole point. If there is a God, he's either a big jerk or he's a negligent parent. No way all this bad stuff happens in a world ruled by the *loving God* you religious people pray to."

"That's one way to look at it. But doesn't the idea that there's just *nothing* after we die scare you?"

He smiled, and his head moved in an ambiguous way—somewhere between *No* and *I pity you for your childish beliefs.*

"You know what scares me?" Aaron said.

I shrugged. "What?"

He moved his queen—*Qh4*. "How bad you are at chess. Checkmate."

I looked down at the board, replaying the four-move defeat in my mind. Aaron began resetting the board for another game when a thud shook my trailer—think of the feeling inside your car when the guy next to you at the stoplight is playing his hip-hop music loudly. A second later the low growl of the Alarm Red siren began.

Mortar attack.

We grabbed our body armor and helmets and ran outside. Fifty yards away was a concrete bunker. We spent the next hour there listening to several explosions around the base, each answered by the almost subsonic *booomp* sound of our guys' return fire.

I leaned against the bunker wall with my helmet low over my eyes and prayed that God would deliver us through the attack. *"A big jerk or a negligent parent,"* Aaron had said. I wouldn't want to believe in that God either. But something was nagging at my soul in the darker places I didn't let myself look into often. Did I really believe, or did I believe I was *supposed* to believe? Was my faith legitimate, and if so, how would I respond to Aaron's statement about who God is?

Before I found the answers, the all-clear alarm sounded. The attack was over. We stepped out of the bunker, and I automatically said "Thank you, God" under my breath.

"If there's really a God, thank him for me too," Aaron said. "I have to make rounds. Rematch tomorrow?"

I nodded. "Sure. I can use the humility."

He walked away into the night. I went back to my room since my only patient was on his way to Germany by then. Attempts to sleep failed because every time I tried, I heard either Aaron's *"big jerk"* line again or the roar of the F-16s taking off for their night patrols.

I thought about my recent life: a brother paralyzed by a stroke, my marriage on life support when I deployed to Iraq, my grandfather's death two weeks before I left, and months of seeing the worst things that can happen to a human body, all while being shot at every day. I missed my kids, was still rattled by the near-miss mortar from a few hours before, and wanted to go home. The Bible is full of stories about how much God loves me and wants to take care of me. But on that night in Iraq, Aaron's logic, like his chess skill, seemed hard to defeat. As much as I wanted to default to my "it's gonna be okay" baseline, it didn't ring true right then.

Whoever said there are no atheists in foxholes probably never actually went to war.

10

Rats in the Cellar

Surely what a man does when he is taken off his guard is the best evidence for what sort of a man he is? Surely what pops out before the man has time to put on a disguise is the truth? If there are rats in a cellar you are most likely to see them if you go in very suddenly. But the suddenness does not create the rats: it only prevents them from hiding.

—C. S. LEWIS, *Mere Christianity*

East Alabama Medical Center
Opelika, Alabama

Two weeks after Joey's surgery, he had an appointment to see me in the office to have his stitches removed. I'd told Lisa his story and that he reminded me of the kid in Iraq we called Lucky because he'd been hit in the head by a bullet that was falling from the sky and had lost much of its velocity. The kid had a skull fracture but little brain injury. Joey, with his crushed skull and brain hemorrhage that led to early diagnosis and possible cure of his brain tumor, was the new Lucky.

But winning the Mega Millions life lottery by being spared from GBM was just the beginning of Lucky Joey's big win.

Joey's blessings continued when the feds dropped the charges against him. Compassion for his medical plight, a pesky pro bono lawyer alleging excessive force, and some apparent question about the lack of a warrant for entering Joey's meth lab congealed into Agent Keaton's departure from the ICU a few days after Joey's surgery.

The morning of Joey's appointment, Lisa and I stepped off the elevator at our office building and looked into our waiting room. I touched Lisa's arm and motioned with my head. "That's the guy I told you about. Joey."

"The poor guy who got his head bashed in?"

"Yeah. That's his sister sitting next to him."

Joey's bruises had healed, and his face was no longer swollen. He wore a black T-shirt with white letters spelling out *SUCK IT.*

He and his sister, Louise, sat in one corner of the waiting room; Samuel and Christy were on a sofa next to them. A few other patients waited, reading magazines or Kindle books, their faces a mix of the things we worry about in waiting rooms.

Am I going to be okay?

When will the pain go away?

How much work will I miss?

Will I need surgery?

When we walked into the office, Samuel looked up and smiled. "Hey, Doc. Good to see you two."

"Hi, Samuel, how are—"

"How long do we have to wait out here, man?" Joey said before I could finish greeting Samuel.

Lisa smiled, slipping into the graceful customer-relations role she comes by so naturally (one of the many things she did incredibly well in running our practice). "Won't be long, sir. The nurse will call you back shortly."

Samuel pointed at Joey's head. "Hey, looks like we had the same barber."

Joey turned toward him, looking as if he'd swallowed acid. "That ain't funny. I have a *brain tumor*," he said, stretching the words out to fill the space between them.

Samuel smiled. "Join the club, brother. Mine's a GBM, glee-o-blast-o-ma," he said. "Grade IV. What's yours?"

Joey's right eye closed partway. "Something I can't pronounce. Don't matter though. I'm gonna die."

Louise threw up her hands. "What's wrong with you? You can't say that. Doc already told you you've got a great prognosis."

Joey shook his head. "I been dying my whole life. That's how it goes for me. Besides, I looked it up on the computer. Sixty percent five-year survival. I've never won anything that had sixty to forty odds."

Samuel smiled. "Have a little faith. Old Dr. Google tells me my five-year is about 9 percent."

"So you're screwed too," Joey said.

Samuel's hazel eyes and broad smile in that moment have stayed with me over the years. He looked at Christy for a beat, put his hand on her knee, and then focused on Joey's face. "Me? Shoot, no. Coach Bear Bryant said quitting's the easiest cop-out in the world. I'll never give up. Nine percent's about nine times more than I need. You hang in there, brother. The good Lord and Doc will get you through this."

A few minutes later I stepped into exam room number 5 to see Samuel and Christy. Christy looked up at me through red eyes as I closed the door. She wiped her face with a tissue. "I'm sorry, Doc. That man, he just upset me."

"It's okay," I said. "I'm trying to change his attitude."

I pulled up Samuel's latest scan and opened the prior study next to the new one. Just like three months before, I felt their eyes watching for my reaction as I read the study.

"No new disease," I said. "And those new spots we saw last time"—I pointed at the screen—"here and here have gotten a little smaller."

This is a critical moment in the relationship between doctor and patient. I've seen it dozens of times, and it's always the same. Apparent good news on a scan in the setting of an incurable disease is a Gordian knot: Do I go with the joy they want me to feel, allow the notion to set in that maybe he's the one who will be cured? Or do I play the realist? Whatever GBM seems to be doing, it's always *really* growing somewhere. At some subcellular level it's in there mutating, plotting, preparing to pounce and pile-drive his nervous system into oblivion. No matter how I tug on this, it won't come undone.

I proceeded carefully. "How's the drug trial going?"

Samuel smiled. "It's been good. Hasn't made me sick at all, and Dr. Grimes says she's encouraged."

Christy touched his arm. "Tell him about the—"

"I'm really feeling great," he said.

Christy cleared her throat. "Tell him."

Samuel smiled with one side of his mouth, but his eyes didn't move. "It's not his specialty. I don't want to bother him."

"What is it?" I said.

"He's been having nosebleeds," Christy said.

Samuel waved his hand. "It was just a little."

Christy cocked her head.

"Okay," he said, "it's happened three times. Once I sneezed and it bled for a few minutes. The other two times I woke up with some blood on my pillow."

Surgeons keep a list of all the things related to our operations that could possibly happen to our patients. We receive all kinds of phone calls after people go home from surgery, and part of the art of medicine is knowing when to worry about a particular complaint, when to reassure patients, and when to tell them to see a different doctor about the problem.

When I perform a carpal tunnel release on a patient's wrist and she calls me three days later to tell me she's having chest pain, I can be sure the problem is not a complication of the surgery. But chest pain is always worrisome, so I tell the patient to go to the emergency department immediately and see a doctor.

After back surgery, if a patient calls to say he can't smell anything, I know it has nothing to do with his operation and it's not likely to be important. I tell him that if it's still bothering him in a few days, he should call his regular physician. Most things stop on their own, usually after we quit worrying about them.

I knew nose-bleeding was not directly related to Samuel's tumor or the surgery I'd performed six months ago. It would have been easy to tell him to see an ear, nose, and throat guy or to call his primary-care doctor. But a subtle nudge in my gut told me to worry. Samuel was getting a drug designed to shrivel up the blood vessels that tumors recruit to supply themselves with oxygen. I remembered reading somewhere that hemorrhage was a potential complication, but Samuel was the first patient I'd taken care of who was on the drug.

I put my hand on his shoulder. "When did it start happening?"

Samuel shrugged. "Four days ago."

The problem with brain imaging—really with any kind of medical testing—is that it is static. It represents a moment at which what you're seeing was true. Telling your patient he is okay based on a static picture is accurate only if you understand this point. Samuel's scan was six days old.

"It's probably just your sinuses," I said. "But let's be safe. I'll get you a CT scan of your brain and sinuses. That way we'll know there's no bleeding in your head."

Samuel smiled. "All right, Doc, but it'll have to wait. I'm taking this little lady to the beach this weekend." He winked at me. "A little grown-up time without the kids, if you know what I mean."

"Samuel!" Christy said.

As we go through our lives, we tend to think of things in phases—school, career, retirement. We think of those times in the context of our family: our kids being born, us raising them, and the years beyond. We feel young and think we have a lot of time, until one day we wake up and realize we're not young anymore and don't have that much time after all.

In this moment I could see all those perceived timelines passing between Samuel and Christy. What would you feel if you knew ahead of time that the next vacation you took with your spouse would probably be your last one?

He reached over and pulled her close. "Doc's a big boy, babe. He can handle a little straight talk. Right, Doc?"

I smiled and shook my head. "You're a piece of work. I want you in the hospital first thing Monday morning for that scan. And call me if you have any more trouble."

"Whatever you think, Doc. But it's really not a big deal."

I took another look at the monitor. His tumor really was smaller. Maybe this new drug would finally be the one. Maybe Samuel would be my miracle cure, the answer to all my prayers about GBM. He looked good—the swelling and discoloration gone from his scalp, his hair starting to grow back, his muscles strong, and his University of Alabama tattoos and *Roll Tide Roll* T-shirt as loud as ever.

"I'm sure you're right," I said. "But let's be safe. I'll call you after I see the scan."

"Okay, Doc, if you say so. Hey, I got a question." He looked down for a moment, and when he looked back at me, his eyes were glassy.

"Shoot," I said.

"That guy out there"—he waved his hand in the direction of the waiting room—"he said I'm screwed. You don't think so too, do you?"

Christy made a soft *humph* sound with her mouth closed.

I shook my head. "His name is Joey. And he thinks everybody's screwed. It's how he looks at the world. You worry about you, okay?"

He blinked twice and slowly nodded, measuring me. "Right. I'm gonna pray for him. It's a hard life if you believe the world's out to get you. Scary place to live."

Samuel took Christy's hand and waved goodbye as Lisa walked them out of the office. I wrote his progress note in the computer: *Six-month recheck, tumor size reduced, neurologically intact. Wound healed. Complains of nosebleeds X3. Plan: CT scan on Monday (patient traveling this weekend). Will discuss with oncology. Potential complication of the trial drug? Follow-up three months with new MRI.*

I saved the note, wrote myself a reminder to call Dr. Grimes about Samuel's nosebleeds, and headed off to see Joey in room 4. The other rooms were full as well, more people living out their stories of brain tumors, trauma, back pain, or aneurysms. The various maladies of the nervous system brought folks from three states to my office every week. All of them believed I could fix them.

I knew that, at least in Samuel's case, I could diagnose and to some degree delay the progression and ultimate outcome of his disease, but I could not cure it. If there were a solution to his problem, it would come through radiation, a chemotherapy drug, a clinical trial, or—more likely—prayer.

How many prayers were wafting upward from the rooms in my office that day? Was anyone listening to them? Or did God have a return-to-sender filter for prayers about GBM?

Samuel looked healthy that day. And he'd told Joey to have a little faith. Jesus said if we had faith even as big as the tiny mustard seed, we could move mountains.[11] This big country boy, himself terminal with humankind's most fatal disease, trying to boost the morale of a guy not half as sick. Amazing.

I made a mental note not to have Samuel and Joey in the office at the same time again; a bad attitude is as contagious as a virus in a waiting room, and Samuel needed all the hope he could maintain. If he gave up on himself, nothing could save him.

Joey sat in the exam chair with his arms folded, scowling like a kid who'd been put in time-out. Before I could say hello, Louise spoke up. "Joey has something to say to you."

"I'm sorry for what I said to that dude," he said without making eye contact.

I sat on a stool and rolled in front of him. "You made his wife cry."

He sucked in his lower lip; his jagged front incisor looked like the granite face of the Matterhorn. He sniffed. "Didn't mean to. It's just this . . . this really sucks."

We talked while I removed his stitches. "Your wound is healing well," I said. "And since your tumor is only grade II, the oncology doc isn't recommending any additional treatment right now." One of the sutures was buried in his scalp, and I had to press the scissors into the tissue a little to cut it.

"Hey, that hurts, man," Joey said. Louise moved to stand at his side. She took his hand to help him through the pain while I dug out the rest of his stitches. "But what happens next?" he asked.

"We're going to repeat your MRI scan every three months for a couple of years and then less often after that."

He nodded. "And what if it comes back?"

I looked into his eyes. "Then I'll take it out, and we'll radiate it."

"Probably kill me," he said.

"Probably deserve it," Louise said. She giggled at her own joke and patted his shoulder.

"Shut up, Lou," he said.

I bandaged Joey's head and said goodbye. As I opened the door, Louise said, "Doc, hold on."

I turned and she stood face to face with me. Her pale skin stretched thin over her bones, and her pulse bounced over her clavicle. "Gramma told me to thank you for saving Joey's life. We're all she's got left 'cept Jesus."

"Tell her I said hello and she's welcome."

"She also told me to tell you she's praying for you. Lord knows you need it, having to take care of my idiot brother."

Joey raised his hands. "*Shut up,* Lou! Doc, tell her to shut up."

"You two are like eight-year-olds," I said. "I'll see you in three months."

"Doc?" Joey said.

"Yes?"

"Tell that dude I'm sorry for what I said."

"I will," I said. "And I'm praying for you, Joey."

He blinked once. "Don't bother. I got Gramma and Lou all over me for that. Pray for that other guy. He seems to believe in it."

A few minutes later I wrote my progress note for Joey's visit: *Two-week post-op after evacuation of intracerebral hematoma, repair of skull fracture, and resection of incidentally discovered right frontal grade II astrocytoma. Neurologically intact, currently no symptoms. Repeat MRI three months.*

I went on seeing patients, a typically busy morning of a typically busy week. I thought about the things I believed . . . and the things I knew.

I believed that God could heal Samuel, even though he had never chosen to heal a patient with GBM in my experience or in the collective experience of any neurosurgeons I'd known or read reports from. I believed that God had been merciful to Joey, but I didn't really understand why. Joey shook his fist at God, lived a life of bad choices, and had a me-against-the-world attitude, yet his tumor was found early and possibly cured.

And I knew that poor Samuel, the nicest guy in the world, was going to die. I knew it. Did it make sense to pray about that, to pray for God to do something he never does? Was I misleading him by encouraging him to go through the trials, take the drugs, deal with all the side effects when I already knew what was going to happen?

Regardless of what happened, though, it was becoming clear that I was learning something from Samuel. C. S. Lewis wrote about how the sudden trials of life can reveal the rats in the cellars of our character.[12] Samuel's problems had shone a bright light into who he really was, and I didn't know whether I would have stood up so well if it had been me. Joey certainly hadn't.

But seeing Samuel handling it so faithfully and with such strength made it much harder for me to play the all-knowing doctor with him. Somehow, despite having gone through this with many other families, this case—this sweet-hearted giant—had really gotten under my skin.

I knew Samuel had a strong faith, and I believed it would never waver.

I knew that nice people often die from cancer but scumbags somehow often survive it, and I believed that was completely unfair.

I knew Joey was a lifelong doubter, and I believed he would never change.

I knew I needed to call Dr. Grimes about Samuel's nosebleeds, although I believed she would tell me not to worry.

I didn't know at the time—and I wouldn't have believed it if you'd told me—that I was wrong about essentially everything.

11

Side Effects

As the two-thousand-year-old saying goes, you can have eyes
and still not see.
But a hard life improves the vision.

—ALEKSANDR SOLZHENITSYN, *Cancer Ward*

The problem of neurology is to understand man himself.

—DR. WILDER PENFIELD

Oncologists are first scientists, with a deep and broad grasp of the various
areas of scientific endeavor relevant to the understanding and treatment of
human cancers. They can casually tell you, for example, the three-month survival
advantage of a group of mice exposed to a given chemotherapeutic agent compared
with placebo controls for any tumor you mention, off the top of their heads, over
dinner.

Oncologists are pragmatic but eternally optimistic, accustomed to loss but ever
quixotic, and always ready to mount a fight against whatever ails you despite knowing better than anyone what the literature says about your chances of survival.

They are also among the best doctors in the world. That's of necessity because
their patients are the sickest of the sick. This is true both because of the world in
which they live—constantly battling cancer's indefatigable desire to kill their

patients—and because of the methods with which they carry out their business. The treatments they prescribe often create such horrific physiological aberrations that oncologists must be masters at managing infections, depressed immunity, fevers, anemias, and a plethora of other issues equally capable of mortally wounding the patient. It doesn't do much good for a chemotherapy agent to reduce a patient's tumor volume by 80 percent if it also suppresses her white blood cells so much that she contracts a fungal infection that melts her brain.

This produces among them a personality I've seen elsewhere only during my military career, in fighter pilots and airborne rangers: a core value that no matter the danger, they will press forward into the fight and give it their all.

Oncologists live in the gray zone between *Primum non nocere* ("First, do no harm") and *Melius anceps remedium quam nullum* ("It is better to do something than nothing"), the guiding principle of surgeons and other doctors who cannot stand by and only *think* about their patients' problems.

The best of them are something more than scientist and soldier. They are deeply human. Parental. Believers. Advocates for life who say, "We will get through this together."

But even among such a bright, talented, and dedicated group of doctors, Dr. Wilma Grimes stands out. She's six feet tall with silver hair—think Emmylou Harris—and carries herself with a regal elegance reminiscent of a young Katharine Hepburn.

She's unflappable in a crisis. I once stood at the end of a patient's stretcher with her when the patient coughed up a blood clot that sailed through the air and onto the front of her white lab coat. Dr. Grimes never moved; she kept her hands in her pockets and said to the patient, "I bet that feels better."

So when I called her the day Samuel told me about his nosebleeds, I knew she would tell me whether to be concerned and would know what to do.

My call went to voice mail, but a moment later she sent me a text message:

In a meeting. What's up?

I replied:

Our patient S is having nosebleeds. Anything to worry about?

Thirty seconds later my phone rang, and her tone of voice answered my question. "Lee, get him to come in right now. Tell him it's urgent. With this experimental drug any kind of bleeding has to be taken very seriously."

"I'll call him," I said. "But he said it's only happened three times. Once after he sneezed and twice on his pillow in the morning."

She was silent for a second. "We'll hope it's nothing, but he needs to come see me today."

I hung up and tried Samuel's cell, hoping to catch him before they left for the beach. No answer.

Lisa pulled up Christy's number. Also no answer.

They didn't have a home phone.

I called both cell phones again and left messages for them to call as soon as they could. And I sent them a text:

Dr. Grimes wants to see you today. She says it's very important.
Please call.

With no other way to contact them, I went back to seeing patients. That afternoon I submerged myself in other people's problems. Brain tumors and aneurysms are the reason most neurosurgeons entered the specialty, but the much more common pathologies of the human intervertebral disk pay the bills. I listened to the stories, investigated the causes, made the diagnoses, and scheduled tests, treatments, and procedures.

But I kept thinking about Samuel. He never called back.

That night while we were having dinner, Dr. Grimes texted:

Have you heard back from S?

I wrote back:

No. Has not returned calls.

The next morning Lisa and I were watching *SportsCenter* when my cell phone rang. It was Christy.

I answered, "Christy, why didn't you guys call back yesterday?"

"Sorry. We had our phones off. What's going on?"

"Dr. Grimes wants Samuel to come in as soon as possible. She's concerned about the nosebleeds."

"I understand, Doc. But we're having such a good time. He says he feels great, and he wants to stay here this weekend. We'll get the scan on Monday, okay?"

We got off the phone, and all day long I thought about what I would do in Samuel's situation. I couldn't blame him for wanting a weekend off from dealing with his brain cancer. I needed a weekend off, and I didn't have something catastrophic brewing in my cerebrum. Lisa and I had a date scheduled for that night, and I was looking forward to it. What if I knew there were only a few more months left to enjoy her company?

I didn't have much time to wander down that trail of thought because my beeper went off.

Call Dr. Stinson in the emergency department.

———————

Human behavior never stops fascinating me. I was drawn to neuroscience in part because the brain is the only organ that is more than it seems to be on the surface. Kidneys and livers and hearts have discrete and well-defined purposes. Brains, however, *do things* like form, store, and retrieve memories, send and receive signals, make hormones, and regulate movements. But somewhere in that box of electrical signals lies *you:* your personality, your moral code, your *mind*. While two people with essentially identical brain imaging can be totally different—in their behavior, their attitudes, their *selves*—any two hearts of the same weight and the same electrical signals and cell health will pretty much behave identically. This is why you can swap hearts out like car batteries.

But even when brains *look* the same, they don't produce the same person.

And even when someone's brain looks normal on a scan, it doesn't mean the person is good, smart, wise, talented, happy, or capable of making good decisions.

When I reached the ED, Stinson ambled up, all knees and elbows as he pulled off a surgical gown. An operating mask hung off his face, and a blue surgery cap sat too high on top of his head, the way "surgeons" on television wear them. If it were black, you could have imagined Honest Abe's stovepipe hat, but instead it just looked silly.

"What in the world are you doing?" I said.

"I put a central line in your patient. Car accident. The moron broke his head open again. I already told the operating room desk you'd need a room."

"Which patient?"

He handed me a chart, patted my shoulder, and stepped past me to toss his gown and gloves into the trash. "I gotta run. We've got theater tickets."

"Don't tell me *Our American Cousin* is playing at Ford's," I said.

Stinson shook his enormous head. "*Fiddler on the Roof* at the Fox in Atlanta. You should see it. Do your Gentile soul some good."

"Watch your back," I said.

"Like I've never heard that one before. See ya. Tell your guy he's running out of lives."

Stinson walked away, and I looked down at the chart: "Wallace, Joey."

Joey sighed deeply and wiped snot from his face with the back of his hand. He looked as if he'd just had a long nap, and he smiled with one corner of his mouth when he saw me at the foot of his bed.

"Hey, Doc," he said.

His right eye was swollen shut, and his wound—the one I'd only recently re-moved sutures from—was bleeding. I could see the stark white of underlying skull through a laceration that ran perpendicular to the incision line, visible because the gauze-and-tape dressing Stinson had placed on it was now in Joey's right hand. Exposed bone meant Stinson was right: surgery was necessary. No date for me that night.

"You pulled off your bandage, Joey."

He looked at his hand with the quizzical face of an infant when he sees his own hand move by, unaware it belongs to him. "Bandage? What happened?"

His left hand moved up to his neck, where Stinson's central IV line was taped down. I grabbed Joey's hand and pulled it away. "Easy. Rip that out and you'll lose a lot of blood."

"I don't know how I got here," he said.

I glanced at the chart. As I suspected, Stinson had given Joey a dose of Versed to sedate him while he placed the line. Versed is a great short-term anesthetic, but it also creates short-term amnesia. As we say, "Versed means never having to say you're sorry."

His left eye glazed over again, but the half-life of Versed is short, and it wears off quickly. He should have been awake by then.

I looked at the chart and saw the urine drug screen: plus signs next to cocaine, benzodiazepines, THC (marijuana), methamphetamine. Blood alcohol level was three times the legal limit for driving. Concussion plus drugs equals intermittent consciousness.

He blinked and his eye cleared again. "I don't know how I got here," he repeated.

"You crashed your car."

Joey's lazy smile faded; a look crossed his face as if he remembered the accident. "I had a fight with Gramma and Lou."

A nurse pulled back the curtain. "Doctor, the operating room is ready."

"They won't shut up about me going to church," Joey said.

"Give him some antibiotics and some more Versed, please. I'll see you upstairs," I said to the nurse. She nodded and walked away to get the medicine.

"They think I have a problem." Joey sat up in the bed and reached for his wound, but I pushed him back.

"Joey, you need to relax. You're going to hurt yourself. If you don't stay down, I'll have to have them restrain your hands."

"Tell them to get off my back, Doc. I'm sick. They shouldn't give me such a hard time."

I've noticed something about addicts over the years. At some point they realize the choice they're making to get high rather than deal with real life. Then they have to justify it to themselves, which usually involves blaming someone or something else for whatever it is that makes them "need" their drug of choice. After that, their lives become about alliances: find the people who will take their side and enable them, and either ignore all others or see them as the enemy.

I wasn't going there with Joey.

"You're lucky to be alive. I'm sure they're just concerned for you." I looked at my watch. "Listen, we've got to get you upstairs and put your head back together."

"They're always telling me I've got a drug problem," Joey said. "But they don't understand how much *pain* I have." He sucked his cheeks in as if he tasted something sour. "They don't know how bad I *hurt*."

The nurse came back in with the medications I'd ordered. She reached up to the IV bag and began to infuse the Versed into Joey's line.

"Tell them . . ." Joey's left eye began to glass over again. "To leave . . ." His speech began to slur. "Me alone . . ." His head fell back onto the pillow, and he was out.

I made eye contact with the nurse, who shook her head. "He's a piece of work."

I looked down at Joey, whose face, despite his bloody head and a lifetime of bad choices, bore the peaceful look of a child with no cares in the world.

Versed means never having to say you're sorry.

———

As trauma cases go, Joey's was straightforward. He'd cracked the screws off the piece of his skull I'd repaired a couple of weeks before, when the DEA agent clubbed him. The skull flap had been driven down onto the surface of Joey's brain and had caused a small amount of bleeding that had already stopped by the time I got to it.

I'd just repaired his skull again and closed his scalp, which now had a jagged, star-shaped wound instead of the clean semicircle I'd created before, when my cell phone rang. My OR nurse, Karen, answered it for me while I put in the last few stitches.

"Dr. Warren's phone," she said.

I saw Karen's face change. Phone calls are like playing Russian roulette when you're a surgeon. It could be your wife calling to check on your dinner date, your plumber calling with a bid on that leaky faucet, or any of the other thousands of reasons normal people's phones ring.

But Karen's been working in surgery with me for years, and those calls don't drain her face or widen her eyes. This one did.

That's the other kind of call surgeons receive.

"Doc, you'd better take this," she said.

———

Fear has its own conversational rhythms. Stuttering breaths, molars clicking as the jaw spasms between waves of tears, speech rising in pitch and then crashing when the air runs out, a quick shallow breath, then starting over again.

"Christy, take a deep breath," I said. "I can't understand you."

I heard her draw the air in as she gathered herself. The tone lower now, more controlled: "I came in to check on Samuel. He was taking a nap. There's blood everywhere in the bed. I can't wake him up."

———

Two hours later the flight medics unloaded Samuel and rolled his stretcher into the ED. When I see this happen, I always flash back to Iraq, watching young men roll into a hospital after bombs or bullets crashed into their brains and slammed our destinies together. Samuel's war was just as real, against a different enemy.

His left pupil was blown, a sign of devastation in his brain stem.

The CT scan showed a massive hemorrhage in his left frontal and temporal lobes, which had shifted his brain from left to right and trapped the fluid in his ventricles. Draw straws to decide how he would die: hydrocephalus, brain-stem compression, continued hemorrhage.

The drug trial's most feared complication: hemorrhage.

His face and his lower body were also covered in blood from the massive nasal and rectal hemorrhages he'd had at the same time the arteries in his brain were exploding. His blood count was dangerously low, which could kill him all by itself even if I could save him from his brain bleed.

Christy had to drive from Florida, so she would be another hour. I had to get Samuel to surgery immediately, or he'd be dead before she arrived.

Maybe anyway.

I looked down at Samuel and prayed. *Please not tonight, God.*

⸻

The ICU is a place where, in every room, desperation and hope slug it out to see who'll be the champ. Beeping monitors, hissing ventilators, and humming IV pumps push their notes into the air, mingling with the stale hints of iodine and body fluids and waning faith. Overworked nurses are spread too thin, trying to keep up with the promised *intensive care* in this unit.

And I stood at the end of Samuel's bed, next to Christy and Dr. Grimes, explaining what had happened in the operating room.

"The clot is out and the pressure's off his brain," I said. "We gave him six units of blood, and now his vitals are stable."

Christy wiped her eye, but it was already dry. With a shudder she said, "What happens now?"

"We wait," Dr. Grimes said.

Christy's face was vacant, as if the plug in the bottom of her emotional sink had been pulled and all her feelings had drained out. I've seen that same look in people who have survived traumas in which their friends died and in soldiers who've seen their buddies killed. "There was so much blood," she said.

I squeezed her shoulder. "We'll be praying. I'll call you if anything changes tonight."

I walked out of Samuel's room and stuck my head into Joey's, which was the next bed down the hall. His head was wrapped in a white cotton bandage, and he was sleeping soundly. The nurse was adjusting his IV pump, and she looked up and saw me in the doorway.

"Hey, Jackie," I said.

Jackie is a retired army colonel with twenty years of ICU nursing experience, and she's been running the neuro ICU unit at our hospital since she left the military. She keeps things on her unit squared away, and she's about as tough as they come. But on this night she had slumped shoulders, and her scrub top was partly untucked on one side. She looked up at the sound of my voice and shot me a look.

She raised a finger to her mouth—"Shh"—and stepped toward me, then pushed me out into the hall.

"I finally got him settled," she said. "Wake him up and you'll answer to me, Major."

She's the only person who still calls me Major, probably to remind me that she outranks me.

"Yes, ma'am. Rough night?" I said.

She nodded. "He's not the most pleasant guy. Seems to think we're all trying to hurt him. I'm gonna keep him sedated overnight," she said, not asking. "I'm sure you don't mind."

"Of course not. But the guy next door's a lot sicker. Call me if his brain pressure goes up."

She held up both hands and her jaw fell open. "Like you had to tell me that. Now get out of here before you wake up my patient, Major."

I went to the nurses' station and logged in to the computer to write a few orders. Then I walked toward the exit of the unit, thinking about my two patients: Samuel sinking, Joey rising.

Desperation and hope, next-door neighbors.

Sometimes in the quiet of the night, you can stand still in the hallway of the ICU and feel the negative-pressure circulation moving air around you in the hallway. If you pay attention, you can almost hear, amid the beeps, hisses, and hums, another current: the prayers flowing around all those rooms, from families and loved ones and conscious patients, from nurses, and sometimes even from doctors. They flow and mix and waft generally upward and out to wherever they go.

I stood there that night, near two brains I'd seen and touched and tried to save, and wondered whether anyone was listening.

12

Stupor, Coma, Science, and Faith

Faith is the assurance of things you have hoped for, the absolute conviction that there are realities you've never seen.

—HEBREWS 11:1, Voice

Faith is the great cop-out, the great excuse to evade the need to think and evaluate evidence. Faith is belief in spite of, even perhaps because of, the lack of evidence.

—RICHARD DAWKINS

The definitive text on disorders of human consciousness is Plum and Posner's *Diagnosis of Stupor and Coma*. I had to basically memorize it during my training because brain surgeons and neurologists have to figure out what's happening inside a person's head when we can't wake the person up. MRI scans and electroencephalograms can tell you a lot, but they take time and aren't always available.

Plum and Posner have taught generations of budding brain doctors how to rapidly figure out what and where the problem inside the person's skull is, determine the prognosis, and know whether anything can be done to improve things.

The cerebral cortex is the top of the nervous system, the outermost part of the brain. It's what you imagine when you think of a brain, the folds and wrinkles of the cauliflower-looking thing you've seen in pictures before. The stuff that happens there produces interactions, personality, and basic outward behaviors. When the cortex is working, a person is awake and able to participate in an examination.

I stood beside Samuel's bed the next morning with a penlight in my hand, Plum and Posner in my head, and gnawing fear in my gut. Samuel had been chemically sedated overnight to let his brain swelling go down, and an hour earlier, I had asked his nurse, Jackie, to stop the drugs so we could see whether he would awaken. She would go through the exam with me and document it in Samuel's chart.

The two-minute neurological examination basically works from the top (the cerebral cortex) down to the bottom (the medulla oblongata) of the central nervous system to determine how badly injured someone is. Since the cortex processes and interacts with a person's environment, we start the exam by observing whether the patient has his eyes open.

Samuel's were closed.

"Open your eyes, Samuel," I said.

No response.

I put my hand on his chest and rubbed gently. "Samuel, wake up."

Nothing.

I pinched the skin in his armpit a little, trying to stimulate his brain enough to rouse him, and he did not move or open his eyes.

When I pinched a little harder, he flexed his arms a bit at the elbows and slightly pushed his feet down as if he were pressing the gas pedal in a car.

Christy grabbed Samuel's right hand, and he squeezed her fingers slightly; then she leaned down and kissed his cheek. Samuel moved his head toward her a few millimeters and then, almost imperceptibly, began to purse his lips as if he wanted to kiss her too.

"Samuel, honey, I love you! Wake up, baby," Christy said.

This is one of the dirty tricks of the nervous system: certain conditions produce movements that mimic responsiveness, which is very confusing for loved ones and seems awfully cruel at times like this. I am the guy who has to explain to the family what's really happening.

"Christy, he's not really responding to you," I said. "Those are reflexes."

Her eyes flashed as the joy turned to confusion—or was it anger? "But he held my hand."

"I know, but let me finish the exam and I'll explain everything to you."

She folded her arms. I leaned over and lightly stroked Samuel's cheek. He turned toward my hand and began the lip-pursing, sucking motion again. I stroked his right palm, and he flexed his chin muscles. I placed my fingers in his right palm, and he grasped them but did not do so when I tried his left side a second later. I tapped him gently between the eyes, and he blinked every time but never opened his eyes. I pinched his armpit again, and he again flexed his arms and pushed his feet down. *Rooting, suck reflex, palmomental sign, palmar grasp on the right, glabellar sign, decorticate posturing.* I checked off the findings on my mental list and heard Plum and Posner talking it over in my head.

I lifted his eyelids and used my light to look at his pupils. "Left pupil is six millimeters and sluggishly reacts to direct and indirect examination; right pupil is normal."

When I touched his eyes lightly with a cotton swab, he blinked vigorously. "Corneal reflex intact."

I turned his head from side to side while I held his eyes open. His eyes moved to keep looking forward. "Doll's eye reflex intact."

I turned to Christy. "I'm not hurting him, but I have to check his gag reflex. He won't feel it."

I inserted a tongue depressor into Samuel's mouth. I pressed on the back of his tongue, and he gagged hard and coughed over the breathing tube several times. He pulled in several breaths beyond what the ventilator was giving him. "Cough and gag intact; spontaneous respirations intact."

My examination was complete.

Now I had to explain it to Christy.

"He's showing what we call frontal release signs. When we're babies, we grab anything that touches our hands, and we try to feed anytime our faces touch our mothers' breasts. When we're threatened, we try to defend ourselves by pulling our arms up. When something hits us in the face, we blink our eyes to avoid injury."

Christy nodded slowly. Her arms were still crossed.

"When we grow a little, our frontal lobes begin to suppress all those infantile reflexes. It wouldn't be good for us to turn our heads and suck every time something touched our faces. But if you have a frontal lobe injury, especially on the left side, you can lose that suppression, *release* the reflexes. That's what Samuel's doing."

"But he held my hand," she said with less excitement than before. Her eyes shot back and forth between Samuel and me.

"I know. It's hard to understand. But it's just a reflex. He doesn't know we're here right now."

She put her hand on Samuel's shoulder.

"The good news is that his brain stem is doing everything it's supposed to," I said. "His pupils are almost back to normal. The left side is still sluggish, but it's a lot better than it was yesterday. His other signs are normal, and he's breathing on his own beyond the machine support. Right now it looks like the injury is only in his frontal lobe and upper midbrain. We have to wait, give him more time to see if he will improve."

She drew in a deep breath and sighed heavily. "He has to. He's strong, and he has a lot of faith. And we need him, Doc. I need him. Please keep praying for him."

"I will," I said. Plum and Posner chuckled inside my skull. *Do you really think God will rewire this guy?*

She opened her mouth as if about to speak when her phone rang. She looked at the screen. "It's my mom. She's watching the kids. I'd better take it. I'll be back for afternoon visiting hours."

She clicked to answer the call as she walked away. I heard her say, "Mom, Samuel held my hand!"

Jackie shook her head. "She can't accept reality."

"It's hard for families. Those movements seem so purposeful, so interactive. Folks always want to believe it's intentional."

She made a *humph* sound. "We believe what we want to believe, don't we, Major? I have to check on my other patient."

After Jackie walked out, I looked down at Samuel and remembered what my atheist friend Aaron had asked me in Iraq: *"You really think there's something after this*

life? That we're more than a skin sack of nerves and bones and electrical im-
pulses? What scientific evidence do you have to support those ideas?"

This is where things get hazy for me. Science has a process—called the scientific method—of investigating things to determine their nature. It's supposed to
start with a hypothesis: "I propose that this is true." Then we're supposed to test the
hypothesis to prove or disprove it, then change our hypothesis based on the results
of those tests. After rigorous testing we can eventually develop scientific laws and
become convinced that something is true. But if we're real scientists, we are obliged
to remain open to further modification of those truths as our ability to look deeper
improves.

Even though the scientific method gives a great framework for learning things
and it holds up over time if we apply it consistently in our search for knowledge,
scientists don't always use the method when it comes to the question of how we all
got here.

Seriously, ask most scientists about the origin of life and they'll say something
like "There was a big bang, and over millions and millions of years, gradual changes
happened in every conceivable combination until one day the right mix of mole-
cules combined to form life."

Then ask, "What caused the big bang?"

They'll say, "We don't know yet."

And if you say, "I think it was God," they will reply, "There is no God. It just
happened."

"How do you know there's no God?" you might ask.

"Because I'm a scientist," they'll say. "I believe only in things I can test and
prove. Obviously, there's no God."

And therein lies my problem as a person of faith who is also a scientist: Scientists like my friend Aaron and even famous ones like Richard Dawkins or Sam
Harris want us to start with the assumption that there is no God and make all our
decisions about life based on what we can test, observe, and explain without invok-
ing the supernatural. According to that approach the biggest single question—How
did we get here?—should be answered only by surmising that everything started
spontaneously, with no God out there lighting the candle.

Essentially, naturalists say, "Obviously there's no God because we can't observe, test, or define him. So we reject any supernatural explanation for anything, and everything has to be explained in natural, scientific terms."

Naturalism has been the religion of scientists ever since Darwin.

I say "religion" in the sense that, in order to stake your entire worldview on a belief system, you've got to have faith in it. You have to believe it, even though you have no absolute proof, and those beliefs have to hold up over time, even when they seem unlikely or when doubt creeps in.

And since the question of how we all got here is beyond science's ability to test and prove, the study of the origin of humanity and life and the universe clearly involves some aspects of inquiry outside the realm of science. So other disciplines, such as philosophy, history, and even theology, have valid claims to aspects of inquiry and knowledge that fall outside science.

Just as it would be silly for a scientist to say, "I do not believe in Julius Caesar because I cannot prove he lived," rational thought tells me it's ridiculous for me to think the same of God. I can't prove God exists, and neither can another scientist prove he does not.

It's not about science.

It's about faith.

I looked down at Samuel and saw his strong muscles and his Bama tattoos and smelled his stale ventilator breath and wondered whether he was more than, as Aaron had put it, "a skin sack of nerves and bones and electrical impulses" and whether in his body somewhere there really was a spirit, a soul, that would live beyond his body's life. It seemed so much easier for me to let him just be a big carbon pile randomly assembled through millions of years of accidents and mutations and lucky breaks.

Then I wouldn't have to admit what I was really feeling: I did believe in God, despite my academic pedigree.

And I did believe Samuel was more than the sum of his parts.

God was real to me, which made me really mad at him right then. Samuel was the good guy. If anyone was a worthless pile of parts, it was Joey. Yet Joey was sleeping off his latest brush with death as if it were just another party weekend. Samuel was probably dying.

Some people use the tragedy and madness of the human condition as a reason to not believe in God, the "I can't believe in a God who would let that happen" argument.

But not liking someone isn't a valid reason to believe that person doesn't exist.

Even for a person of faith, it's hard to understand why bad things happen in life. And some of the most hard-core doubters might agree there is no science that can explain why nice people so often get malignant cancers or die in horrible accidents while their scumbag neighbors run meth labs and survive brain tumors and multiple head injuries.

But faith can't explain that either, at least not in a way that's very palatable. Jesus said it rains "on the righteous and the unrighteous,"[13] but GBM seems to rain on good people a lot more often. People say there's a reason for everything, but I couldn't see the reason for this. I didn't like it.

Plum and Posner reminded me that Samuel's coma meant he would need a tracheostomy and a feeding tube soon. If he survived a few more days like this, he would need long-term life support and all the other things that "vegetables" require to keep them alive.

Science offers no comfort for those facing the harsh realities of life.

God seemed equally unavailable to reassure me that any of this made sense.

My beeper buzzed.

Call Dr. Stinson in the ED.

I put my hand on Samuel's chest and said a little prayer for him.
And one for myself.

13

The Living Dead

A drowning man will catch at a straw.

—well-known proverb

Weirdest thing I've ever seen," Stinson said. He handed me the chart, and I flipped it open while he tore into a bag of Fritos.

"Andrews, Robert," the chart said. He was a fifty-five-year-old man who had never been seen in our ED before. This was strange, since according to his intake form, he lived in Auburn, less than five miles from the hospital.

"His wife's got some records, but she only wants to give them to you. True believer, that one," Stinson said. "I gotta go see a kid with appendicitis in room 8. Let me know what you think about Mr. Andrews." He popped a handful of Fritos into his mouth and headed off to the other side of the ED.

I walked into Mr. Andrews's room and saw something I'd never seen before, which is saying something at this point in my career.

The first thing I noticed was the helmet. He had a silver apparatus on his head that might have been made of aluminum foil, with dozens of wires coming out of it, all connected to some sort of controller that sat on the bed next to him. His eyes were open, but he was staring at the ceiling and did not move when I spoke to him. He had a feeding tube in his nose, the end capped off and taped to his cheek.

His wife sat next to him in a chair, talking into a cell phone. She looked over at me and held up one index finger in a "hold on a second" way. Next to her on a table were multiple three-inch-thick binders, all with boldface type on their sides: EMORY, UAB, DUKE, UCSF, SLOAN KETTERING, MD ANDERSON, and several others.

Mr. Andrews was a still-breathing skeleton. Imagine the concentration camp survivor photos or African relief commercials you've seen; he was that thin. I waved my hand in front of his face, and he didn't blink. I clapped my hands and got no response.

As in the old cliché, the lights were on but no one was home.

Mrs. Andrews clicked off her phone and stood. "I'm Sandra. His wife." Her eyes were pale green like sea glass, set deep in an etched, joyless face. She blinked when she talked, but her eyes were as lifeless as her husband's.

"I'm Dr. Warren." I pointed at the helmet on Mr. Andrews's head. "What's this?"

She shuffled through the binders and handed one of them to me. The label read GLIO-WAVE 6000.[14]

"It sends alternating currents through his brain to kill the cancer cells," she said.

I had never heard of such a thing. "Where did you get it?"

She looked at her feet. "It was our last hope. And the last of our money, eighteen thousand dollars. I sold his car to buy it. He won't need a car anyway, at least for a while." She reached down and grasped her husband's hand, but he didn't squeeze hers. I could see all the tendons in his hand and the pulse in his fingers through his translucent skin.

I nodded. A familiar burn began to work its way up my spine, the heat of disgust at the part of the cancer industry that profits from families' hopes. "Why did you bring him in tonight, ma'am?"

She took a tissue from the bedside table and wiped a little drool from her husband's face. "Last week I took him for his last anti-glioplastin treatment at the Center for Cancer Cures[15] in Dallas, and they told me that the tumor is no longer responding. They said he would have to move up to their Level V treatment or he would probably die."

"What's Level V?"

"They said that Dr. Karpowski has discovered an anti-glioplastin protein that works in 95 percent of people with glioblastoma. But it's extremely expensive to make, and so they have to charge fifty thousand dollars for the treatment. I've already taken out a second mortgage, spent all our savings, and borrowed everything I can. There's just nothing left."

"Okay, but why the hospital? Why today?"

"Usually when I speak to him, he responds. Today he's not, so there must be something wrong."

"How does he usually respond? Does he speak?"

She shook her head. "No, he hasn't spoken in a long time. But when I talk to him, he usually moves his right thumb a little. He likes my voice." She brushed his face with the back of her hand and looked into his eyes. "Don't you, baby?"

No response.

"See? There's something wrong—I know it. Can you help us, Doctor?"

This man weighed no more than ninety pounds, and since he was at least six foot two, his weight alone should have told Mrs. Andrews that there was indeed something wrong. As far as I could see, his not moving his thumb was far less surprising than his being alive at all.

"I'm not sure, Mrs. Andrews. I need to know his history. Can you tell me everything he's been through?"

"It's all here in these binders. Start with this one," she said, handing me one labeled MEDICAL HISTORY OF ROBERT Q. ANDREWS 2006–PRESENT.

"Okay," I said, "I'll read through this while we get him an MRI and see what things look like inside his head."

She nodded. "Thank you. I've heard you're good. I just always thought he should go to major medical centers for his treatments. But I would like it if you can be his doctor now."

"We'll have to remove the helmet for the MRI," I said.

A single tear fell from her right eyelashes and ran down her face. She looked at her husband and then back at me. "Just for a few minutes, right?"

"Right," I said. "Just while he's in the scanner."

She wiped her cheek. "Because they said it only works if it stays on all the time."

I nodded. "Ma'am, I can't help him if I don't know what's happening inside his head."

She slowly turned to the machine and held her hand over the power switch. Then she looked at her husband and finally turned back to me. "Okay, but hurry."

I put my hand on her shoulder. "It will only take a short while. I promise." I asked a nurse to order an MRI for Mr. Andrews and went to the doctors' lounge to read through the binder. In my mind I kept seeing Mr. Andrews's lifeless eyes and bony hand, and I remembered what my old chief, Jed, used to say: *"There are some things worse than being dead."*

Mr. Andrews's medical history told me a lot about Mrs. Andrews.

Her record keeping was impeccable, with detailed reports and copies of every encounter, test, procedure, and bill generated over the course of Mr. Andrews's illness. In each phase of his care, Mrs. Andrews had written a brief summary, including how she felt he had been treated, how they were feeling emotionally, and what was to happen next.

It started out fairly typically: He was an accountant, and he'd caught himself making mistakes with numbers. Subtle things but errors he would normally not make. Then the headaches, and before long it was clear to both of them that something was wrong.

Then doctors, scans, a biopsy, and a diagnosis: glioblastoma.

That's when his care became unusual. Because his wife was not going to allow him to die.

"It looks like swiss cheese," the technician said. "How's this guy still alive?"

"I have no idea," I answered. I was sitting in the MRI control room, watching the monitor as Mr. Andrews's images came across the screen. Every *clack-clack-clack* of the scanner generated more data, which the computer turned into a picture of the freak show that used to be a human brain.

Magnetic resonance imaging, or MRI, is not an X-ray technology. There's no radiation involved at all, in fact. It's a marvelous application of particle physics, electrical engineering, differential mathematics, and computer science to molecular and cell biology. Basically, if you put a human body into a very strong magnetic field, almost all the hydrogen atoms in the body would line up with the field. And the few that do not line up can be exploited to give us a picture of what the tissue they make up looks like.

Using math equations that are beyond the scope of this book (by which I mean *I* don't understand them and cannot explain them), the computer can translate this information into highly precise images of the inside of the human body.

And the images of the inside of Mr. Andrews's head were horrifying.

Most of his brain was gone. I could see holes from previous surgeons' work, vast sections of his neuroanatomical landscape that had been carved away by the scalpels and ultrasonic aspirators of guys like me who thought they were helping him. And there was even more damage from the radiation and chemotherapy and all the other things this poor man had been through. On top of that, the MRI revealed that Mr. Andrews had active tumor on both sides of his remaining brain.

The tech's question was unanswerable. I had no idea how this patient was still living. But it was obvious why he was a shell of a human.

Most of his brain was dead.

I started rounds the next morning on the regular nursing floor. Neurosurgery is a split-personality specialty, since 75 percent of our time is spent taking care of non-life-threatening spine problems like ruptured disks and pinched nerves. Those patients, for the most part, are relieved of their pain after surgery and are very happy. We hear a lot of "Thank you" and "I feel so much better." But to keep us from becoming too full of ourselves or thinking we could fix almost anything, God gave us brain surgery.

I rounded on my five postoperative spine patients from the previous few days of surgery. As usual, rounds were fun, with lots of smiles and "You're a miracle worker" comments from people whose arms and legs weren't numb or painful anymore. I sent them all home, and I was confident they would fully recover and get back to their lives.

It's a great feeling being able to help someone who's in so much pain. To know

I have a skill that offers people so much improvement in their quality of life brings me great joy. But once I signed the last discharge summary, it was time to go to the ICU, and my mood darkened.

———

My three patients were in consecutive rooms, 17 through 19. I went to Joey in bed 17 first. Jackie was standing outside Joey's room, her eyes glued to her cell phone.

"Good morning, Colonel," I said. "Updating your Facebook status?"

She quickly slid the phone into the pocket of the crimson scrub blouse she wore, and her face chameleoned into the same color. "Hardly." She straightened herself to her full height—about an inch taller than me. "This guy wore me out last night. I was texting the nursing supervisor to tell her I'm taking tomorrow off. Between him and your other guy, it's been a long shift."

I nodded. "You deserve it. How's he doing?"

"One of the unhappiest people I've taken care of. His head hurts, he hates his family, everyone misunderstands him, and he thinks he has a cold."

"A cold?"

She nodded. "Yeah, he's blown his nose a thousand times overnight. Keeps ringing his call bell for tissues."

I knew in my gut that the odds of Joey having a common cold two days after getting his head crunched in again were slim to none. Runny noses after head injuries make neurosurgeons nervous.

Jackie and I stepped into Joey's room and saw him sitting up, watching a rerun of *The Beverly Hillbillies* on television and eating his runny scrambled eggs. It never stops surprising me how yellow hospital eggs are. It's a color not found in nature and always makes me wonder what they're really made of. Joey had tissues stuffed into each nostril, and the bandage I'd wrapped around his head the night before lay on the bed next to him.

"Mornin', Joey," I said.

His eyes darted toward me for a nanosecond and then back to the television. "Jethro Bodine reminds me of you," he said.

"I have no idea what you're talking about," I said.

Joey flashed a wry smile. "He said he was either gonna be a double naught spy when he grew up or a brain surgeon."

I shook my head. "And to think I could have been James Bond. What's going on with your nose?"

"Won't stop running." He pointed his fork at the screen. "Ooh! *Smokey and the Bandit*'s coming on next!"

I pulled on a pair of exam gloves and stepped up to Joey's bed. "Let me pull those tissues out."

He turned his head toward me but kept his eyes forward, like an owl. "I love that show. Why does that sheriff care 'bout Bandit haulin' some beer around anyway?"

I slowly removed the tissue from each of Joey's nostrils. They were soaked with a bloody yellow-tinged liquid. I asked Jackie for a four-by-four gauze, which I then held under Joey's nose. "Lean forward a little for me, Joey."

When Joey leaned over, pinkish fluid dripped out of his nose. "Dang, that makes my head hurt, Doc. Lemme lie back down. Feels better that way."

I nodded to Jackie, who pressed the button to make Joey's bed flat. I looked at the gauze and saw that the fluid had separated into two circles, a bloody center with a yellowish zone around it. Just as I'd feared.

"Halo sign," I said to Jackie. "Can you get me a sterile sample cup, please, and set him up for a skull base CT scan?"

"Sure thing, Major." She turned and walked out of the room.

"What's a halo sign?" Joey said.

"It means you probably have a spinal fluid leak."

"What's that mean?"

"Your brain makes a couple of cups of fluid every day. It circulates through the brain and all the way down your spine and back and keeps everything protected and cleaned out inside your nervous system. It's called cerebrospinal fluid, or CSF, but we often call it spinal fluid for short."

"Why's it coming out of my nose?"

"When you hit your head again, you most likely cracked the base of your skull. That can allow CSF to leak from inside your head into the sinuses above your nose. Then the only place for it to go is to drip out."

"Great. So now I gotta keep Kleenex stuffed up my nose forever?"

I chuckled. "No. If it's really CSF, we can stop it with a procedure called a lumbar drain."

Joey's face fell. "More surgery? I'm already sick of this place—and all y'all. No offense."

"None taken. It's not a big deal. We can do it right here in the ICU while you watch TV. If we don't stop the leak, you'll get a nasty infection called meningitis."

"Could I die from that?"

I nodded. "Yes. It's really dangerous. But let's not get ahead of ourselves. I need to send some fluid to the lab to test for CSF and get a special CT scan of the bones at the base of your skull to check for a fracture. Then we'll talk about the procedure."

"Wouldn't mind that anyway," he said.

"What? The procedure?"

"No, dying. Gonna die from this stupid tumor anyway."

I put my hand on his shoulder. "Joey, don't be so negative. I already told you that your tumor is under control for now. Who knows what will happen, but you have a good prognosis."

His shoulders slumped a little, and he was quiet for a few seconds. Then he shook his head. "Dang it! Bandit's in trouble."

"I'll see you in a few minutes, Joey," I said.

"Not if I see you first," he said.

———

Bed 18 held Samuel. His nurse was Carl, who was starting a new IV in Samuel's left arm. Carl is one of the smartest and most compassionate nurses I've ever worked with. I smiled. "Good to see you, my friend. How's Samuel?"

Carl looked up from the IV. When I saw his face, I knew the news wasn't good.

"His brain pressure's been okay. But he hasn't had any sedation all night, and I'm not seeing any improvement in his exam. GCS is 3T."

GCS stands for Glasgow Coma Scale, the most common way health-care providers communicate about how a patient is doing neurologically. We examine three things: eye opening (E), speech/verbal communication (V), and movement (M). You can have a minimum score of 1 in each area and a maximum of 6 for movement, 5 for speech, and 4 for eye opening, so the lowest possible score is 3, and the highest possible score is 15.

If a person has a breathing tube in, we use a *T* for "tube" in the verbal score, indicating that the one point the person receives for speech is because of the tube.

Samuel's GCS of 3T, which I verified with a quick exam of my own, meant he scored E1 since he did not open his eyes at all, V1T since he couldn't talk, and M1 since he didn't move during my exam.

A dead person in the morgue has a GCS of 3. The desk my computer is sitting on while I write this book has a GCS of 3. In the absence of chemical sedation, it meant Samuel's brain wasn't working well at all. He was in a deep coma. GCS 3 is the score of near brain death. It's the score of people in a vegetative state, the score that meant I needed to call Christy.

"Better send him down for a CT scan," I said. "I need to make sure there's nothing else I can treat."

"I'll take care of it," Carl said. "Call you when it's done."

"Thanks. Would you please also call his family and ask them to come up?"

He nodded and walked away to order the scan.

I put my hands on Samuel's chest and prayed for him. His chest rose and fell mechanically in time with the ventilator. His skin was warm, and he looked like Samuel. But I knew from his GCS that most of what made him Samuel had been eaten away by his GBM, surgery, radiation, and the massive brain hemorrhage he'd had.

I knew all that, even as I prayed to a God I believed in for something I believed—or maybe just hoped—he could still do.

Until the CT scan was done, there was nothing else I could offer Samuel.

———

Jackie stepped out of Joey's room and followed me into Mr. Andrews's room. The first thing I noticed was the smell. There is an unmistakable odor around people with neurologic injuries who can't care for themselves. When you're in a coma or otherwise impaired and cannot brush your own teeth or drink water, your throat begins to accumulate stuff you normally would swallow, gargle, rinse, or otherwise clear out yourself. Other people can swab out your mouth and brush your teeth, but there's only so much they can do for you.

The result is that after a day or so you start to smell bad.

Nurses call it neuro breath.

Mr. Andrews's lips were dry and rutted with deep cracks like the surface of a desert. His mouth was open, and he took rapid, deep breaths that reminded me of a dog panting, except that every thirty seconds or so he would stop breathing altogether for a few seconds. His Glio-Wave 6000 brain helmet controller beeped in rhythm with his heart monitor. His eyes were closed, and his body was so thin I wondered why he didn't float away.

"How long's he been Cheyne-Stoking like that?" I said.

Jackie shrugged. "All night for me. The other nurse signed him out to me last night, and she said that's how he's been since she got here yesterday morning. Worst neuro breath ever too."

Cheyne-Stokes breathing—the rapid, deep panting pattern followed by short periods of no breathing at all—is a common sign of serious brain injury. We see it in head injury patients and people with brain tumors when they're near death. In his case it wasn't surprising, since most of his brain was gone and I was already wondering how there was enough neuronal activity to keep his body going. But it was a significant change from when I'd seen him the day before, so it was concerning.

"Not a good combination, Cheyne-Stokes in someone with a filthy mouth," I said. "He's blowing that smell all over the room. You want to do some mouth care for him, for all of our sakes?"

"Love to," she said, "but I can't. His wife told us nobody messes with his mouth except for her."

"Why?" I said.

She stepped closer to the bed and lifted her hand to his face. "Because of this."

When she gently touched his upper lip, he pursed his lips and made a vigorous sucking motion for a few seconds.

"That's just frontal release, the sucking reflex," I said.

Her lips formed a little O, and she shook her head. "I know that, Major Obvious. But his wife thinks he's trying to kiss our hands, and it makes her mad. Last night she called Sandi from second shift a tart. She demanded a new nurse and filed an incident report saying Sandi was flirting with her husband. That woman's crazy."

I shook my head. "She's not crazy; she's just desperate. He's dying, and on some level she has to know it."

"Right," she said, "but the helmet, the twenty-five binders of medical records she insists we all read before we can be his nurse . . . it's too much. When's she gonna face reality? It's inhumane what she's doing to this poor man."

"Look, I don't disagree with you. But at least Mr. Andrews isn't aware of what's going on. Based on his MRI, the parts of his brain that could understand anything are all gone. He's not really in there. It's amazing his body keeps going. Don't be too hard on his wife; some people build their whole lives around their spouses. He's not going to last much longer, though. Then she'll have to come to terms with it."

"If you say so. But can you at least tell her to let us clean his mouth up?"

"Get her to come up. I'll handle it. Be back in a few."

She sighed. "Thanks."

The Glio-Wave 6000 beeped.

Mr. Andrews didn't notice.

14

Level-of-Care Choices

Neurosurgeons do things that cannot be undone.

—FRANK VERTOSICK JR., *When the Air Hits Your Brain*

Joey's skull base CT scan showed a tiny fracture line that extended across the roof of his orbit into an area called the cribriform plate. This bone is perforated with multiple tiny holes, through which pass the hairlike fibers of the olfactory nerves. These nerves allow you to smell things, but the thin bone of the cribriform plate they traverse from the nose to the brain creates an opportunity to leak spinal fluid if you happen to crack your skull in just the right way.

The combination of fluid dripping from the nose and a visible skull base fracture meant Joey almost certainly had a CSF leak. The definitive test to prove it—involving an enzyme called beta-2 transferrin—takes three days to get back, since it must be sent out to a reference lab in another city. But if Joey had a CSF leak, he'd have meningitis by the time the labs came back.

I had to do something now.

"My head's hurting again, Doc," Joey said.

"That's because when you sit up, your brain is sagging when the fluid around it drains out your nose. I have to put a drain in your spine to stop the leak."

Jackie lowered the head of Joey's bed again, and he screwed up his face.

"Wait," Joey said. "That don't make no sense. You say the problem is I have a leak, but you want to treat that by taking more fluid out? Ah, man! I missed the end of the movie 'cause you distracted me. Nurse Jackie, did you see what happened?"

She shook her head. "Sorry. I was listening to the major."

"Great," Joey said.

He clicked off the television.

"That's a good point, Joey. Let me explain. When you're leaking spinal fluid from your nose, the fracture can't heal because it's too wet. Like when the seal of your coffee mug gets wet and it keeps leaking."

Joey nodded. "You say the weirdest things. You really think I have a coffee mug?"

"So if I put a drain in at the bottom of your spine and we keep you flat for a couple of days, we can divert the fluid away from the fracture. Most of the time it will heal and stop the leak."

Joey raised an eyebrow. "Most of the time? What happens if it doesn't?"

"Then we have to go back to the operating room."

"And what if we don't do nothing?"

"Then you get a terrible brain infection and die. Is that what you want?"

Joey turned his head and looked out the window. He thought for a few seconds and then sighed. "Like I said, I'm a dead man walking anyway. Don't much matter."

"Joey," I said, "you have to get a better attitude about all this. You're doing great, and we're all working hard to help you. Do you want to just give up? What about Louise and your grandmother? They certainly want you to hang in there."

He slowly nodded. "Okay. Do it."

Christy stood at Samuel's bedside with his brother, Brooks, and the hospital chaplain, Pastor Jon. Brooks had his hands resting on Samuel's chest, and his glassy brown eyes were streaked with red. Christy looked washed out, an almost-transparent version of herself, with a look I've seen too many times—the look of someone whose hopes have been completely replaced with a clear sense of what's really happening.

Pastor Jon had his left arm around Christy's shoulders, and his right hand held a little olive wood cross. He is famous in the hospital for those crosses because anytime someone is sick or in trouble, that person gets a cross from Pastor Jon. I've even got one, which I wear on a cord around my neck in the operating room to hold my wedding ring close to my heart when I'm in surgery.

Pastor Jon wrapped the cord around Samuel's right hand and left the cross in Samuel's grasp. When the wood hit Samuel's palm, he gripped it tightly. I saw Christy's face clinch for a microsecond, and I thought she was going to think he moved intentionally.

"Christy, that's just—" I said before she held her hand up to stop me.

"Frontal release. I know," she said. "After we talked, I googled it. I know he's not doing that on purpose, Doc. I—" Her breath shuddered for a few seconds. "I know. I understand."

Brooks looked up, a doppelgänger of his big brother. "Doc, what did the scan show?"

I held up my iPad, which I'd used to open Samuel's CT from that morning. The radiology tech had run the scan with IV contrast, which I had not ordered since I was looking only for bleeding or a stroke. But the contrast proved useful, as I was about to show Samuel's family. "It's best if I let you see it."

We gathered into a small circle, and I zoomed the scan to fill the screen.

"He hasn't bled any more, and that's good," I said. "But the brain around the area of his hemorrhage has died. He has several areas of cerebral infarction, which means he's had a bunch of strokes. A lot of his brain is dead."

"That's really my brother's brain?" Brooks said. It's a common question, as people desperately hope I'm showing them the wrong patient's scan and maybe their loved one's isn't as bad.

I nodded and pointed to the identifiers in the corner of the screen. "Yes. That's the first thing I check. It's really him. But there are two more things I need to show you."

Christy held Brooks's hand so tightly her skin turned white. Her eyes bored into the screen and she made no sound.

I scrolled through the scan. "This is his brain stem. He's had a terrible stroke from the top of his midbrain down through his pons. That means he's not going to wake up."

Christy rocked back and forth on her feet, slowly nodding as silver lakes formed in her eyes. "You said there were two things," she said.

I swallowed the acid that had crept up into my throat. "There are." I scrolled the scan up to a large white area in the middle of Samuel's brain. "The contrast scan showed this. It's new tumor growth, a lot of it. It's in both sides of his brain now and his corpus callosum."

All four of us stared at the screen for what seemed like an eternity. The glioblastoma stared back at us, as if to remind us it had won. Under Grossman's microscope the GBM cells form islands of tumor surrounded by lakes of cellular derangements and necrotic tissue. But on my iPad screen GBM showed the same picture writ large: the tumor was alive and well, laughing at us as it swam in an ocean of dead brain that used to program Samuel into the vibrant, faithful man I'd come to know, dead brain caused as much by our attempts to kill the tumor as by the tumor's own work.

"What do we do now?" Brooks asked. "More surgery?"

Christy shook her head and cleared her throat. "No. We do not. I talked to that poor woman, Mrs. Andrews, in the waiting room. She told me all they've been through. And she still believes her husband's going to wake up. I hope he does. But I asked her something, and I can't stop thinking about what she said."

"What did you ask her?" Pastor Jon said.

She wiped a tear that had fallen onto her cheek. "I just wondered, since she said he hadn't spoken or opened his eyes in over a year, if she was fighting so hard to save him for his sake or for hers."

Christy took a few stuttering breaths, then said, "My question seemed to confuse her. It took her a long time to answer, but then she said, 'I guess for me. I can't stand the thought of losing him.'"

She pinched the bridge of her nose and squeezed her eyes shut. Pastor Jon pulled a handkerchief from his pocket and placed it in Christy's other hand. She wiped her face and steadied herself before she spoke again. "I'm not doing that to my Sam. I see his body lying there, his big muscles and his beautiful face. But that's not him. It's not him, Doc. No more surgery. He's had enough."

We went on to discuss the end-of-life decisions Christy had to make for Samuel. Once a family has determined their loved one would not want any further treatments, the medical team requires two separate clarifications so we know we are acting in accordance with the patient's wishes. This is easier if a patient already has a living will, but in neurosurgery there are too many young people involved, too many late-night car accidents, strokes, aneurysms, tumors, and gunshots. Most of us do not make end-of-life plans until we are, well, closer to what we anticipate will be the end of our lives. And when someone without a living will winds up on life support and it becomes clear we cannot save him, family members are left with big choices.

The first is what happens if the patient's heart stops beating. On television, doctors rush in and perform a code, which frequently involves heroic bedside procedures, like CPR and shocking the heart, and some brilliant decision-making by the incredibly handsome doctor. The patient wakes up and usually looks none the worse for wear, moments after supposedly having no heartbeat.

In real life it doesn't play out that way.

Resuscitation is a nasty endeavor. Because the heart has stopped, it is very difficult for the code team to start IVs, and many patients end up with large IV lines in their necks, groins, or both. CPR breaks ribs. Patients lose continence of their bladders and bowels. They vomit.

In the end, even when we bring people back, only a small percentage of those patients survive to the end of the hospitalization; research suggests that only 16 percent of cancer patients who are saved by CPR are alive thirty days later.[16]

So when we have a chance to discuss these matters with a patient's family before a cardiac arrest happens, we need to know whether the patient would want us to do that.

In Samuel's case he had a universally fatal malignant brain tumor and a severe stroke from a massive brain hemorrhage. If his heart stopped and we were able to restart it, all those things would still be true. Restarting his heart would not change anything about his diseased and damaged brain, other than making it worse because of several minutes of decreased blood flow during his cardiac arrest.

The decision a family makes to *not* have us do CPR on their loved one is called a DNR order—do not resuscitate. That means if your body tries to die—if your heart stops—we let you die.

DNR orders are fairly easy to understand, and families usually do not struggle too much in making this decision. Their loved one either would or would not want us to do everything possible to save him.

Christy didn't hesitate for one second when I asked her whether Samuel would want us to resuscitate him.

"No, Doc. Do not do that to him. Make him DNR," she said in a firm, hushed voice.

The next decision I asked her to make—whether to leave him on life support or withdraw it—was much more difficult. It always is. She needed some time to think about it, so I went to check on Mr. Andrews. I needed to have the same conversation with his wife.

———

I stepped into Mr. Andrews's room but stopped short when I saw Mrs. Andrews. She had her back to me and both hands on her husband's face. She was leaning over the bedrail and speaking to him quietly.

"Come on, Robby. Wake up for me, baby. I need you." She leaned farther and kissed him gently. Mr. Andrews pursed his lips in response, and she held her face there for a long time. "I miss you, Robby. Come on. You've missed so much. Darren and Amy are about to have the baby—you're going to be a grandpa. It's a boy, Robby. They're going to name him after you. Don't you want to see him? Who's going to teach him to fish? Who's gonna . . ." She sniffed, straightened up, pressed her face into the crook of her elbow, and let out a deep sigh.

Mr. Andrews continued with the sucking motion, kissing the air, for another thirty seconds while she continued to softly exhort him. The only other sounds in the room were the twin beeps of the heart monitor and the Glio-Wave 6000. I stepped closer and placed my hand on her shoulder. Jackie came in behind me as Mrs. Andrews turned to face me.

"I'm sorry. It's just so—" she said before I cut her off.

"It's okay. I know it's hard. We need to talk about a few things."

She stiffened, and I could see her jaw muscles flexing, fibrillating as she clenched her teeth. "I agree," she said without really opening her mouth. Her eyes narrowed and she seemed to get a little taller. "Why aren't you doing anything to help my husband? I brought him here because I heard you were the best. But so far all you've done is let these tramp nurses behave inappropriately."

"Hang on a second, lady," Jackie said. She pointed her index finger and was winding up to say something else, but I held up my hand, and she closed her mouth.

"Mrs. Andrews, the nurses haven't done anything wrong. All of us are trying to take care of him, and I've already explained to you what's happening to your husband. He's not trying to kiss them; it's a brain reflex caused by the massive destruction of his frontal lobes. I know it makes you angry that this disease is wrecking your husband's brain, but it's not the nurses' fault. You have to let them do their jobs."

She stared into my eyes forever, and then she suddenly seemed to deflate. She slid into the chair at her husband's bedside and cried uncontrollably into her hands for a while. I stood there with my hand on her shoulder, Jackie at my side, and waited for her to compose herself.

Finally she was able to speak again.

In short, clipped bursts interrupted by rapid breaths, she said, "I'm sorry. You're right. I'm not mad at the nurses. I guess I'm mad at God. How could he let this happen? Robert's such a good man. We're in the prime of our lives. Then I heard that girl Louise—she sits out there with all those *drug people*—in the waiting room talking about how her brother is probably going to survive his brain tumor. A meth head! Why does he get to live? It's not fair."

I pulled another chair up next to Mrs. Andrews and sat. She put her head in her hands and rested her elbows on her knees. "I know. It isn't fair at all, and I'm so sorry your family has to go through this. But it's time to make some decisions."

She looked up. "This is when you tell me it's time to let him go?" Her nostrils flared with each breath she took in, and she stared at me like a jury judging a killer. I was Osama bin Laden, Ted Bundy, the 9/11 hijackers, public enemy number one.

I shook my head. "No. It's not my job to tell you what to do. I'm here to tell you what you need to know so you can decide what your husband would want us to do."

Her mouth opened and she made an *uhh* sound. "What he'd *want* you to do is apply some of the talent you used to save that *gentleman* down the hall and do something for him instead of just watching him die. How about that?"

I straightened in my chair.

People say a lot of things when they're hurting, and doctors have to swallow most of them whole. React emotionally and you lose any chance to keep the conversation focused on what's best for the patient, because when people lash out, it's usually an attempt to divert their energy to something they can control—like attacking another person—instead of dealing with the problem that's making them feel out of control.

Knowing the reasons people say those things doesn't make them hurt less though. And having to go through this type of emotional abuse as we face diseases and injuries we can't always fix is one of the reasons a lot of surgeons begin to develop an armor around themselves. We project indifference, untouchability, as if we can float above the humanness of these situations and remain rational, clinical, robotically unhurtable.

We really can't.

"Mrs. Andrews, I know you're struggling here. But there's nothing else we *can* do. Even if I could somehow cure him of his cancer, which I cannot, he's lost so much of his brain that he would still never wake up. And he's so malnourished that his body is literally eating itself. He has lost most of his muscle mass, his joints are frozen from a year in bed, and his kidneys are starting to shut down. You've done a great job trying to take care of him, but he is near the end."

I saw it in her eyes: she flew in her mind across time and space, through the years she and her husband were together, the babies, the home they made, the triumphs and the trials they endured. I saw her reliving them. Her breathing steadied and her eyes filled with even more tears. Her face fell, her shoulders slumped, and I could see the painful parts cross her mind: the diagnosis, the fear, the false hope she'd been sold across the country as she accompanied and then assisted and then pushed her husband into cancer clinics and to modern-day snake-oil salesmen dressed as doctors.

And then, just like that, she was back with me.

"You said there were decisions we have to make. What are they?"

I cleared my throat. "Well, his Cheyne-Stokes breathing indicates that his brain stem is beginning to fail. And his labs show that his nutritional status is terrible. His body is shutting down from his inability to eat. The next thing that will happen is that he'll start having trouble breathing, and then he'll start sucking saliva into his lungs. That's called aspiration, and it can lead to pneumonia and death. And when his kidneys stop working, he'll go into multisystem organ failure. Dialysis might buy him a little more time, but once things start sliding down into organ failure, the fatality rate is very high."

She interrupted me. "You said there were decisions, but you're just telling me how he's dying. What decisions do I need to make?"

"The nurses said they already talked to you about making him DNR so that if his heart stops, we don't try to resuscitate him. So far you've been against that, but we need to ask again. And beyond a DNR order, we have to decide how much longer and at what level we're going to treat him. There's something called comfort measures, which means we stop actively trying to save him and instead do things to make sure he's not hurting at all while his body goes through the natural process of dying."

Her mouth opened, and she shook her head. "So you're telling me to just give up? Just let him go, let my husband lie here and die? That's not much of a decision. What other choices do I have?"

"Well, if you think he would want to keep fighting, keep trying, then we need to do some things to protect him. If we want to get him more calories so his body isn't so starved and possibly save him from organ failure, he needs a surgical feeding tube placed. If you want to do that, then at the same time we should give him another way to breathe to keep him from aspirating. We can cut a hole in his throat and give him a tracheostomy, which will prevent the pneumonia and suffocation he's bound to develop as his brain stem gets worse."

"So he dies, or he has to have two more surgeries? I've already told you we're out of money. I don't know how I'll pay for it. Doctor, I don't know what to do. I can't live without him." Just then her cell phone rang. "Hold on. It's my mother."

"Mom, I can't really talk," she said into the phone. "The doctor's here. Robby isn't doing well."

She listened to whatever her mother was saying, and suddenly her face lit up like a child at Christmas. "Are you sure? Mom, that's a miracle! Thank you so much. I'll call you in a few minutes."

She clicked off the phone and looked at me with a huge smile on her face.

"My mom borrowed money from her life insurance policy for me to take Robert to Dallas for the Level V anti-glioplastin treatment, including a medical flight! Dr. Karpowski said it could cure him, and if we came next week, they would be able to start treating him immediately."

"Mrs. Andrews," I said, "he's far too weak to travel. Without the feeding tube and the tracheostomy, I don't think he would survive the flight."

Her smile never faded. She stood and took her husband's hand and said to him, "Robby, this is what we've been praying for. We're getting you back."

Then she turned to me. "Doctor, give him the procedures he needs. I'm taking my husband to Dallas as soon as he's a little stronger."

"I did some research on Dr. Karpowski," I said. "Did you know that none of the treatments he's offering are FDA approved?"

She smirked. "I would expect you to say that. Traditional hospitals and doctors don't want people like Dr. Karpowski to succeed, because if he cures these tumors, there won't be any patients for you to make money off of."

I shook my head. "Ma'am, that isn't true. It's just that there is no published scientific data to support the things he claims his drugs will do. I've seen so many people spend all their money on these pseudoscientific treatments, and I've never seen any of them work."

She chuckled condescendingly. "Whatever. I'm going to save my husband. Get those procedures done, and we'll leave when he's ready. That will give you more time to spend with your drug-addict scumbag patient."

She turned back to Mr. Andrews. "I'll be back, honey. I'm going to call Dr. Karpowski. I love you."

She pushed past me and left the room. I turned to Jackie. "Call the general surgeon. Trach and a feeding tube. Let me know when it's done, please."

Jackie nodded. "Unbelievable."

Mr. Andrews's oxygen tube slipped out of his nose a little and landed on his upper lip. He sucked away, kissing the air over and over. The Glio-Wave 6000 beeped, the heart monitor answered, and Mrs. Andrews's misplaced faith hung in the air like bad perfume.

I looked at what was left of Mr. Andrews's body, ravaged by weight loss, multiple neurosurgeons having their way with his brain, radiation, chemotherapy, and having been dragged around the country and exposed to a host of ill-advised and poorly studied treatments. And now my lone contribution to his care would be ordering yet another surgeon to place two more holes into Mr. Andrews than God gave him.

15

End-of-Life Decisions

"Would you tell me, please, which way I ought to go from here?"

"That depends a good deal on where you want to get to," said the Cat.

"I don't much care where—" said Alice.

"Then it doesn't matter which way you go," said the Cat.

"—so long as I get *somewhere*," Alice added as an explanation.

—Lewis Carroll, *Alice's Adventures in Wonderland*

I stepped into the staff restroom in the ICU, locked the door behind me, and turned on the cold water in the sink. In the mirror I saw a guy wearing the costume of someone who had all the answers. My lab coat identified that guy as

W. LEE WARREN, MD
NEUROSURGERY

But the man inside the coat was just *me,* a kid from Oklahoma who knew the truth. I'd completed the training, received the certificates, passed the boards, and earned the title, but I knew the truth about GBM. The truth is, it didn't matter how steady my hands were, how sound my clinical decision-making was, how expertly the oncologist and radiation oncologist had done their jobs, or how much Christy had prayed and begged God for something other than this to happen. GBM wins—every time.

The guy who'd earned the white coat was supposed to be unflappable, indefatigable, unwavering in his quest to defeat this disease. But I knew the kid inside the coat was also supposed to believe in something bigger than medicine, surgery, ionizing radiation, and chemotherapy. I went to church, read my Bible, and raised my kids to do so. I believed God could and sometimes did make fools out of the experts who think they know everything. I was the person who encouraged others that it would be okay, because I had faith.

But in my head and my heart, I knew without any doubt that the prayers for Samuel to survive were answered with a no before they were even uttered.

I'd seen the end of him when I saw his first MRI.

And so it had come to pass, as it always does with this disease, except in a few cases here and there at Duke or UCLA or some other university when the luckiest of the lucky patients with just the right tumor genetics and locations meet just the right surgeon at just the right time to somehow survive GBM's otherwise universally fatal assault. Samuel wasn't one of those people.

In the next few minutes, I would be standing next to Christy, helping her make a decision that would most likely lead to Samuel's death today. I remembered the first time I'd been in such a situation, while I was a junior resident in Pittsburgh.

I splashed cold water on my face, and in my mind I was ten years younger, standing at the bedside of a local pastor, my hands locked with his family members' as we sang an old hymn, "It Is Well with My Soul," at the pastor's request.

He'd made the decision to not have a feeding tube or tracheostomy, to stop trying to fight his GBM. His tumor was in both of his occipital lobes and had mercilessly stolen his vision and subsequently his strength and ability to walk as it marched forward in his brain. His body looked a lot like Mr. Andrews's toward the end, but somehow his powers of speech and cognition remained intact until the very last days of his life. One of the last things he'd said was that he wanted his family—and me—to sing hymns and pray over him as he died.

He was the first GBM patient I'd ever cared for. My professor, Dr. Julian Bailes, had assigned me to stay with the patient and his family as much as possible until he died. I didn't understand it at the time, but now I know that Dr. Bailes wanted me to learn exactly what this disease does to people and their families. As hard as it was to go through that—most neurosurgeons make the proclamation that the patient is dying and then leave the family to deal with death's realities while they go off to conquer more manageable cases—I now know it was one of the greatest blessings of my training. When I said to myself as I initially reviewed Samuel's MRI, *I've seen the end of you,* it was because of the pastor and my experience of watching him die.

When I see those scans, GBM's characteristic white-and-black initial foothold in someone's brain, I don't just see in my mind the tumor. I see the progression, the weight loss, the disability, the dementia, and the bedsores and malnutrition. I see the spouse's tears and the kids' confusion and the seemingly unanswered prayers.

I see it all in a flash because of the pastor and too many subsequent patients.

That day back in Pittsburgh, we sang and prayed for two hours.

When peace like a river attendeth my way,
When sorrows like sea billows roll,
Whatever my lot, thou hast taught me to say,
"It is well, it is well with my soul."

One by one the pastor's wife and children said their goodbyes, as did I. I'd grown to love him, love them, over the nine months from his diagnosis to his last day. I'd been in all his surgeries, placed his brain pressure monitor, saved his life twice from blood clots and hydrocephalus, and gone to church with his family to pray for him.

Once, I'd tried to get off his case, but Dr. Bailes wouldn't have it. "You need to see this through, Lee," he'd said. "If you understand this disease and what it does to people, you'll be a much better surgeon. And a better person. Your future patients need you to experience this, and so does this family, this patient. You have to stay with him all the way."

So I'd been there, singing.

No pang shall be mine, for in death as in life
Thou wilt whisper thy peace to my soul.
It is well, it is well with my soul.

But even then I'd recognized that it wasn't well with *my* soul. He was a pastor, one of God's people. Surely his prayers meant something, and those of his family must have meant something, right? Yet GBM achieved its evil intent, stripped a church of its leader, a family of its husband and dad, and a young brain surgeon of some innocence.

The pastor took his last breath, as if he'd planned it that way, right after we sang the last lines of his favorite hymn.

> And, Lord, haste the day when the faith shall be sight,
> The clouds be rolled back as a scroll;
> The trump shall resound, and the Lord shall descend—
> Even so, it is well with my soul.[17]

That day in the ICU restroom in Alabama, I remembered something else Dr. Bailes told me: "The only way to kill a GBM is to let it die with the patient."

All three of me—the scared Okie who wasn't sure whether the things he believed were really true, the angry doctor who was tired of this disease killing his patients, and the supposedly know-it-all neurosurgeon who was about to go ask Christy whether she wanted to place her husband on comfort measures—stuffed ourselves back inside our white coat, dried our faces, and headed out to prove Dr. Bailes right once again.

And all of us wished we were still making rounds on our routine postoperative spine patients, hearing them tell us how great we were.

———

Christy stood at Samuel's bedside, her body twisted and bent so she could rest her forehead on his. She cupped his face in her hands and spoke to him quietly, her voice broken in grief even though she'd run out of tears. Brooks stood to her left, his hand on her shoulder for support, and Pastor Jon stood on the other side of the bed.

The two men turned their eyes to me when I entered the room, but Christy stayed engaged with Samuel.

I stepped around the bed and stood next to Pastor Jon. Christy stood and opened her mouth as if to speak, but no words came. She shook her head slowly and finally said, "No. No, Doc. Don't make me do this."

I reached over and took her hand. "There's no rush, Christy. We can keep him on life support as long as you think that's what he would want."

She jerked her hand back and her eyes flashed. "What he would want? You think any of this is what he would want? He wants to be home with his family!"

With that, her emotional dam seemed to break. Another outpouring of tears came from some internal reservoir, and she fell back onto Samuel's chest, sobbing and grabbing handfuls of his gown. Brooks put his hand on her back and tried to comfort her.

Pastor Jon said, "Lee, maybe you should come back in a little while."

———————

I walked out into the hall and sat on a chair in the nurses' station. I leaned forward and rested my head in my hands and tried not to feel anything for a moment. Down the hall I heard Joey yelling at the television. Various beeps and clicks and phones ringing and ventilators whooshing filled the air. But above it all I heard Christy crying.

These are among the most excruciating moments of a physician's career, the times we have to ask a family to speak for their loved one. Inevitably, no matter how carefully I explain that they're not *choosing* to let the person die, they believe telling us to withdraw life support is tantamount to killing their family member. It's not, I tell them. They're choosing to no longer allow us to intervene in the disease process if that's what the person wants. We are no longer going to artificially fight back, but sometimes the body keeps going. We're not doing anything to force the person to die, but we're not going to force her to live against her wishes anymore.

That explanation of what withdrawing life support means is 100 percent accurate, but families never buy it at first. In their minds they are absolutely faced with making the decision of whether their loved one gets to live or die.

And it is unbearable for most of them.

So here was Samuel, with an incurable, growing tumor and having suffered multiple strokes and a massive brain hemorrhage from a medicine we were using to try to save him. And here was Christy, the grieving not-quite widow.

I had served my time as Samuel's surgeon; there would be no more trips to the operating room for him, no more opportunities for me to intervene directly in his disease process with my hands. No, now I played the role of counselor, adviser, and guide. I was supposed to have the answers, know what to do, help her decide. We had talked about everything; I had told her and Brooks all I could about Samuel's condition and his prognosis and what would likely happen if they decided to remove the breathing tube versus pressing on with a tracheostomy and feeding tube.

I say "what would likely happen" because that is accurate. When we pull the tube, not everyone stops breathing. Some people live when we think they will die. Some people, like Mr. Andrews next door, live a lot longer than we think they will.

But despite that lack of certainty, there are well-defined and utterly necessary branch points in the care of trauma patients. We need to establish what their wishes would be if their bodies actually tried to die, as in the DNR orders Christy gave and Mrs. Andrews refused. And then, after people have been on artificial respiration and IV or nasal tube feeding for a while, we come to a point at which the methods we're using to keep them alive begin to hurt them.

Breathing tubes start to erode the vocal cords and can lead to infections in the throat, lungs, and sinuses. IV feeding (also called total parenteral nutrition, or TPN) is not as effective as feeding people through a nasogastric (NG) tube and can cause blood clots, liver disease, infections, and bowel issues, among other things. But leaving an NG tube in place has the same set of problems as long-term artificial respiration—including ulcers, skin breakdown, infections, and electrolyte imbalances.

If we believe that a person has a good chance to make a meaningful recovery, we offer the family these choices—tracheostomy and gastrostomy (a surgically placed feeding tube in the stomach)—so our treatments are less likely to make the patient worse instead of better. We trade one set of problems for another, though, because once we perform a tracheostomy, we can essentially keep a patient on a ventilator forever, and with a gastrostomy tube, we can nourish the person effectively forever as well. Thus, if it turns out the patient never actually does improve— never wakes up—then we've created a situation in which he isn't likely to pass away during the acute phase of his injury and can thus be expected to live months or even years in a vegetative state.

That's when I remember my old chief's adage: *"There are some things worse than being dead."*

It makes perfect sense to offer these life-extending treatments to someone who has an injury that can potentially heal. But trauma and tumor are not the same thing.

Samuel didn't have a head injury that would someday heal. He had a menacing, evil, rapidly advancing form of humankind's most malignant cancer marching through his brain, laying waste to his cerebral circuitry like Sherman pillaging farms on his march to the sea. Add in the devastation piled on by surgery, radiation, and hemorrhage, and it made little sense to draw his demise out much longer.

At least to me.

But it wasn't my decision.

———

I walked back into Samuel's room and stood across the bed from Christy.

She straightened and turned to me. Her eyes seemed dull and empty. She clenched her fists but then relaxed them, and her hands dropped to her sides.

She was out of fight.

Her voice, almost a whisper, held none of the fire and faith I'd always seen in her. "We're gonna let him go, Doc. He's had enough."

"I think that's good," I said. "He won't suffer. We will keep him comfortable."

Even as I said those words, I hated myself for them. It wasn't *good*. He did suffer—he doesn't get to grow old with his wife, see his kids grow up, hold his grandchildren. I know as a Christian I'm supposed to anticipate the wonderful nature of a painless eternity in heaven, and I do.

But right then it didn't feel so heavenly.

I spent a few minutes explaining what would probably happen once we took Samuel off life support. We had already had the conversation once, and Christy had no questions.

"Are you ready?" I said.

Christy nodded slowly. "Can you just give us a few minutes with him?"

I nodded, then turned to Carl, the nurse. "Once they're ready, give him five milligrams of morphine, and then pull the tube. I'll be back in a few minutes. Call me if you need me sooner."

I walked down the hall and placed Joey's lumbar drain. He griped and cussed and wouldn't hold still, but eventually I finished the drain, and he settled back down to enjoy the movie he'd been watching.

Just as I pulled off my gloves, Carl stepped out of Samuel's room and waved me over. "He's going fast, Doc."

I walked into Samuel's room. His mouth, set free from the tubes and tape that had obscured his face moments before, was agape in what interns call the O sign. His eyes remained closed, and his breathing was rapid and shallow.

Carl had lowered the rails for Christy, and she sat on Samuel's bed, her head resting on his chest, her arms wrapped around him in one last embrace.

Brooks stood on the other side, Pastor Jon next to him. The olive wood cross hung around Samuel's neck; I guessed Christy thought he would want it there after the tube came out. Carl had shut off the monitors, so the only sound in the room was Samuel's labored breathing in the heavy atmosphere of desperation and sorrow.

"The kids are with Mama," Christy said.

Samuel drew in a deep breath, held it for a long time, and then exhaled completely. It was his last breath. I watched for a few seconds, then stepped over and placed my hand gently on his neck. He had no pulse.

"Carl, may I borrow your stethoscope, please?" I said. He handed it to me.

I listened to Samuel's chest. Nothing.

I handed the scope back to Carl. "He's gone, Christy."

She never moved.

Brooks, giant clone of his brother, leaned over and put both hands on Christy's back. "I'm so sorry, sis."

Christy said, "Thank you, Doc. Can you leave us alone, please?"

I nodded. "Of course."

As I left the room, I heard Christy say, "I love you so much, Samuel."

Brooks said, "Roll Tide, big brother. Roll Tide."

16

Why Bother Praying?

Prayer does not move God to do things he is disinclined to do. . . .
Prayer is God's way of bringing our priorities into line with his.

—JOHN PIPER, "Hallowed Be Thy Name"

I left the ICU and walked downstairs to the chapel. I've found over the years that if I want to be alone, hospital chapels are a great place. Whether in Oklahoma City, Pittsburgh, San Antonio, Landstuhl in Germany, Al Udeid Air Base in Qatar, Balad Air Force Theater Hospital in Iraq, or my hospital in Alabama, somehow the chapel is always empty. So when I'm out of answers or even just out of gas, sometimes I go there to sit, think, pray, or cry.

It's funny to me how people know to go to the emergency department when they're bleeding, but they forget about the chapel when their souls are hurting. Somehow it helps me—the quiet and the low lights and the palpable residual tapestry of softly spoken prayers, hopeful requests, and tearful cries for help from other folks with other problems at other times.

As a medical student in Oklahoma City, I hid in a chapel until I could stop crying after the first time I witnessed death, a twelve-year-old girl from my hometown who died of a fungal infection in her brain following chemotherapy for a malignant tumor called medulloblastoma. In Pittsburgh the chapel was my place to collect my thoughts when the task of becoming a brain surgeon seemed insurmountable. In Qatar I went there to ask God for the strength to get on the plane moments later to go to war—and to keep me alive during it. And in Iraq I sat with Chris Coppola, a pediatric surgeon with the best hands and biggest heart of any surgeon I'd ever known. We talked and cried and prayed and raged after we watched his patient Maria die, a baby whose only crime was being born in a country at war.

When I entered the chapel on the day Samuel died, I wasn't sure I wanted to talk to God yet. He'd spared Joey again. And at least Mr. Andrews got to see his kids as adults before GBM obliterated everything human about him.

No, I didn't trust myself with what I would say to God yet.

So I called Lisa.

"Samuel just died," I said.

I heard her breathe. When I hear Lisa breathe, in my mind I can see her face. I know all her sounds and how they reflect what's going on in her heart. I saw the tears forming, saw her lip trembling, heard the little stutter in her breathing before she said, "I'm so sorry, honey."

My heart connection with Lisa is the pinnacle of my emotional accomplishment as a human being. I can *feel* her emotional state. She can be lying in bed next to me, silent in the dark, and I can know when she's sad, anxious, angry. Somehow I know it. It's as real as feeling the wind change direction. I have an instinctive ability to recognize every subtle movement of her face, look in her eye, change in her posture, pattern of her breathing.

That day I knew she would be feeling sorrow for Christy and for Samuel and their kids. And she would hurt for me and with me since she lived the practice of neurosurgery both emotionally as my wife and professionally as the administrator of our practice. She knew our patients, loved them, worked tirelessly to make their experience in our office and throughout our care of them as good as it could be. She is, entirely, my partner.

"I'll come over and see Christy. Be there soon," she said. "I love you."

"I love you too."

When she hung up, I was left alone in the chapel, still unsure how to start unpacking all the things I wanted to say to God, whether I really believed he would listen anyway, whether there was actually anyone out there at all.

I thought about my connection with Lisa. How I knew what she was doing at that very moment. She would be hurriedly wrapping up whatever was happening at the office, stopping only to gather our staff and pray for Christy. She would go into the bathroom and wipe her eyes, compose herself, and walk to the car. She would be worried about Christy's kids, and she would do what we all do when we hear of someone else's tragedy—she would feel simultaneously glad it didn't happen to us and afraid it could.

How was any of this fair? Samuel wasn't a drug addict; he wasn't the pawn of bad habits or unwise choices like so many other patients I'd seen die. Trauma is always tragic, but it is seldom entirely random.

Not to diminish the sadness, but is it a true accident if someone is hurt because he drives under the influence or doesn't wear a seat belt or if someone falls off a balcony and breaks her neck while high on meth? Those things are awful, but they're not usually random.

On a human level, an injury conjoined with some aspect of preventability, causation, or intentionality gives us something to understand. *I know why Cousin Tim is paralyzed—he was drunk and dove into the lake at night. He hit his head on the bottom and broke his neck. That's really sad.* We don't usually shake our fists at the universe or God or chance when we can wrap our minds around the *why* of something. We're still sad and surprised, but at least we have something or someone to blame.

Even when processing many cancers, strokes, and such things as heart disease, we can often find a *why* to help us philosophically process the pain. *Dad's been smoking two packs a day since he was thirteen. No wonder he got lung cancer.*

But GBM is random.

Among all cancers its cause is one of the least understood. It doesn't run in families; even with identical twins the likelihood of both twins having a GBM is the same as the chance of you and me both having one. It's not tied to a particular environmental toxin, age group, geographical location, predisposing condition, or genetic makeup.

All of which makes it sometimes feel as if God just shuffled all our names in a hat and drew one out. Samuel Martin, your name came up. You get to have a glioblastoma. Good luck with that.

I sat in the silent chapel and stared at the stained-glass wall behind the pulpit. *The Last Supper* spread out in bits of colored glass in front of me, Jesus and the disciples eating before he went out to die on a cross. The sentence hadn't been spoken out loud yet; Jesus still had a few hours before Pilate would convict him of crimes he did not commit, and subsequently he would go to the cross and be cruci-fied for the sins of humankind. But even as they shared that final meal, the outcome was already determined.

I thought of the day I met Samuel and Christy, his first MRI scan, and the familiar feeling I get when the picture tells me the story before the biopsy's even done. I'd seen the end of him, just as surely as Jesus Christ was a dead man walking from before the virgin birth. God's eternal plan to redeem us from our sins de-pended on Christ's willingness to go through with that horrible death. I believe that with all my heart, and I know if he hadn't been willing to make that sacrifice, we would all be lost.

But even Jesus, who surely had a more eternal perspective than I do, prayed for relief from his coming torture and death. In the garden, moments after the Last Supper I saw depicted in the chapel's stained-glass art, he said, "May this cup be taken from me."[18]

Of course, God, as he is prone to do, either did not answer Jesus's prayer or said no.

As in Samuel's case.

A voice from the back of the chapel interrupted my thoughts. "It's beautiful, isn't it?"

I turned to see Pastor Jon behind me. "What?"

"The picture. It's beautiful."

"Yes. But it's not doing much for me right now," I said.

He sat next to me, put his arm around me, and hugged me as my dad used to when I'd lost a game or a girlfriend. "You've had a rough day. The nurse told me there were two other tumor patients in the ICU as well?"

I nodded. "One guy's got a lower-grade tumor. He'll live a long time. The other man is hanging on, but I don't know how."

"How are you?" he said.

"I'm all right," I said. "I just come in here sometimes to think."

Pastor Jon took his arm from around me, stood, and turned to face me. He dropped to one knee and put his elbow on his leg like Rodin's *The Thinker* and leaned in close to me. "Remember where we are? Tell me—how *are you*?"

His words hung in the air, passing judgment on my superficiality.

I shook my head. I didn't have time for this and wasn't accustomed to anyone

cornering me. I was the doctor, after all. I asked the questions, at least in this building. Yet Pastor Jon's question seemed to penetrate me, to pass through a slit in my
white-coat armor. His question wasn't the meaningless phrase we utter twenty
times a day in the hall to people from whom we expect or desire no answer: "How's
it going?" "How you doin'?"

Pastor Jon meant it. And he would have his answer.

"Honestly, I'm pretty mad right now."

He nodded. "Tell me about it. Talk through it."

"It's just—watching Samuel die. It's so unfair. He was young, happy, in love.
He was productive, a good guy. Went to church, tried to do right, loved his wife. I
don't understand why guys like him always get the worst cancers. It's never the
scumbags, the drunks, the bad people. It feels like GBM was designed to kill nice
people."

Pastor Jon had a faraway look, as if he were walking the halls of his memory. "I
know. I've been doing this for forty years. I've seen pediatric cancers, ruptured aneurysms, heart failures, drive-by shootings . . . you name it. And in every case we
say the same words: 'He was so young.' 'She was just standing there.' 'He was such
a good person.' If you push too far into trying to decide which deaths are senseless
and unfair and which ones seem about right, you'll drive yourself crazy."

He stood, walked over to the altar, and lit one of the little prayer candles. Its soft
yellow glow added little to the dim chapel light, but it drew my eyes as it flickered
and spat its few photons into the void, fighting against the darkness like the train in
The Little Engine That Could.

He sat back down next to me.

"It's just the longer I practice," I said, "the harder it is for me to be sincere about
praying for these people."

He cocked his head. "What do you mean?"

"When I first met Samuel, I looked at his MRI and I just *knew.*"

"Knew what?"

"Everything. I knew it was a GBM. I knew what his brain would look like in
the OR. I knew he'd get radiation and his hair would fall out, that he'd stop eating
eventually. That something would happen—a complication of chemotherapy, an
infection, a blood clot, something—and he would die. I looked at his scan and said,
'I've seen the end of you.' And I had."

"And what does that have to do with praying for him?"

I shook my head. "Everything. I'm supposed to be his doctor. To tell him the truth. And when I saw his first scan, I already knew the outcome. How can I tell him to keep his faith, keep fighting, be strong, when *I know*? I'm a Christian. I believe. But there are some things I just already know. How can I pray about that?"

I looked up at *The Last Supper,* the twelve disciples around the table with Jesus. In Scripture, Judas, the betrayer, and Jesus had a moment in which they both knew what was about to happen. Jesus knew what Judas was going to do, and Judas knew that Jesus knew. But then Jesus blessed the meal and carried on as if everything were normal. As if it were okay. He prayed even though he *knew*. In that moment it probably made no sense whatsoever to Judas.[19]

And that day in the chapel, it made no sense to me.

Pastor Jon squeezed my knee with his right hand. For a few minutes the only sound in the room was our breathing. Then he spoke in a tender, quiet voice.

"I think I know what the problem is."

"What?" I said.

"You think your prayers are valid only if the outcome is what you want. Like it counts only if you get what you ask for. You think since you're a doctor, if your patient dies, it means God wasn't listening to you. You also think it's not fair when someone you think is good dies young and someone worse gets to live. And you think we're supposed to know what to ask for when we pray. Does that about sum it up?"

I nodded. "When you say it out loud, it sounds bad. We're not supposed to question God, are we?"

Pastor Jon made a *humph* sound. "You haven't read Psalms lately, have you? Or Job. Or Jeremiah."

"What do you mean?"

"The Bible's full of examples of people doubting, questioning, being mad at God. And his being okay with that. Job questioned God for most of the book. It seems like half the Psalms ask God where he's been and why he's not answering. And the prophet Jeremiah literally said to God, 'I would speak with you about your justice: Why does the way of the wicked prosper? Why do all the faithless live at ease?'[20] He wrote that during a time when people were trying to murder him, when the world seemed really unfair to him. Stuff like that—it's part of why I believe the Bible's true."

"I don't understand," I said.

Pastor Jon smiled with half his mouth. "It's the only religious book in which the people are honest when they doubt and God says it's okay. If I were writing a book I wanted people to believe was from God, I'd fill it with a bunch of commands and rules and stories about how powerful God is. I wouldn't put in there that people can shake their fists at him and he'll still love them. And I certainly wouldn't make it seem like you can do everything right and still suffer. I'd make more enticing promises than that."

My pager's shrill beeping shattered the quiet of the chapel. I was secretly glad because Pastor Jon's interrogation had made my head hurt.

"I gotta go. Thanks for being here," I said.

He stood and squeezed my shoulder. "I'm always available. You've got a tough job, but don't forget you're not alone."

I nodded, then walked out of the chapel to return my page. Judas and Jesus and the others stayed behind, silent witnesses to the countless prayers, tears, and fears wafting around in the room with the candle smoke and my vaporous faith.

———

Joey's lumbar drain stopped his leak, and he left the hospital a few days after Samuel died. By visiting his room each day, I'd been exposed to multiple sitcoms and old movies, along with reality shows about rednecks, survivalists, doomsday preppers, and pawn shop enthusiasts. By the time Joey left, I found myself subconsciously humming the theme song from *The Dukes of Hazzard* and wondering whether my grandfather's Civil War–era musket would be worth hauling down to Depend-a-Pawn after all.

Mr. Andrews, for his part, continued to be dragged from clinic to clinic by his wife. Over the next few months, our office received records requests from three other cancer centers around the country, evidence of Mrs. Andrews's persistence in her goal of keeping her husband alive at all costs.

———

That summer we rented a house on Kiawah Island in South Carolina. Another chance to play together in the ocean and deepen the bonds of our blended family. Our oldest daughter, Caity, was working and couldn't make it, but we had everyone else together again for a week in the sun.

One of the highlights was our morning runs on the beach. Lisa and I would go out for a 10k at sunrise, and her dad and the boys would join us for a few miles. Josh and I discovered that something had changed since the last time we all ran together: neither of us could keep up with Mitch anymore. He'd become a strong runner as he approached his high school years.

Mitch didn't need Josh to swim out to rescue him from the surf anymore either. He'd improved as a swimmer, but I noticed this also came with more risk tolerance. Mitch would go farther out, bodysurf in taller waves, and generally tackle rougher conditions than I was comfortable with.

My two sons, one of biology and one of choice, grew much closer on that trip to South Carolina. They were growing, no longer boys, and they didn't need me as much. And when we raced in the sand, no matter how hard I tried, I couldn't catch either one of them.

It was good to be away from work for a while, reconnecting with one another and enjoying the beautiful Atlantic coast. Having time alone with both boys and two of our girls gave me a fresh perspective on what was going on in each of their lives and helped me focus my prayers for all of them. Our family had so many moving parts, trying to keep up with everybody sometimes felt as futile as chasing my two fast sons down the beach.

At breakfast on the last morning of our vacation, Lisa opened our hometown paper on her iPad and read me Mr. Andrews's obituary. As sad as it made me to hear the words, I'd known it all along.

Nobody beats GBM.

Mr. Andrews's case took longer to verify, but in the end I was right. When I see the scan and the pathology and when the diagnosis is certain, there are some things I just know.

But back at work the next day, I met Eli, a thirty-five-year-old electrical engineer who taught me that I really don't know anything.

17

Clean Margins

Brain surgery is a terrible profession. If I did not feel it will become different in my lifetime, I should hate it.

—Dr. Wilder Penfield

The phone rang as soon as our office opened that Monday morning. "Doc," our receptionist, Shelby, said, "it's Dr. Patel. He says he's got a favor to ask you."

Dr. Patel is an internal medicine specialist, and he rarely calls me unless someone's really sick or in a lot of pain. I picked up the phone.

"What's up, buddy?" I said.

"Hey, Lee," he said, "I'm seeing a young electrical engineer who's got a weird complaint I can't figure out. He has no neurologic problems I can see and no headaches. But he says he's making math errors that he never makes. He's apparently some sort of math genius, but he's having trouble lately. The neurologist is out of town, so I thought I'd pick your brain about it."

"Did you do an MRI?" I asked.

"No. I'm not sure there's really anything wrong. Insurance won't approve it from me without documentable symptoms. I was thinking maybe you could see him and tell me what you think."

I've learned over the years to listen to Dr. Patel because his instincts are spookily accurate. Practicing in a small town, we all have to see some patients who might not exactly be in our specialty. This results in my often seeing someone who really needs a neurologist. Some surgeons get hung up on seeing only surgical patients, but I've found that choosing to help out a colleague or a patient pays more dividends than standing firm on my superspecialist principles. Especially for a doctor and friend like Patel.

"Sure, I'd be happy to see him," I said.

He chuckled. "And that, my friend, is why you're the best neurosurgeon in town."

"Right. And I'll remind you that I'm the only neurosurgeon in town."

"It's still true," he said before hanging up.

———

Eli Bailey wore a tweed sports coat over a red Burberry polo shirt. On his left lapel was a script *A* pin, the way professional folks often show their support for the University of Alabama, as opposed to the elephant logo or tattoos of various sorts worn by the school's more blue-collar fans. He had round glasses, a receding hairline, brown eyes, and a kind look. When I entered the room, he smiled pleasantly and extended a hand.

"Hello, I'm Dr. Warren," I said as we shook hands.

"Eli Bailey," he said. "Nice to meet you."

I pointed at his lapel pin. "War Eagle" I said, settling the question of my sports loyalty before it came up.

He shook his head. "Great. My doctor's an Auburn fan."

"I'm just giving you a hard time," I said. "You guys kill us almost every year."

Eli screwed up his face. "How can time be hard? It's a mental construct."

I laughed. "Good point." He was a pretty serious guy apparently.

"And I've never killed anyone."

His expression was stolid, with no hint that he was joking. *Weird.*

I decided to move on.

"What's going on with you? My friend Dr. Patel says you're having some trouble with math?"

"Not with math in general. It's just that I usually know the answers to equations out to five decimal places before I use the calculator. My work is very precise, and lately I've been missing the fourth and fifth place."

I thought to myself, *How many people in the world can do that?*

"Isn't that what calculators are for?" I asked. "To solve complex math problems so we don't have to do them in our heads?"

He frowned. "I'm not talking about complex equations, Doctor. I'm talking about simple multiplication. I've never had these problems before, and it's worrying me."

I nodded. "I can tell. I'm going to try to help you get a handle on this, okay?"

He sighed loudly. "Doctor, you can't put a handle on a fear. You say the most inane things!"

I thought, *Either this guy's a jerk, or he's the most concrete person I've ever met.* But something was bothering me, something way back in the corner of the mental closet where I'd stored most of my neurology knowledge after residency.

Math problems and the inability to understand metaphors . . .

He'd failed to get what I meant by "hard time," "you guys kill us," and "get a handle," three idioms most people would easily understand. And his math problem, even though most normal people would never even be able to guess the answer to the first decimal place, was significant for such an intelligent person. I remembered a phenomenon I'd seen once before, and just as a hunch I decided to look for it.

"Mr. Bailey, hold up your left index finger for me," I said.

He confidently showed me his right thumb.

"No, your left index finger."

He looked at his hands and then held up his left thumb.

"How long have you been having trouble telling the difference between left and right?" I asked.

"Wow," he said, "I hadn't noticed that until now."

"Are you having any trouble with reading or writing?"

He shook his head. "No. In fact, I just wrote a report for my boss this morning."

"And you're not having headaches or any other type of symptoms?"

"No, just the math and apparently these other things you've discovered. Can you help me, Doctor?"

"I hope so. You need an MRI," I said.

The angular gyrus of the parietal lobe in human brains is involved in processes related to language, spatial relationships, memory retrieval, attention, and number processing. When you read something and you hear the words in your head as language, that's your angular gyrus. When you hear someone ask "What's two plus two?" and you think *Four,* thank your angular gyrus.

It's also in charge of our ability to understand figures of speech and metaphor. Both of which were problems for Eli.

Eli had a cluster of neurologic findings that reminded me of Gerstmann syndrome, named after the Austrian neurologist Josef Gerstmann. Just as Harvey Cushing had died in 1939 on the day my dad was born, Josef Gerstmann died shortly after I came along in 1969, so maybe my family has some kind of connection with giants of neuroscience. It was Gerstmann who first discovered that trouble in the angular gyrus caused finger agnosia (problems knowing which finger is which), alexia (trouble reading), agraphia (trouble writing), and left-right confusion.

Patel recognized the math issue and trusted his instincts enough to call me. Although I'm no neurologist, my habit of teasing Bama fans had revealed that Eli couldn't get metaphor, which then led to the recognition of his other Gerstmann-like signs.

Based on his clinical findings, I believed Eli had a problem in his angular gyrus.

But when I saw the MRI, I knew.

Multiple forms.

That's why they decided to call it glioblastoma multiforme.

From one patient to the next, this tumor takes on many shapes, sizes, locations, and behaviors. It's never the same, never consistent, except in its near-universal ability to steal, kill, and destroy quality and length of life. I've seen tiny tumors kill in weeks, huge bilateral butterfly GBMs take several months, and total brain GBMs called gliomatosis cerebri that kill their victims slowly, grinding them down into bits of malfunctioning humanity like Robert Andrews, their families carting them around to for-profit clinics all over the country, trying anything, everything, to snatch them back from the brink, always failing eventually.

I was sitting in the MRI control room, watching Eli's scan come across with a radiologist we call the Oracle, although his real name is Sandy Jackson.

The form on the screen, Eli's tumor, was cystic. A perfect round ball, bright on the edges and dark in the middle, the size of a walnut. I could see in my mind what it would look like in surgery—aggressive dark red cells bumping into fuzzy, swollen white matter. I saw the yellow fluid inside the cyst that would drain out, leaving the capsule of the tumor to collapse and come out more easily.

I saw the pathology slides with Grossman whistling under his mustard-tinged breath, his sandwich crumbs on the microscope stand. I heard his terminal trifecta announcement and saw the twelve-month clinical course of Eli fading into oblivion and dying despite our best efforts.

I knew what would happen.

I'd seen the end of him right there on the MRI screen.

"It's in his angular gyrus," Sandy said.

Sandy Jackson is best known for his noncommittal reports. Surgeons groan when they realize he'll be reading their films because they know it'll be up to them to decide what they really show. He never wants to make the wrong call on anything, so his reports are so vague as to be mostly useless. The flip side of this is that he is incredibly thorough and never misses anything. He's actually one of my favorite radiologists because I know that somewhere in the midst of all those qualifiers is the absolute truth, which is always better than having no confidence in the report at all. He might not tell you what he thinks he's seeing, but you can bet he will describe it.

Once, I had a patient who had fallen fifty feet and had a terrible spine fracture. Sandy's report read,

Patient has what I think is a linear anomaly extending front to back through the L3 vertebra. This is possibly a fracture, although it could represent imaging artifact, infection, a nutrient blood vessel, or perhaps it might also be a congenital deformity. I am pretty sure, based on how it looks, that it might be related to the patient's fall, although certainly it could be many other things. Neurosurgical consultation, I think, is recommended.

After that case I casually mentioned to Sandy that I imagined him sitting in the dark, his eyes closed, hands on the monitor, visualizing the MRI scans and awaiting a prophetic vision of what they showed, scrying into the flickering monitor like the Oracle of Delphi with a crystal ball. He thought it was hilarious and mentioned it to some of his colleagues.

The name stuck, and Sandy became officially known throughout the hospital as the Oracle.

"Yep. Cystic tumor, young guy, angular gyrus. It explains his symptoms," I said.

The Oracle nodded and touched the screen. "It could also be abscess, stroke, an old blood clot, or a metastatic tumor."

"It could," I said. "He's thirty-seven, so stroke is unlikely. And he's never had a head injury or any other reason to have a hemorrhage. He's healthy, not diabetic or an IV drug user, so I doubt abscess. He deserves a scan of the rest of his body, though, just to be thorough."

It's dangerous in medicine (or in anything, really) to let the most likely thing be the only thing you think of. Occam's razor notwithstanding, just because Eli was statistically most likely to have a GBM did not, in fact, mean he *did* have a GBM. A CT scan of the rest of his body would rule out other malignancies.

The Oracle was right about that, but Occam won out. The CT was negative.

Eli's tumor was not the result of anything happening outside his head. Parsimony prevailed, and the simplest answer proved to be true.

Just as I'd thought.

When I told Eli and his parents the news, he said, "I've done the research, Dr. Warren. If this is a GBM, I'm done for, right?"

"Eli! We did not raise you to be so fatalistic," his mother said. "Have faith."

He clinched his jaw once and said softly, "Mom, I'm being realistic, not fatalistic. It has nothing to do with faith. It's published actuarial data."

I put my hand on Eli's shoulder. "Hey, let's not get ahead of ourselves. It's not a

GBM until the pathologist says it is. It could be lots of other things," I said, channeling the Oracle.

Eli nodded, but we both knew I was full of it.

———

The phone rang in my operating room twenty minutes after I sent the first biopsy of Eli's tumor to the pathology lab.

The nurse put the phone on speaker, and I heard Grossman crunching and then swallowing something. I swear, that man is always eating.

"What you got, G-man?" I said.

"This is Dr. Grossman," he said.

He's a great pathologist, but he has no sense of humor.

"I know, Grossman. It's a nickname."

"I don't like nicknames. Looks like a glioblastoma. Pretty low mitosis rate though."

"Great," I said. "Thanks. I'll send you more tissue in a few minutes."

"I'll be ready."

The nurse hung up the phone, and I went back to work.

Eli's tumor was mostly fluid filled. Some GBMs make cysts, which can make a small tumor much larger on MRI, since most of the tumor volume is just juicy, goo-like material instead of solid cancer. The other thing I noticed was that the tumor had very well-defined edges. Most GBMs sneak out into the surrounding brain, making it hard to know when you've removed the whole thing.

Once I drained the cyst, the tumor collapsed and came out easily. I had the whole thing in my hand, very unusual for GBM. I looked around in the cavity for a few minutes using the operating microscope, and I noticed a dark area in front of where the tumor had been.

That's where you're going to come back, I mentally said to Eli's tumor. I carefully dissected the dark material and removed it, until all the surrounding tissue looked normal.

I sent the tumor and the extra tissue to Grossman's lab for more studies.

In the recovery room Eli woke up moving both arms and both legs and within a few minutes was asking questions.

"How'd it go?" he said.

"Perfectly," I said. "No trouble in the OR, tumor is all out, and we'll have the final answer from pathology in a couple of days."

He nodded. "Is it GBM?"

"Yes. The preliminary diagnosis is GBM. But we don't do anything until the finals are back. Sometimes the pathologist changes his mind."

Eli cocked his head and raised one eyelid. "Doc? I'm smarter than that."

"It's true. Not often, but sometimes. So let's not focus on anything but getting you over the surgery for now, okay? How are you feeling?"

He smiled. "Like a million bucks."

It wasn't until that night at dinner with Lisa that it hit me.

Eli had used a metaphor.

———

Three days later I sent Eli home. He was well, having no headaches, and begging to leave the hospital. He smiled as I walked into his room and said, "Guess what?"

"What?" I said.

"I did some practice math last night. I got five decimal places!"

———

The next morning I opened my email and saw the pathology report from Grossman. As expected, it was glioblastoma.

His tumor did offer a few surprises though. The first line of the description of Eli's tumor read,

Grade IV astrocytoma/glioblastoma multiforme is present on all slides.
Low rate of cell division, however.

The punch line was that while Eli's tumor was in fact a GBM, it wasn't as malignant and rapidly dividing as they typically are. His was on the low end of the cell growth–rate spectrum.

Even more surprising was the last line:

Margins are clean. No evidence of tumor in the additional biopsy
specimens examined.

The dark material outside Eli's tumor had no malignancy in it. I had removed
the entire GBM with clean margins.

At the moment Eli was cancer-free.

A couple of weeks later, the tumor genetics came back from the outside lab.
Grossman emailed it to me, and I read it in my office:

MGMT receptors are methylated.

That meant Eli's tumor was likely to be sensitive to temozolomide, the best
chemotherapy drug for GBM.

I read the report, feeling happy that things looked positive for him. But then I
reminded myself that happy feelings in GBM care are transient and relative.

Cancer-free for GBM patients means "don't get your hopes up."

It comes back every time.

I closed the email and walked to my office door with Grossman's words stuck
in my mind. *"Margins are clean."*

That won't last long, I thought.

I turned off the light and left the office.

18

Even Before You Start

From the beginning I declare how things will end.

—ISAIAH 46:10, Voice

Being on call in a trauma center is like playing the slot machines at a casino. Sometimes you drop a quarter in, and—*bing bing bing*—you win a hundred bucks. And some nights when you're on call, you have a nice dinner with your family, go to bed, and wake up the next morning realizing you didn't get called all night.

You hit the trauma jackpot.

It's such a good feeling because it means not only that you got a good night's sleep but also that nobody got hurt overnight.

But they say in gambling that the house always wins.

And the same can be said for trauma.

Gamblers invariably take their hundred-buck jackpot and, fueled by the adrenaline from hitting it big on that first pull, keep putting those quarters back into the machine until they finally go back to Tuscaloosa or wherever they're from down a couple hundred dollars.

And doctors who take trauma calls inevitably spend more nights in the ED, standing around the scanner trying to figure out which parts of their patients are broken after this particular crash or fall or shooting or stabbing.

Sometimes you have a few nights in a row of no calls, and when that happens, your sense of impending doom builds until you can almost picture the drunk guy out there deciding that 2:00 a.m. on a stormy night is a good time to climb a ladder to clean out the gutters on his house. Or the redneck who's about to utter those famous last words, "Hey, y'all, hold my beer. Watch this."

I was on such a winning streak for months after the last time Eli came in for a follow-up. His six-month post-op MRI scan was still clean, with no evidence of tumor recurrence, and all traces of his Gerstmann syndrome had vanished.

The ED had been exceptionally quiet, and then I committed a terrible violation of the law of trauma call: never ever talk about how quiet the ED has been.

Lisa and I were having dinner, and I was relaxed and happy and enjoying the soft glow of candlelight on her beautiful face. We held hands and talked and laughed, and I breathed in the warm aromas of her lovely meal and my utter contentment in such moments with her.

"I love you so much, Lee," she said. "This is a perfect night."

I smiled and kissed her hand. "I love you too. And it is a perfect night. I'm so glad that this stretch of call has been so easy. No one's even called me from the ED in weeks."

Lisa's lips parted, and the realization of what I'd just done sucked the air from the room in an almost audible fashion. She started to speak, and I could see her diplomatically editing what she was about to say—*Nice job ruining the evening, buddy*—to something more consistent with her kind and gracious character.

"Oh, honey, you shouldn't say things like that."

Three hours later I'd almost fallen asleep when my phone rang.

"Hello?" I said, knowing before I heard the reply that it was Stinson.

—————

I spent that evening trying to save a young man who had shot himself in the head with a .357 Magnum. Gunshots to the head rarely end well, and they always take me back to Iraq.

There, blood and sweat and hatred and fear swirled in the OR when we worked frantically to undo the destruction of brain and bone caused by snipers and small arms and IEDs. But in the civilian world, when we're treating a self-inflicted gunshot victim, the operating room smells mostly of despair. We're treating someone who was obviously struggling with the hardships of life. And if we save the person, we'll be adding yet more pain and mental anguish to a life that is now dependent and disabled. It's a desperate situation because people who survive gunshots to the head are almost always left with a host of lifelong medical problems, worsened depression, and severe cosmetic deformities.

Knowing all this, we in the operating room bear a heavy load while we work.

On the one hand, I do not believe that anyone can be sane and suicidal at the same time. Thus, despite the self-inflicted nature of these injuries, I work hard to save these patients because I want to give them a chance to survive and find the answers to the questions that drove them to this dark decision.

But at the same time, I can see and feel in the shattered bones the pain they must have been in, and I know they will feel that pain magnified and multiplied a thousandfold if they survive.

Yet we try; we struggle with the brain swelling and the bleeding and the inevitable postoperative complications and family conferences because in the end it is a neurosurgeon's job to try to save lives.

And sometimes we win.

That night we lost. The patient was too hurt, too broken, too late. He died in the ICU shortly after surgery. My best efforts, even the prayers I uttered under my breath as I worked, failed.

I spoke to his family, and they told me he'd struggled with depression and anxiety since he was twelve. And now he was gone at twenty-two.

His mom had a Bible in her hand.

"I'm so sorry," I said. "We did everything we could."

She wiped away a silver tear. "We knew this was coming. Everything we've done to help him feel better has failed. It's like he was created to be sad. We've prayed more for him than for all three of our other kids combined, but it was like those prayers were answered with a no before our son was even born."

I didn't know what to say, but I knew a little about how she felt. We'd had some of the same thoughts about our son Mitch as he grew up. As funny, smart, and caring as he was, he'd always felt uncomfortable in his own skin. I felt this mother's pain and resolved to work even harder to help Mitch.

Sometimes the situation is so sad and the loss so profound that the only thing to do is acknowledge it. There's no sense to be made of it, no explanations to be proffered, no philosophical or religious declaration to give it a context people can relate to and be comforted by.

Any of those statements—"He's in a better place now," "I guess heaven needed him more than you did," or "At least he didn't suffer"—are so unhelpful as to be offensive in those moments when you're staring at a mommy who just lost her boy or a daddy whose spitting image just blew his own brains out. I knew—and they both knew—that in a few minutes they would stand at his bedside, and the bandages covering the mess he'd made of his once-handsome face would be their last memory of a life they created together and desperately tried to help.

Her husband never lifted his eyes from the floor. "He did it in my office. At my desk with my gun. He told me once that he thought he would have been happier if I hadn't worked so much. He felt like my job kept me away too much, like I wasn't there for him."

Moments like these illuminate so clearly the things we should have done that we often speak them out loud, then wonder why they eluded us when we could have done something about them.

I searched my mind for some way to respond, but all I managed was a weak reiteration of "I'm sorry."

The next month was the busiest stretch of civilian trauma call I'd experienced in my career. Car crashes, motorcycle wrecks, a ten-year-old shot through the spinal cord with his dad's hunting rifle, a drunken ATV driver with a massive brain hemorrhage, a lady who jumped off a bridge, and an old man who tripped over a dog toy and fell down his basement stairs kept me in the ED almost every night and in the OR almost every day.

Wartime trauma hospitals are desperate places, but at least the injuries are usually understandable—enemies with an open intent to kill one another. In the civilian world it's all about bad things happening to people who didn't deserve it or who put themselves in situations they shouldn't have been in or who had freak accidents that make us all shake our heads and say, "Thank God that's never happened to me."

I don't think I ever said the words "I'll be praying for your family" more frequently than I did during those few weeks, and I'm certain there was never a time when I was more doubtful it would do any good.

Many nights, during the few hours I had at home to talk about it with Lisa, I circled back to the grieving mother's desperate statement: *"It was like those prayers were answered with a no before our son was even born."*

Trauma patients often present a compressed version of the "I've seen the end of you" feeling I get when I look at a new brain-tumor patient's scan. With GBM I can see the end—the surgery, the chemo, the radiation, the progressive disability and ultimate death—from the beginning. With trauma the primary injury is often perfectly displayed on the initial CT scan, with the end of the story plainly written from the moment of impact.

And I often find myself in the chapel, staring at *The Last Supper,* thinking back through the previous few hours' work, trying to find something we could have done differently but already knowing the answer. The die is cast when the bullet hits the brain, the crowbar crushes the skull, the horse steps on the neck, the truck crosses the median. It's often over before I meet the patient, and my job is to give the family a sense that we tried.

There's a scene in the Mike Myers movie *Austin Powers: International Man of Mystery* where the villain, Dr. Evil, is arguing with his teenage son, Scott. Every time Scott tries to speak, Dr. Evil shushes him, cuts him off before he can get the argument out of his mouth. This goes on until finally Dr. Evil shushes him and says, "Shh, even before you start. That was a preemptive *Shh.*"[21]

And that's how I felt that month.

My daily morning prayers on behalf of the patients I would meet that day, the quiet moments before starting each case, my pleas when I look at a scan and ask for help for the coming operation—all shushed before I got them out of my mouth, over and over as if God were saying he'd already considered my requests and denied them before I was even aware I would ask.

In the movie the shushing before poor Scott can speak is hilarious.

In real life it's soul crushing.

And as if the multiple trauma deaths we had during that bloody month weren't bad enough, near the end of it I met a man named Rupert Chang, who gave me a chance to shush someone else's prayers.

19

First, Do No Harm

He ground my face into the gravel.
  He pounded me into the mud.
I gave up on life altogether.
  I've forgotten what the good life is like.
I said to myself, "This is it. I'm finished.
  GOD is a lost cause."

—LAMENTATIONS 3:16–18, MSG

Rupert Chang was thirty-seven years old, a high school creative writing teacher with three kids and a wife named Grace. I met Rupert and Grace when they came to my office after Rupert's ear, nose, and throat doctor found something he wasn't looking for.

Rupert had suffered for years from chronic sinus infections, so he wasn't surprised that year when he felt it coming on again—the pressure behind his eye, the sense of cloudiness in his thinking, the nagging pain that wouldn't respond to his allergy medicine or Tylenol. Every year, it seemed, he had to go see Dr. Medina to have his sinuses checked, and he knew he'd have to have sinus surgery eventually.

The headaches were particularly bad that year, and Rupert and Grace decided this was the year to stop fooling around with his annual attacks and finally just get it taken care of.

Dr. Medina ordered a sinus CT scan in preparation for the surgery that could eliminate Rupert's struggle with chronic sinusitis once and for all.

Except that the scan did not show only sinusitis. Dr. Medina looked at the images and realized that something else was there. He could see only a little bit of the brain—the bottom of Rupert's frontal lobes—just above the sphenoid sinus, but what he saw did not look normal.

He ordered an MRI, and the next day Rupert and Grace were in my office.

Rupert had a kind face—I can see it as I type these words—a pleasant grin, closely cropped black hair, a nice blend of his parents' obviously Anglo and Asian genetics. Grace was Korean, a tiny woman with a big persona whose smile on this day covered only the lower half of her face. Her eyes tracked my movements and held the same fear I'd seen in Christy's the day I met her and Samuel.

Rupert's neurological exam was completely normal. He had no symptoms other than the headache and mild brain fog he'd had numerous times before when the green Alabama pine pollen covered the entire state and everyone's lungs and immune systems had to react to it.

I pulled up his MRI on the monitor and pointed to the bright areas.

"Every part of your brain is lit up on this scan," I said. Whereas Samuel and Eli and even Mrs. Knopf had discrete lesions—one identifiable area that was obviously tumor—Rupert's whole brain looked the same.

It was all tumor.

"This looks like a condition called gliomatosis cerebri," I said.

"What does that mean?" Rupert said, reaching for Grace's hand.

"Well, we have to have a biopsy to be sure," I said, "but it's basically a cancer that shows up in your whole brain at the same time. This could instead be infection or something else, and that's what we'll pray for, but it's highly suspicious for cancer."

If GBM is a tumor in the brain, gliomatosis cerebri is a brain that has *become* a tumor. It's as if the entire brain decided to become malignant at the same time. I looked through Rupert's scan and couldn't find any area on either side that didn't have some abnormal tissue in it.

Grace nodded slowly. "So there's no chance this is related to his sinuses? Can we try antibiotics?"

I shook my head. "No, ma'am. It's all in his brain, and even if it is an infection, we would have to biopsy it to know how to manage it. I don't see any way to treat this without going to surgery to get a sample of it."

Rupert cleared his throat, looked at Grace, and then turned back to me.

"Then we'd better schedule it, Doctor. I want to know what I'm dealing with."

The Changs wanted to take the weekend to pray and spend time with their family. They were devout people and had handled the news that Rupert likely had a brain tumor with grace and resolution. They returned to the hospital on Monday morning, and I met them in the preoperative holding area to go over the risks of surgery and obtain an informed consent from Rupert.

"This will be a short operation," I said, "thirty minutes or so, and most of that time will be waiting for the pathologist to confirm that we have a diagnosis."

They nodded.

"The scan shows that the safest place to biopsy is in your right temporal lobe, where the tumor looks to be right on the surface. I'll shave a little of your hair and then make the incision here"—I pointed to the skin just above and in front of Rupert's right ear—"and make a quarter-sized hole in the bone with a drill."

Rupert raised an eyebrow. "So I'll have a hole in my head?"

"No, I'll reinsert the bone and secure it to your skull with a small titanium plate."

He looked at Grace and pointed at his head. "When my hair grows back, my part just ain't gonna look right," he said, mimicking Cousin Eddie from *National Lampoon's Christmas Vacation*.[22]

Grace sighed heavily and shrugged. "We watched that movie yesterday. He's been practicing the line since last night."

I laughed and shook my head. "I'm glad you've got a good attitude about this. Once I take the bone off, I'll open the dura—it's like a leathery covering over your brain—and then I'll just take a tiny bit of the tumor to send to the pathologist. He'll look at it under a microscope and then call me to tell me what it is. As soon as I'm sure we have a diagnosis, I'll close everything up and you'll be done. One night in the ICU to make sure there's no bleeding, and then we'll know how to treat this disease. Understand the plan?"

He looked at Grace and then back at me. "Got it."

"Okay," I said. "Now let's talk about the risks."

I'm so practiced at this conversation that I've honed it down to about three minutes. And most of the things that *could* happen are so rare as to be almost not worthy of mention. But it's my job to make sure people know what they're signing up for, so I always mention them.

"Anytime we put you to sleep and open your skin, no matter how minor the procedure, there's a risk you could die. I've never lost anyone in the operating room, except in Iraq, but it's possible. You could develop an infection, lose enough blood to require a transfusion, have a seizure or a stroke or be paralyzed. You could develop memory loss, personality changes, weakness, numbness, lose coordination, go blind, lose hearing, develop a spinal fluid leak. We could fail to make a diagnosis, and you have to remember that this is just a biopsy and that I'm not able to remove the tumor or cure you here today. Do you understand?"

Rupert and Grace both nodded, and Rupert said, "Geez, Doc. You make it sound dangerous."

I smiled. "It *is* dangerous, but we'll get you through it. Most of these things never happen, but I have to tell you about them. And the risks of the procedure are less than the risk to you if we do nothing. Any questions?"

Rupert gave me a thumbs-up. "Let's do this."

I took a marking pen and wrote a purple *W* for "Warren" on his right temple, the mark that our hospital requires surgeons to place on the body part we intend to operate on before the patient goes to sleep. It's designed to make sure we are operating on the correct site and side of the correct patient, and it's the last thing I do before the nurses take my patients from holding to the OR.

I prayed with Rupert and Grace, held both their hands, and then left the room. As I walked out, I heard Grace say, "I love you, honey. It's going to be fine."

———

An hour later I was looking down at the taut red surface of Rupert Chang's right temporal lobe. The craniotomy had been straightforward, the dural opening routine, and now I was ready to take the biopsy and prove what I already knew—that Rupert had gliomatosis cerebri.

I thought about the conversation I would soon have with Grace and her family in the waiting room and what I would say to Rupert in the ICU later that day. Dr. Grimes would get involved, and we would have to call radiation oncology because this wasn't a disease I could cure in the operating room. Rupert's face looked peaceful—no one looks stressed out when anesthetized, which is why people think alcohol and drugs are a good idea when they're having a hard time—but I knew that the next few hours and months for him would be anything but peaceful.

"Bipolar," I said to Nate. He handed me the electrocautery forceps, and I carefully coagulated small surface blood vessels in a one-centimeter square of the brain. This would make it safer to cut out the piece and send it to the lab for Grossman to confirm what I already knew.

"Microscissors," I said. I took the tiny scissors from Nate's hand and made a delicate cut in the pia mater on the surface of Rupert's brain. So far so good. Now all I had to do was remove the specimen.

"Tumor-grasping forceps."

Nate handed me the instrument, and I reached down and removed a chickpea-sized piece of tissue. When I pulled it out, a tiny artery underneath it started to bleed. This is very common and nothing to worry about.

"Gelfoam," I said, and Nate passed me a small collagen sponge soaked in a chemical called thrombin, which helps the body form blood clots.

It didn't work, and red arterial blood quickly soaked the Gelfoam.

I tried the bipolar, but the one-millimeter artery just disintegrated and retracted into the white matter of Rupert's brain. Brain tumors trick the brain into creating new blood vessels to help them grow, but this neovascularity is never normal. The tumor arteries are thin and malformed, not as robust as normal arteries. And sometimes they are so fragile that when you try to cook them, they just fall apart.

In about three seconds the situation turned from Rupert having a tiny bleeding surface artery into an arterial hemorrhage developing inside his right temporal lobe.

From routine to significant in the amount of time it took to pass off the specimen to the tech so she could take it to the pathology lab.

"Bring in the microscope," I said to the circulating nurse.

I've learned over the years that using a microscope can often turn something hard into something easier because light and magnification make it much less difficult to find the problem when I'm dealing with tiny structures.

The nurse pushed the microscope up to the table, and I pressed the button to unlock it and swing it over Rupert's head. Within a few seconds I had a much clearer picture of what was happening, and it wasn't good.

"These vessels are like wet tissue paper," I said.

The brain began to swell, so I had to resect part of the temporal lobe to get down to a larger part of the artery and try to control it. But every time I tried to coagulate the vessel, it would crumble and retract farther. The disintegrating vessel pulled back past a branch point and then another, and suddenly there were four or five bleeders and major brain swelling. Over and over I chased the bleeding arteries with the same result. The temporal lobe began to bulge outside the edges of the skull opening I'd made.

"Heart rate's dropping," the anesthetist said. This meant Rupert's brain pressure was rising. The situation was rapidly deteriorating.

Rupert was in trouble.

As I'd once had to do for Samuel, my only option was to perform a temporal lobectomy. I again called on my training, on the dozens of epilepsy lobectomies I'd performed under the instruction of Professor Jack Wilberger, my mentor and friend. I removed the temporal lobe quickly, but the bleeding would not stop. All of Rupert's arteries were diseased and weak and would not close with any of the numerous techniques I'd mastered over the years.

"Pressure's getting pretty high up here," the anesthetist said.

I fought Rupert's bleeding brain for several more minutes. I tried pressure, Gelfoam, cautery, multiple hemostatic agents, and carotid artery pressure, but nothing worked. Ultimately I made a decision to clip off the middle cerebral artery upstream from the bleeding.

This stopped the flow, but I knew it would also cause a stroke to the other parts of Rupert's brain that received blood from the artery.

The vital signs stabilized, and things seemed to settle down. I prayed that Rupert had good collateral flow from the other brain arteries I had not clipped; some people depend entirely on one artery for some parts of their brains, while others have numerous vessels that contribute to the flow. Those people can handle losing one of their arteries to a clot or, in this case, to a surgeon-applied clip.

Only time would tell us whether Rupert had collaterals.

About the time I got the skin closed, the phone in the OR rang. It was Grossman. "Looks like gliomatosis cerebri. Nasty one too. Every cell in the specimen is malignant."

I didn't go into it with Grossman, but the diagnosis wasn't Rupert's biggest problem at the moment.

I bandaged Rupert's head and lifted his eyelids. His pupils were blown—maximally dilated—which meant his brain stem was damaged. I knew the bleeding was stopped, and there wasn't a chance I'd put any pressure on the brain stem while I was inside his head. So there were only two possible explanations for his dilated pupils. Either the temporal bleeding had caused obstruction of his CSF pathway, resulting in hydrocephalus, or the hemorrhage had extended into his midbrain and directly injured the nuclei of his third cranial nerves. They are the control centers for the oculomotor nerves that serve to constrict the pupil, elevate the eyelid, and move the eye in most of the directions you can look (other nerves control the ability to look to the side or down and in).

The only way to know was to send him to radiology for an emergency CT scan. Once I had a picture of the deep parts of Rupert's brain, I would know whether there was anything I could do about it.

I ordered the scan, and Nate, the anesthetist, and the OR nurses rolled Rupert's stretcher to radiology while I went out to talk to Grace and Rupert's other family members.

She was sitting on a couch on the other side of the waiting room as I entered. Head down, she was no doubt praying for her husband and maybe even for me and my team as people commonly tell me they do—"We're praying for you too, Doc! That your eyes will be sharp and your hands steady!"

She looked up as I approached, and a look of relief crossed her face. But she instantly recognized that I wasn't smiling, and before I got halfway to her, she was on her feet and rushing toward me.

"What happened? You look worried," she said.

She clasped both my hands, and I said, "We should sit down."

She shook her head. "No. Tell me here. What happened to my husband?"

I looked into her deep brown eyes and did what I had to do. It's my job to shoot straight with people no matter what.

"When I took the biopsy, his brain began to bleed. The blood vessels were so diseased that they wouldn't coagulate like normal arteries do, and I had to clip off a major brain artery to get the bleeding stopped. He's had a lot of brain swelling and has most likely suffered a major stroke. He's getting a CT now, and in a few minutes I'll know if there's anything else I can do for him."

Her eyes spilled over with tears, but she never broke her gaze. "Did you get the biopsy result? Is it really brain cancer?"

I nodded. "Yes. Gliomatosis cerebri. But what happened in the operating room today is much more life threatening right now."

"Then why are you here with me?"

"I had to tell you what was happening," I said.

She squeezed my hands even more tightly. I can feel her grasp as I write these words, her strength and resolve as she spoke. "Go try to save him, Doctor. We can talk later."

"I'm so sorry," I said.

"Don't be sorry. Be fast. Do what you can for him."

The images scrolled onto the CT scanner's monitors slowly, one cut at a time, and they told a horror story of neuronal destruction and brain damage.

In between the already-present tumor and brain swelling was blood—a lot of new blood. While his arteries were bleeding, a branch must have been pointed toward the inside. It looked very similar to what we see when a person ruptures a brain aneurysm. All the places where we normally see CSF were now filled with blood. Rupert had blood in all his basal cisterns, the tiny wells of CSF around the brain stem that contain all the blood vessels that bring oxygen to that important territory. He had blood in his ventricles and was rapidly developing hydrocephalus.

And most of the right side of his brain was already dark, a sure sign he was having a massive stroke.

"Get him to the ICU. He needs a drain immediately," I said.

I went back to the waiting room to find Grace. She and her family were on their knees in a circle, right in the middle of the room, praying and calling out to God audibly.

I told Grace about the scan and that Rupert needed a ventriculostomy drain if he was to have any chance to survive. This would allow me to drain some of the blood and fluid out of his brain and lower his intracranial pressure to improve the blood flow to the brain and help him fight the swelling. I told her that he would be in the ICU any minute and that the nurses were already setting up for me to do the procedure. But I needed her consent, and I needed it right now or we would lose him.

She nodded slowly as I spoke, her face pale and her grip on my hands slack. "Go. Do it. Do your best."

The drain went in easily, and within a few minutes Rupert's brain pressure was back to normal. But despite the rapid intervention, he never woke up.

After three days on the ventilator with no signs of spontaneous brain activity, Grace brought us a living will Rupert had signed at home the day before his surgery. In it he clearly articulated his wishes should he ever be on life support with no chance of meaningful survival.

In his own hand Rupert had written, "I do not wish to be kept alive artificially if my doctor has determined that my quality of life will be impaired or that my underlying brain cancer cannot be cured. I wish to be allowed to die and do not consent to feeding tubes, breathing tubes, emergency intervention, CPR, or any other treatment designed to prolong my life if my overall prognosis is terminal or if I would have serious or permanent neurological deficits."

We took him off the ventilator, and he immediately died without taking a single breath on his own.

Through it all Grace never lashed out, never blamed me, never said anything other than to direct us to try our best and to thank us for doing so.

She asked to be left alone with his body, and she was gone when I returned to the ICU an hour later to check on her. I thought I would never see her again.

When there is an unexpected surgery-related death in most hospitals, it triggers a protocol to review the issue. This includes a mandatory autopsy.

It took a week to get the results, but in addition to the obvious stroke and hemorrhage the coroner noticed in Rupert's brain, one paragraph stood out:

Gliomatosis cerebri is widely present in the cerebral tissue, with over 96 percent of examined brain exhibiting malignancy.

Most people in the world never have the experience of directly contributing to the death of another human. Doctors, even those of us who work with deadly diseases, rarely experience the loss of a patient that is directly tied to something we do—thankfully. Our oath begins with the mantra *Primum non nocere*—"First, do no harm."

I take that very seriously, and in the weeks following Rupert's death, I was in a deep hole of self-doubt and anger at what had happened. The fact that he'd had a terminal disease did not make it more tolerable to me that he had died as a direct result of my operation.

The Department of Surgery held a peer review of the case, as we do for every perioperative death. All the surgeons in attendance said they would have done everything exactly as I did, and it was ruled an unavoidable death. I even discussed the case with several neurosurgery peers across the country, and all of them said they couldn't find a single thing I did that they would change.

One of my friends, a brain surgeon of the highest caliber and whose judgment I trust implicitly, said, "Lee, this tumor was like a booby trap. He never had a chance. Without the biopsy he would have died in a month anyway. This wasn't your fault."

Even though I knew that was true, the feeling of guilt associated with a surgical death—even an unavoidable one—lands squarely on the shoulders of the person holding the knife. You want your surgeon to have that kind of conscience, and I certainly did.

The hard part is to keep going, to take care of your other patients, to not let the pain wreck you. Or, worse, to let it make you doubtful, because a surgeon who loses self-confidence is completely unsafe.

I kept thinking about Rupert and the prayers his wife and family were uttering on his behalf while I was operating on him. God must have been saying *Shush!* the whole time, because the answer was no. It was always no, even before Rupert had the sinus scan in Dr. Medina's office prior to his surgery.

The answer to all the prayers spoken for Rupert Chang—from the ones his parents prayed for his safety and his future as he was growing up to the ones desperately cried out in the ICU by his wife and kids and relatives as he languished in a deep coma for seventy-two hours after I'd clipped off his middle cerebral artery—was a definitive no.

I struggled to make sense of it, especially in the context of the horrible month of trauma and bloodshed we'd had in our hospital. So much pain, so many tears, so many families meeting the doctors in conference rooms to discuss end-of-life issues. So many loved ones having conversations with Pastor Jon and the other hospital chaplains in so many corners of the hospital, all grappling with why God said no to them and their faithful prayers.

I had no answers.

Lisa, my constant adviser and confidant, was equally unable to provide context or solve the puzzle.

Gliomatosis cerebri, GBM, head trauma, and a host of other deadly outcomes raged through our hospital and ravaged my faith that month and left me almost ready to say aloud something I'd been secretly feeling for a long time—I wasn't sure what I believed anymore.

And on top of all that, one day Lisa and I entered our office and found a note from our receptionist on my desk. It said, "Grace Chang, her parents, and her children want to meet with you."

20

Voices

Any man's death diminishes me, because I am involved in
mankind, and therefore never send to know for whom the
bell tolls; it tolls for thee.

—JOHN DONNE, "Meditation XVII"

The next afternoon I'd finished making rounds and was walking down the
hall toward the hospital parking garage. The weight of the day pressed
down on me like a sixteen-ton load, so when I passed by the chapel, I decided to go
in and sit for a few minutes.

As usual it was empty and dark, which was perfect because I had some things
I wanted to say to God.

That morning I'd spent two frantic hours trying to stop the bleeding inside the
head of an eighteen-month-old baby. Like many babies, he'd had a rough morning
during which he'd been crying nonstop. Unlike most babies, however, his crying
wasn't met with the comforting cuddles of a loving mother. Instead, his mom's
drunken boyfriend had shaken him until his brain bled. I'd been in my office seeing
patients when Stinson had called and said, "This kid's not going to make it to Birmingham. He needs surgery now. Will you come and see him?"

Our hospital was not equipped to handle pediatric intensive care, but my experience in Pittsburgh, San Antonio, and Iraq had made me comfortable with pediatric neurosurgical emergencies. I pulled up the scan. Stinson was right: The baby's

large subdural hematoma was shifting his brain from left to right. He was in serious trouble. By the time we could spin up a chopper and have the kid airlifted to Children's of Alabama, he would already be dead.

I canceled the rest of my office schedule for the day and ran to the car. While I drove to the hospital with my hazard lights on, I called Jim, my pediatric neurosurgery colleague in Birmingham.

"We'll have the Life Flight medics in the OR with you," he said, "and as soon as you get his brain decompressed, we'll fly him straight here to take care of him post-op."

Procedurally, the case was typical—no different from the dozens of other pediatric brain surgeries I'd done except for the specifics of the case. No bullets from insurgents, skull fractures from falling off a changing table, or scalp lacerations because Mom didn't bother with a car seat, but the same swollen brain, multiple bleeding arteries, and sense of rage I always feel when I'm taking care of babies whose injuries are the fault of adults who were supposed to protect them. And it always strikes me how tragic it is that this is a typical thing for neurosurgeons—trying to save the delicate and precious nervous systems of patients who have suffered due to other people's negligence or malice.

The baby was alive when the medics wheeled him out of my OR, and I waited anxiously the rest of the day for word from Jim. He finally called just as I was finishing evening rounds.

"Doesn't look good," he said. "We found evidence of multiple previous injuries—broken bones, cigarette burns, retinal detachments, possibly even sexual assault. This boy's been someone's punching bag for a while now."

I sat in the chapel and intended to have it out with God. I didn't understand why he allowed a baby to be born whose primary experiences in this life would be serial abuse and a potentially fatal brain hemorrhage because a man wanted him to be quiet.

The Last Supper and the soft music and the flickering candles gave me the venue I needed to be still and think. I heard the door open behind me. I turned as Pastor Jon entered the chapel. He sat next to me, smiling and avuncular with a Bible in his hand.

"Lisa called to tell me about your day," he said. "She said you'd probably be here."

"She knows me," I said.

"Tell me what happened," he said.

I told him the story, and then I said, "I just don't understand how a God who says he loves us could let that baby be born into that family. How can it be true that he knows everything before it happens but also that he cares about us and wants us to have happy lives? It doesn't make sense to me sometimes."

He listened to me, squeezed my knee, and wiped his eyes with a handkerchief he pulled from his pocket. "I have four children. Two are here, and two are with the Lord."

The phrase *with the Lord* is Christianese for someone having passed away.

I looked over at him. "I'm sorry. What happened?"

He looked forward, his eyes moving back and forth as if he were watching a movie in his mind. "Our oldest daughter died when she was a few days old. Heart defect. And our son was hit by a car when he was twenty-one."

"I'm so sorry. So you know what I mean, then?"

He waved the Bible toward me. "Yes. Anyone who claims that being a Christian means you won't have any trouble in your life is reading a different Bible than I have. Even Jesus promised we'd have hard times."[23]

I nodded. "I know that. But some things in life make me wonder if any of it's even true."

Pastor Jon was silent for a few seconds. Then he spoke again, a little softer. There was a tone in his voice that hadn't been there before, a little waver in his pitch. "Don't get me wrong, Doctor. Burying your baby makes you wonder if what you believe is true. And for most of those twenty years between losing our daughter and burying our son, I wasn't sure what I believed either. I shook my fist at God more days than not. But then, when our son died, it hit me: Knowing the answers isn't my work. Raging against God for putting us into a world full of pain doesn't make the pain stop. My work had to be about learning how to live—and help other people live—in a painful world but still somehow be able to have faith."

"I'm just so tired of all of it," I said. "The last couple of months around here have been awful, and the baby today just put me past the limit. I don't know how you did it, surviving the loss of two kids, when I can't even handle nearly losing someone else's kid. And I'm sick of having to act like I'm hopeful for people when I already know what's going to happen to them."

Pastor Jon looked at me for a while and then said, "You mean like Mr. Chang?"

I'd been so focused on the baby that I'd completely forgotten I'd scheduled the meeting with Grace Chang for the next day. I squeezed my temples. "Yes."

"Lisa told me about your meeting tomorrow."

"I don't know what they want to talk about," I said, "but whatever it is, I don't have any answers for them."

He nodded and put his hand on my shoulder. "Most likely they just want to understand what happened to him."

"That's the thing, Pastor. I'm the surgeon, and even I don't understand what happened. His brain turned into cancer, all the blood vessels were rotten, so diseased that my tiny little biopsy started a chain reaction of vessel disintegration and hemorrhage that ultimately required me to sacrifice a major artery to keep him from bleeding to death in the OR. How can anyone understand that?"

"You're right," he said. "There's no way to make sense of it. And yet it happened, and they're living in the aftermath of it. It's got to be hard for them. I've been praying for them—and for you—ever since I heard about it."

I shook my head. "I don't know why God lets these things happen. It doesn't make sense to tell us to pray without ceasing, to pray about everything in our lives, when some things are already decided before we even become aware of them."

Pastor Jon was silent for a couple of minutes. Then he stood and walked closer to *The Last Supper*. He pointed at Jesus. "Think about what happened after this moment."

"What do you mean?" I said.

"Well, Jesus is God, right? He knew before he ever created the earth that the plan would be for him to go to the cross not long after this scene, the Last Supper in the upper room, right?"

I nodded. "Yes, but I still—"

He waved a hand. "Okay, he knew what the plan was, what God's decision was, but did he go straight from the supper to the cross?"

I thought through the story. "No, he went to the garden to pray."

"And what did he pray?"

"That's when he said 'Let this cup pass from me' and 'Thy will be done,'"[24] I said.

"Exactly. Jesus, who *is* God and who already knew the plan, still prayed that it could be different. He still asked God to change it, to spare him, even though he knew the answer before he said the prayer."

I thought about the countless Bible classes and sermons I'd heard growing up in our small-town Oklahoma church using this story to illustrate Jesus's faithfulness and self-sacrifice. Or to explain that his taking time to pray was an example to us of his humanness, showing that his flesh didn't want to experience what he knew was coming—the unfair trial, the beatings, the humiliation, the nails in his flesh, the asphyxiation on the cross, the excruciating pain of crucifixion. And how despite the human Jesus not wanting it, the God Jesus was faithful and went to the cross anyway.

What I didn't see was how this was relevant to Rupert Chang's brain tumor, his death as a result of the biopsy, or my meeting with Rupert's family.

I felt the dull ache behind my eyes growing. "I'm sorry. I don't get it. How does this help me tomorrow?"

Pastor Jon walked over and sat next to me. He leaned back in his chair and reached into his pocket. He pulled out one of his little wooden crosses, like the one he'd given Samuel on his deathbed. He held it up and rubbed his thumb up and down it.

"The reason Jesus stopped in the garden to pray, to ask for a different outcome, even though he knew the answer already, was because the purpose of prayer isn't to bend God's will to ours. The purpose of prayer is to bend us to God's will. Jesus was showing us that it's a good thing—in fact, sometimes it's the *only* thing we have—to stop even when things seem hopeless and remember that it's not hopeless to God. He's got a plan, even when it's not obvious to us or when it's not the plan we would choose."

I held up my hand. "Hold on. That's awfully convenient, isn't it? To fall back on the 'God has a plan' platitude when things are hard? That's exactly what's bothering me right now, Pastor. I see somebody who's going to die; I know they're dead when I look at the initial MRI. But I'm supposed to pray for them, encourage them to have faith, believe they can make it, when I already know. That baby today, Rupert Chang, all of them—doomed before I ever met them. And when it turns out to be true, we as Christians are supposed to shrug our shoulders and say, 'Well, it's just part of God's plan.' It's crazy, and it doesn't feel right to me anymore. Next you'll tell me to read Romans 8 and remember that everything works out for good."

Pastor Jon looked me straight in the eye. I'd never seen a sterner look on his face. "Listen. I understand you're hurting and you're tired on a level I can't even imagine. I don't know how you doctors do it, being around such difficult things all the time, having to make such tough decisions and have your hands right there on it in the worst moments. But you need to really understand something if you're going to survive this career with your faith intact."

"And what's that?"

"Romans 8:28 is one of the most misquoted and misunderstood verses of the Bible. It *does not* say that God makes everything good for people who believe in him—"

"Yes, it does," I said, interrupting. "My dad quoted that verse to me every time I lost a game or a girl broke up with me. It says that all things work together for good for those that love the Lord."

Pastor Jon smiled softly and shook his head. "That's almost what it says, yes. But you're ignoring the context and the following verses. Go read it and pay attention to what it's really saying, because that verse is one of the only reasons I didn't kill myself after my son died. If I believed that the Bible says everything works out for good all the time, I would know it wasn't true and I would throw this cross out and get another job. But that's not what it says. It says if we love the Lord, he will use everything in our lives to make us more like Jesus, which is always good for us. Big difference."

I stared ahead, looking at all the disciples' faces, wondering whether any of them had been as doubtful as I was right then.

"I have one more question," I said. "You said you thought about killing yourself after your son died. And that Romans 8 helped you through that time. Help me understand that."

He sat down next to me, looked ahead for a moment, and then said quietly, "It was the nighttime, really, that did it. When I heard the voices."

"The voices?" I said.

"Yes. The ones we all hear, the ones that tell us that we're all alone or that nothing will ever get better. Those voices. You have them too."

I thought about it for a moment. "Sure. I never thought of them as voices though. Just negative thoughts that pop into my head sometimes."

He nodded. "Right. Same thing. After my son died, I heard them a lot. I was going to be an old man someday, but my two dead kids would always be the same ages they were when they died. Only two of my four kids would be at my funeral someday. Those voices."

"I'm sorry. What did you do?"

"I challenged them. I remembered what the Bible says, that this life is only part of the story, that I would see those two kids again. And then I remembered something I'd read in *The Pilgrim's Song Book,* an old book by a man named Oswald Chambers. I used to read it every morning, but I'd kind of forgotten about it since our son died. Then one morning, after hearing the voices all night while I couldn't sleep, I opened it, and something he said made a lot of sense to me. 'The remarkable thing about fearing God is that when you fear God you fear nothing else, whereas if you do not fear God you fear everything else.'"[25]

"You're saying that being afraid of God made you less afraid of everything else? That makes no sense."

He shook his head. "Not that kind of fear. Think about your dad when you were little. He seemed so powerful, so strong, so awesome. You wanted to please him, knew he could protect you or punish you or reward you, and you wanted desperately for him to love you and hold on to you, right?"

I nodded. That was exactly how I'd felt.

"Okay, so you get it. A better word than *fear* is *reverence.* You held your dad in such high esteem that you were in awe of him. And when things were scary, you wanted to hold his hand or climb into his arms."

"I thought my dad could do anything."

"And that's what Oswald Chambers meant. God is so big and powerful and mighty and dangerous and righteous that he's kind of terrifying. But he's also good. He promises that everything that happens is redeemable, that he can use it to make us more like Jesus. Compared to that, everything else is nothing. The things I was afraid of—growing old without my kids and the rest of it—weren't as scary when I realized that I was still alive and had a purpose and that God was still there. Believing I was all alone would have been far more terrifying. I told the voices to hush, and ever since, I've held tight to the idea that no matter what my circumstances are, God's bigger. It sounds so simple, but it really worked."

"I wish I could feel that right now," I said. "I've seen so much death lately. So much pain. It feels like there's nothing good left in the world. All these people, these families, so broken. That little boy today, Rupert's kids . . . It's not fair."

Pastor Jon squeezed my knee. "I know. But remember for whom the bell tolls. It's not your job to understand why things happen. It's your job to make the biggest difference you can in spite of what happens."

Another bizarre reference. "For whom the bell tolls?" I said. "Hemingway?"

He chuckled quietly. "No, but that's a good novel. The quote came from an essay by John Donne.[26] It means that everyone dies. Every life ends. So don't get so caught up in the tragedy that you forget to live while you can. You're here to help make things better. To shine a light. Heal when you can, help people deal with the diseases and the injuries they can't handle on their own. That's your work, Lee. And the voices—the Enemy's voice—will always try to make you feel overwhelmed and ineffective, make you question your faith. But every time you make it through one of these situations and help people process it, you're better able to help the next one. A little stronger. More like the guy in the painting over there. And that's a good thing."

Neither of us spoke for a minute or so, and then Pastor Jon looked at his watch. "I've got a couple more patients to pray with tonight. Let me know how it goes tomorrow."

I thanked him, and he walked out of the chapel. The sound of the door shutting behind him reverberated.

I appreciated Pastor Jon's heart, but his words didn't sit right.

The next day I would meet with Rupert Chang's family and try to help them understand his illness and his sudden death, but I had no idea what I would say. In my entire career I'd never met with a family after the day a patient died, nor had I ever heard of any family requesting such a meeting.

They must be mad at me, I concluded. They wanted to look into the eyes of the man they believed was responsible for Rupert's death. And I didn't blame them; I was mad at myself too. But even so, I knew it wasn't my fault. The disease had laid the trap and led me into it. Rupert Chang had been a dead man walking when his parents' chromosomes combined to make the embryo from which he arose, their united DNA producing mutations that led to a tumor suppressor gene being deleted or an oncogene being expressed. All their prayers for their bouncing baby boy to have a long and healthy life were definitively answered no before he took his first breath.

But how could I say those things?

And how could Pastor Jon, who'd buried two of his own children, still believe in a God who is said to be all love, all about giving us an abundant and happy life?

Fear God, or fear everything else.

That night the voices came.

I wasn't a good enough doctor.

God, if he was even real, had let that baby suffer.

The Changs were going to blame me for Rupert's death, when in reality Rupert had never even had a chance.

None of us, really, ever have a chance.

Don't forget, Lee: the bell tolls for thee.

21

Not the Whole Story

Stories are the most important thing we humans can create.

—Shawn Coyne, *The Story Grid*

G race Chang, her three children, and her parents and in-laws sat in chairs across from my desk, dressed as if they'd just come from church. Eight impassive faces with no smiles or frowns or tears to reveal their feelings. The last time I'd seen these people had been moments after I'd told them that Rupert was going to die, before I'd given the order to have him taken off life support at Grace's request. These faces had been full of pain and surrounded by the heavy air of grief. Now they were still, quiet, softened somehow from how they'd looked in my mind the thousand times I'd replayed the scene.

"Good morning, Mrs. Chang. How are you?" I said, then immediately wished I'd chosen different words.

She half smiled. "We are well, Doctor. Thank you for meeting with us."

This was the moment I'd been dreading. I had my speech about Rupert's disease and the inevitability of his death prepared, had his films and the pathology report on my computer in case they wanted to see them. I was as ready as I could be to go back through his entire case.

"Of course," I said. "What can I do for you?"

Grace leaned back in her chair and folded her hands in her lap. She looked at her children and then back at me. "We realize that you are probably feeling bad about my husband's death. It must be very hard as a doctor when you lose a patient."

These people are concerned about my feelings? That's very kind, but it's a strange way to start this meeting.

"You're right," I said. "And thank you for saying that. I do feel terrible about what happened to Rupert. Would you like to go over his case again so I can try to explain it more clearly?"

She shook her head. "That's not why we're here. We understand what happened, and we're grateful for everything you did, especially for praying with us before the surgery."

"I thought you wanted to meet to talk about the surgery," I said. "What is it you wanted to discuss?"

"We just thought you should know this: The night before surgery Rupert prayed that if he really had gliomatosis cerebri, God would just take him home. He did not want to waste away or become a burden to his family. We of course told him he would never burden us, but he said he wasn't afraid of dying. The only thing that scared him was not having a life while he was still alive. After everything happened and we saw the final pathology report, we realized God answered his prayers."

Rupert's father, a professorial older man with silver hair and John Lennon glasses, leaned forward and cleared his throat softly. "Doctor," he said, "my son was an educator, an eloquent man who loved writing, language, and teaching. But his first love was Jesus, and he always knew that this life was only the beginning. Being trapped in a body as it broke down around him would have been incredibly difficult for Rupert, and we are very thankful he was spared such a fate. We believe God prepared those blood vessels and orchestrated this event in order to take Rupert home with no pain or suffering, and we are most grateful for this mercy."

I didn't know what to say. Rupert's death was, for them, an answer to prayer—his as well as theirs. A merciful thing, a blessing. They saw it as a part of God's plan.

My eyes burned and I blinked hard. "I'm so glad you have peace about it. Thank you for sharing this with me."

"Of course, Doctor," Grace said. "But may we ask you a favor?"

"Absolutely," I said. "Whatever you need."

She looked at her children and nodded. Then all of them—the kids, Grace, and the parents—stood and walked around my desk.

"We'd like to pray for you," Grace's father said, "that you will be blessed in the difficult work you do, that the pain of losing a few patients would be balanced by the joy of seeing many saved, and that you would always be reminded that God is operating according to his plans even when he's using your hands."

I was unable to speak as they all placed their hands on my shoulders and my head. Both Rupert's and Grace's fathers prayed over me, asking God to bless me and my family, to help me heal the sick, counsel the dying, and bear up under the trials of my career. They prayed for my family, my children, and my health. I'd never experienced anything like it, and tears flowed down my face. When they were done, all of them hugged me and thanked me for taking care of Rupert.

Grace shook my hand and said, "Doctor, Rupert wrote me a letter that he asked me to read only if this disease took him. In it he said he wanted me to remember that his story consisted of his whole life, not just his diagnosis and his death. He wanted me to remind the kids of the thousands of moments we had together, all the laughter and the lessons he taught us about how to really live while you're alive. And to remember that his life was always aimed toward something higher, which I believe he's living now. He wanted us to celebrate who he was and not to perpetually mourn the brevity of his time with us."

After the door closed behind the Chang family, I sat at my desk for a while, thinking through all they'd said. Rupert had faced his disease and death with a strength I hadn't seen before, and he'd shown us all that his faith wasn't just something he talked about. He must have really, deeply believed that he was going someplace better, that his life was about something bigger, that his family needed to see him live it out even to the end.

The funny thing was, I realized I had needed to see it too. Grace said Rupert wanted his family to understand that his life was a story, and those words nudged something inside me I'd been trying to find.

That night I lay in bed next to Lisa, centered and safe in her arms. I was comfortable, healthy, and happy, but wondering. A few weeks before, Rupert had also been comfortable, happy, and, to the best of his knowledge, healthy too. But now he was gone from this life, either out there somewhere knowing for sure that his faith was well founded, or cold and dead and unaware he'd chosen the wrong side of Pascal's wager.

At the end of his life, he'd held up well, taken it like a man, faced into the headwind of his life's greatest storm, and shown his kids and his wife that all those times he'd told them what he believed in, he really had.

What would I have done?

———

The next morning I was up at three, my first cup of coffee warm in my hands, Matt Redman's "Blessed Be Your Name" playing in my ear, my MacBook Pro in my lap. I start every morning this way, one earphone out so I can hear if Lisa calls out to me or my phone rings.

Sitting at the kitchen table with my laptop, I could hear the ceiling fan, the refrigerator, and the sounds a happy home makes when everyone's asleep. My morning routine helps me order my thoughts and steel myself for whatever may come that day. It starts with worship music and a few minutes of Bible reading and prayer, and I've found over the years—even when I wasn't sure I believed what I was reading—that disciplining myself to adhere to this routine somehow makes my life steadier.

And then I write.

In past years that early-morning time was when I studied, learning physiology or pharmacology or the written parts of how to become a surgeon. But since the war, since realizing Iraq followed me home, the couple of hours before Lisa gets up and the day really starts are when I sit and try to grapple with how to tell myself and the world what all that carnage and chaos really did to me.

On the day after Grace Chang and her family prayed for me instead of telling me how angry they were at me, I was writing about operating in a tent hospital during a mortar attack.

And that's when it all started coming together for me.

We're all getting mortared. We're all exposed, all in a war, all perpetually fighting for our lives. In Iraq some people couldn't handle the strain, and every time the sirens wailed, they would break down and run to the bunkers, abandoning their patients. Others seemed indifferent to the danger, kept on working, never flinched.

So, too, in normal life.

Like Rupert Chang.

Grace said that Rupert's whole life, not just his diagnosis and untimely end, was his story. As I was typing out my stories about battles and bombs and blood-shed, the idea that all those experiences were part of my story—all our stories—started coalescing in my mind.

I heard a noise and looked up to see a sleepy Mitch standing next to me. He wore pajama pants and a T-shirt with a grizzly bear on it—Mitch loved bears—and he had a troubled look on his face. He had grown several inches over the previous year, lean and already taller than me. But in the low light and pajamas, he still looked like my little boy.

"What's up, buddy?" I said.

He rubbed his eyes. "Had a bad dream. I just got up to go to the bathroom."

I pushed my computer away and patted the chair next to me. "Sit down. Let's talk about it."

He sat for a moment and stared ahead into the dark room. He was quiet for a while, and then he leaned his head against my shoulder. "I'm gonna go back to bed."

"Tell me about your dream first," I said.

"It's nothing," he said. "We'll talk later. I need to sleep a little more."

He went back downstairs, and I heard his door close. I took a sip of my coffee and started writing again.

That morning I finished the chapter I was working on, which ultimately became part of my first book, the self-published *Called Out: A Brain Surgeon Goes to War.*

But left unfinished was my realization that what really bothered me about Rupert Chang's death—and all those trauma patients in the horrible month I'd just endured and that punching-bag baby I'd tried to save—was Pastor Jon's reminder that the bell tolled for me too.

Rupert's story wasn't my story, but I was a part of his and he a part of mine.

Another line of John Donne's essay that describes the bell tolling is the equally famous "No man is an island."[27]

And that morning was the first time I actually made the connection.

The thing that troubled me so much about glioblastoma was that I wasn't sure how I would hold up if it happened to me, when just watching other people go through it made me quiver with doubt.

But Rupert made me see that it wasn't about the cancer; it was about the character. I wasn't afraid of *getting* cancer; I was afraid of how I would respond if I did.

Raised in a Christian home, armed with a sturdy knowledge of Scripture and the right answers to whatever questions life supposedly could raise in me, I was taught to have faith, to believe. But a look back through my life gave me pause because the results were mixed.

I'd been drawn to science, and I admitted to myself that sometimes science—whose culture says it is sufficient to supply all knowledge—felt more tangible and comforting than hoping in an invisible God whom the "smart people" taught me doesn't even exist.

I'd been taught that divorce is the fastest way to get to hell, yet my first marriage had ended that way when the rules provided by my church upbringing had proved insufficient to solve the riddle of how to make a tough marriage work.

I'd held up well under the strain of war but come home with lingering doubts about why God would leave us in a world where ideologies create firebombers willing to burn up little babies and where heads of state are willing to send their nations' sons and daughters to foreign lands to die.

In the years since the war, I'd developed a serious case of feeling as if I were still there, which I'd lately begun treating by writing about it.

I'd been raised to believe in the power of prayer, but in my work I kept meeting Samuels and Ruperts and Mrs. Knopfs who implied that some diseases seem to be exempt from the influence of a God who "heals all your diseases."[28]

More than anything, I think I was disappointed in myself that GBM and a month of unprecedented civilian trauma had rattled my spirit and shaken my faith so. After all, I was the one who'd promised God I'd let him be in control after he'd rescued me from intense mortar and rocket fire one day in Iraq. Exposed and alone, I'd been terrified until I finally asked him to help, and I believe he did.

But here I was a few years later, safe and sound in my own home, filled with doubt because no one seemed to survive this particular brain tumor and because Rupert Chang seemed so unfazed by it when I knew—*knew*—I would not have held up so well.

Matt Redman sang about having the kind of faith that would praise God whether life is going your way or not, whether you're suffering or prospering.[29] Easy to sing about, but I'd rarely seen anyone live it out. Until Rupert Chang.

I'd seen the gamut of human responses to death—in combat, in civilian hospitals from all sorts of damage and disease, in nursing homes and private homes and hospices—and I knew that in general people of faith die more comfortably and less fearfully than those who have no real belief that anything comes next; atheists don't often die well.

Rupert Chang died like someone who knew something most of us do not know. I had spent my life professing the same truths that offered Rupert so much comfort as he faced his demise. But as I drank my coffee that morning, I questioned my heart because I didn't know for sure whether such faith would sustain me when it was my turn.

When death came for me or those closest to me, would I be singing "Blessed Be Your Name" or shaking my fist at a God I wasn't always sure I believed in? Would I proclaim and live out my faith or stuff my doubts and fears inside and carry on, like Mitch after his bad dream?

Because as much as I *believed,* I also *doubted.* At that moment I didn't know what I knew or believed.

Rupert said his whole life was his story.

What kind of story was I writing?

22

Believing Is Not
the Same as Knowing

Why, sometimes I've believed as many as six impossible
things before breakfast.

—THE WHITE QUEEN,
LEWIS CARROLL, *Through the Looking-Glass*

D avid Oliver-Smith is a neurosurgeon in Pittsburgh who was one of my professors during residency. He took a special interest in my success and was incredibly good to me during those tough years. Once, he came into the hospital on Thanksgiving Day to take my beeper and cover for me long enough to allow me to go home and have dinner with my family, an incredible act of kindness from a staff doctor toward a lowly resident.

In 1996 I was a first-year resident trying to learn the art of spine surgery, and Dr. Oliver-Smith was probably the first surgeon to allow me to use the Kerrison rongeur in the operating room. Kerrisons are bone-biting instruments used to remove the lamina, the back part of the spinal canal. The procedure—a laminectomy—is designed to remove arthritis and bone spurs that narrow the nerve pathways and cause leg pain and weakness. It is one of the basic, essential skills of every neurosurgeon, one we learn early in our training.

I can see it in my mind as I type these words. Dr. Oliver-Smith had used a nitrogen-powered drill to remove most of the lamina—I wasn't advanced enough yet to be allowed to use the drill—and a yellow ligament was all that stood between us and the patient's pinched sciatic nerve. The yellow ligament, or ligamentum flavum, lies under the lamina and becomes thicker with age. It is part of the pathology in spinal stenosis—the narrowing of the spinal canal I mentioned above—and must be removed to decompress the nerves and complete the operation.

Dr. Oliver-Smith had shown me how to handle the Kerrison properly and had made several bites of bone and ligament to expose the underlying blue-gray spinal sack. The sack contains the spinal cord and all the nerves to the legs, bladder, genitalia, and anal sphincter. And all those important neural structures float in a bath of CSF.

A spinal fluid leak is a feared complication in spine surgery. It can lead to infections and other complications, as I described earlier when I wrote about Joey's nasal CSF leak and the lumbar drain I placed to stop it.

The sack is made of the leathery dura mater, the same stuff I have to open to get into the brain when I grapple with GBM.

Dr. Oliver-Smith looked across at me and said, "Would you like to try taking a few bites?"

He handed me the rongeur, silver and shiny in my young hands. I was Arthur holding Excalibur for the first time. I carefully emulated what he had done and took a few timid nibbles of ligament.

"Good," he said. "Now slip it under the edge of the lamina and take a little bone."

He guided my hands, and together we removed most of the remaining lamina. The dural sack looked more normal and less compressed with every bite we took. He taught me to keep the instrument light in my hands, to learn to feel the tip of the rongeur and sense it as an extension of my arm.

"You're doing great," he said. "Go ahead and take a little bigger bite."

I slipped the Kerrison under the edge of the bone, careful to make sure there was no dura near the instrument as I closed its powerful jaws.

Just as I squeezed tightly on the Kerrison to take the bite, Dr. Oliver-Smith said, "Wait!"

But it was too late. I'd already pulled the trigger and closed the rongeur, and before the *t* in *wait* was out of his mouth, the wound had filled with spinal fluid.

I'd torn the dura.

"That wasn't a safe bite! Why'd you do that?"

I shook my head. "I felt the bone. I believed it was safe. I *knew* it was safe."

He worked quickly and didn't say much for the next few minutes while he showed me how to repair the tear and stop the leak—a lesson he had not planned or desired to teach that day.

I watched, ashamed of my mistake and worried about our patient. Finally he looked up at me. "You believed it was safe, but you did not *know* it was safe. Believing is not the same as knowing. Seeing is knowing. Don't ever take a bite if you can't see the tip of your instrument."

Once the repair was complete and the surgery was over, Dr. Oliver-Smith noticed that the piece of dura I'd torn was still in the Kerrison. He took it out, placed it in a sterile plastic collection cup, and had the nurse fill the cup with formalin. Then he asked her to place a sticker on the cup with the patient's name.

At the end of the operation, he scrubbed out and picked up the jar. He took a pen and wrote on the label, "Dural tear by Dr. Lee Warren, July 30, 1996. Careless rookie mistake."

He handed me the jar.

"Lee, put this in your locker, right at eye level. Every time you open that locker, I want you to remember this patient and this day. And then think carefully before you take a bite with a Kerrison. Give it back to me when you graduate."

I put it in my locker just as he'd said.

We never spoke about it again. Over the course of my residency, Dr. Oliver-Smith became a good friend and close adviser. I scrubbed with him on hundreds of cases, and much of what made me the surgeon I am today I learned from him.

In June 2001, when I'd shaken all the professors' hands at my chief residency graduation dinner, I reached into my pocket and took out the jar with the little floating piece of dura mater I'd stared at every day for five years. I handed it to Dr. Oliver-Smith.

He smiled. "What did you learn from this?"

"That you're kind of a jerk," I said. "But I also learned the difference between believing I was safe and knowing I was safe, and it made me a better surgeon."

In the twenty years since that first dural tear, I've taken hundreds of thousands of Kerrison bites and have calluses on my hands in the places where the rongeur rubs them. Every time I do a laminectomy, I think of David Oliver-Smith, who taught me how to perform it safely.

I don't think I ever told him that he taught me a huge spiritual lesson as well. That's because I didn't realize it until the night after my meeting with the Chang family.

Lisa and I sat in the high school auditorium, watching Mitch perform in the school's production of *Alice's Adventures in Wonderland*. Theater was an interest for Mitch, and he performed in several plays during high school. His hobby became a passion for his little sister, Kalyn, who wound up being heavily involved in theater and show choir and even majored in theater in college for a while.

The play was hysterical, and I held Lisa's hand as we watched our son dressed as a playing card in Carroll's fantastical story.

"This is my favorite part," Lisa whispered as the White Queen and Alice chatted onstage.

Alice laughed. "There's no use trying. One *can't* believe impossible things."

"I daresay you haven't had much practice," said the queen. "When I was your age, I always did it for half-an-hour a day. Why, sometimes I've believed as many as six impossible things before breakfast."[30]

The silliness of the play based on Lewis Carroll's story relaxed my mind enough to remember something David Oliver-Smith had taught me years before: believing is not the same as knowing.

Seeing is knowing.

Rupert Chang was more Moses than Thomas. In the Bible, Moses fled his privileged life in Egypt to be with his own people because he had faith that God would keep him safe. In the book of Hebrews, Moses is said to have "continued strong as if he could see the God that no one can see."[31] But Thomas, one of Jesus's twelve disciples, refused to believe that Jesus had been raised from the dead until he could see the holes in Jesus's hands and side for himself.[32]

Moses believed so powerfully that he behaved as if he knew, as if he had seen.

Thomas doubted. He needed to see it to believe it. And Jesus accepted him anyway, offered him grace—but not without telling him, "Thomas, you have faith because you have seen Me. Blessed are all those who never see Me and yet they still believe."[33]

Rupert said he believed, behaved as if he believed, and died as if he believed.

As if he could see.

As if he knew.

But sometimes these seem to me like impossible things: *knowing* something you cannot see, *believing* something you cannot test, touch, or feel. In those moments I feel like Alice in Lewis Carroll's tale, as if there's no use trying to believe impossible things.

As the days passed, I knew two things for sure.

I knew the next GBM patient was out there, growing a tumor, preparing to have a seizure or speech problem or headache and show up in my office or Stinson's ED for me to see the MRI and say to myself, *I've seen the end of you.*

And I knew that if I was going to figure this whole mess out and sleep at night, I needed to take the White Queen's advice and practice believing impossible things. Because I'd noticed over and over that people of faith have more peace from the moment of diagnosis to the day they draw their last breath, and I wanted that to be real for me. I wanted to get to the place Pastor Jon described, when after his son died, he realized that he'd never figure it all out, never understand the things that happen in this life, but that he had to live it anyway and needed to be able to do it well and happily.

I didn't want to be led around emotionally by the circumstances of my life, like a bull led by the ring in its nose, my faith wavering with each new trauma or tragedy or terminal patient. I'd seen something in Rupert Chang I desired, but I didn't know how to get it.

In the book of Genesis, there's a story about Abraham, who, when he was a very old man with a very old and infertile wife, still believed that God would keep his promise to give them a son.[34] Later Saint Paul wrote, "Against all hope, Abraham in hope believed."[35]

When I first articulated my conundrum to Philip Yancey—how to help a patient hang in there and have faith when I already knew the outcome of the disease—he said, "Write about it, and you'll figure it out."

Yet here I was, writing instead about Iraq and my troubles coming home from the war. But Samuel and Joey and Eli and Mrs. Knopf and Mr. Andrews and

Rupert Chang were under my skin and in my head. I felt like the last person in the world who should be thinking about writing a book on faith, because I often had so little of it.

Despite the horrifying subject matter, writing about the war was easy; I just reported what happened and how I felt about it. But when we try to talk about our beliefs, sometimes it seems more *Alice's Adventures in Wonderland* than something real, honest, and true. And to attempt it with a heart like mine, so full of doubt and worry, seemed unlikely to help anybody else build faith.

Still, Rupert Chang looked into death and stood tall, and his wife and family came to encourage me to hang in there and hold on, praying that I "would always be reminded that God is operating according to his plans even when he's using your hands."

As I remembered Grace's comment that Rupert had viewed his whole life, not just the end of it, as his story, something dawned on me: When we watch movies or read books, we don't focus so much on the trials the characters face or even whether they survive them. We are moved by and remember the characters who face those trials well, who hold up under the strain and live or die true to themselves or their calling. We don't remember all the extras in *Saving Private Ryan* who died on the beach or who survived the final battle. But we remember Tom Hanks's character even though he died on the bridge. We remember him because he was brave, he accomplished his mission, he overcame impossible things to save Private Ryan.[36]

I'd been focusing on the outcome and not the journey. And my up-and-down faith was part of my journey. I didn't know the outcome yet, but Rupert Chang had me thinking more clearly about what's important, what's real, and how the seemingly impossible task of believing right up to the end not only is possible but also has a profound impact on other people's lives.

That seemed worth writing about.

And it seemed like a goal toward which to strive. It could reframe my approach to taking care of people when they face their worst fears, deepest wounds, and deadliest diseases.

And it gave me something else to pray for: that whenever the bell tolled for me, this type of faith in action would allow me to answer it more like Rupert Chang, Moses, and Abraham.

Less like Thomas.

Less like Lee.

And although I didn't yet believe I could get there, I did know it was possible, because I'd seen Rupert Chang do it.

Believing is not the same as knowing.

Seeing is knowing.

23

Haikus Are Easy

You only live twice:
Once when you are born
And once when you look death in the face.

—IAN FLEMING, *You Only Live Twice*

Guess who's on the clinic schedule today," Lisa said. "You haven't seen him in a while."

I swallowed a bite of Nutella-stuffed french toast she'd made for breakfast—the kids' favorite—and wiped my face clean of the heavenly hazelnut delight. "No idea."

"Remember the guy who found out about his brain tumor because a cop cracked his skull?" she said. "He called the office yesterday and said he's been having headaches lately. I told him he'd better come in."

"How could I forget him?" I said.

I hadn't seen Joey Wallace in almost two years. He'd missed all his follow-up appointments after the lumbar drain had stopped his CSF leak, and I figured he'd moved or gotten himself thrown back in jail.

It had been six months since my meeting with Rupert Chang's family, and we were enjoying another long stretch of quiet nights of trauma call—although I wasn't about to mention it to Lisa. I'd learned my lesson.

In those six peaceful months, I'd finished and published my book and even done a bit of public speaking at churches and graduations. In those speeches I told my story of God delivering me from the war and putting me back together. A few thousand people bought that book, and the friends and family members I wrote it for came to understand my experiences in Iraq and what I learned from them.

I looked across the table and smiled at my family. Lisa looked radiant in the glow of the sunlight through the window, and our high school–aged kids beamed like kindergartners with their mouths impossibly full of french toast.

"Kalyn, Mitch, you don't have to eat it all in one bite, you know," I said with a smile.

"But it's so good!" Mitch mumbled around the mouthful of food.

Kalyn said, "Dad, will you be at my concert tonight?"

"Absolutely," I said. "Wouldn't miss it for the world."

Mitch held up a hand as he swallowed hard. "And my cross-country meet is tomorrow."

"We'll be there," Lisa said. Mitch had become a graceful runner since Lisa had watched him run on the beach a few years before and seen in his stride the potential he'd never seen in himself. She has a gift for seeing in others the things they'd never recognized in themselves, and she had led all our kids to explore gifts they might have allowed to lie fallow without her motherly guidance. Kalyn's singing, Mitch's running, Kimber's art, Josh's craftsmanship, Caity's dancing and music—all gifts to the world sparked by Lisa's insight and mentorship.

We had one more year with Mitch at home before he would go off to join Kimber at Auburn University, and as I surveyed my beautiful family, I felt such peace and thankfulness for them. And for Nutella, which is one of God's ways of saying how much he loves us.

"This guy," Mitch said. "A cop hit him? What happened?"

I gave the kids a sanitized version of Joey's story (without using his name, of course)—how I found a tumor because of an injury he sustained while resisting arrest.

"Wow," Kalyn said. "What a blessing."

"It's not really a blessing to get your skull cracked," Mitch said. "Did God allow that to happen to save him from his tumor? Or to get him to stop being a criminal?"

"Do you think God does stuff like that sometimes, Dad?" Kalyn said. "Like he kind of smites you in one way to bring you around?"

I shrugged. "In this case our patient found out about one problem because of another one, which probably saved his life. I like to think I'd see that as a blessing, but our patient doesn't think so. He's pretty mad at God about his brain tumor—and, really, about his whole life."

"I can understand that," Mitch said. "Doesn't seem fair."

Lisa nodded. "If you look at other people's circumstances, it's easy to get upset about your own life. But we have to find joy despite what's happening around us, to keep up our faith even when things are hard."

Mitch looked down at his plate. "For some people it seems like everything's hard."

I smiled. These breakfast theology/philosophy conversations were some of my favorite moments of raising our kids, and I knew there weren't many more years of them left.

"Almost time to go," Kalyn said. "I have a test this morning."

"That's right," Lisa said. "Algebra. You're ready. You've got this."

"What do you have today, Mitch?" I said.

"Literature. We've been studying poetry. We have to write a haiku today."

Kalyn raised an eyebrow. "What's a haiku?"

"A Japanese poem with only three lines," Mitch said. "You have five syllables in the first and last line and seven in the middle. Seventeen syllables."

"Weird," Kalyn said.

"Yeah," Mitch said. "I found some funny ones on the internet." Then he quoted one from memory:

Haikus are easy,
But sometimes they don't make sense.
Refrigerator.

We all laughed at the haiku, which was typical of things Mitch found humorous. But as we went our separate ways that morning, the nonsensical poem rattled around in my brain, along with the warmth of family breakfast and the discussion we'd had about Joey and trouble and life in general.

———

I knocked on the door of exam room 4 and opened it, expecting to see the disheveled, dirty, tattooed Joey I'd come to know.

At first I thought I'd entered the wrong room. The man who sat in the exam chair was dressed in green work pants and a gray long-sleeve shirt. His hair was short, washed, and combed neatly. His earlobes were unplugged; I could barely tell they had been gauged. And when he smiled, I was shocked to see that he must have visited a dentist since the last time we met.

In fact, I wouldn't have believed it was him at all if his shirt hadn't plainly read "Joey."

"Hey, Doc. Good to see you again," he said.

"You too," I said. "You look different."

He smiled. "I know. A lot's changed since last time I was in the hospital."

"Catch me up," I said.

"Started the day I left, before the discharge papers were all finished. That chaplain, Pastor Jon, he came by my room. I told him I didn't need anything, but he asked me if he could pray for me. I told him to pray for himself, believing all that crap. He was real nice, just thanked me and told me he would be praying for me anyway."

Despite how he looked, Joey still pretty much sounded like the man I'd known.

"Anyhow, a couple weeks later Gramma got pneumonia somethin' awful. We ended up in the hospital with her, and she was mighty sick. Pastor Jon showed up, and Gramma made us all hold hands around her bed while he prayed for her. Louise and her husband—"

I held up a hand. "Wait. Louise has a husband?"

"Yeah," he said. "She met this guy, Zane, at church. Nice guy, works as the maintenance man for the pastor. Kind of runs the place. Reddest hair you ever saw. They got married about two months after they met. He's been real good for her."

"That's good to hear," I said.

Joey smiled. "I know. Kind of made me think there might be somebody out there for me. Anyhow, we was about to pray, and Gramma told Pastor Jon she wanted him to pray for me. She said she was old and tired and didn't much care if she made it or not but that he should be praying that I'd get things in my life straight. I told her I didn't need none of that, but she said to hush and not interrupt an old woman when she's talkin' about Jesus."

I laughed. "Sounds like your gramma."

Joey nodded. "Yep. Well, while Pastor Jon was praying, he said something I'd never heard before."

"What was that?"

"He said that God loved me and was proud to be my dad. That God knew about my whole life before any of it happened and that no matter what I had done, God would never stop wanting me to come back to him and be part of his family."

Joey cleared his throat and blinked hard before continuing.

"I thought, *Fat chance,* since even my own dad didn't like me enough to stick around and watch me grow up. And I've been nothin' but trouble to everybody my whole life. But that Pastor Jon, he just kept praying and saying stuff like that, and by the time he was done, something changed. I finally found it."

"Found what?" I said.

Joey wrinkled his brow for a moment and then held up a finger. "You ever done drugs, Doc?"

"No, never. Why?"

"Well, the first time you try meth or get high on anything, you feel something, like a big rush, and everything in your brain kind of feels like it's on fire but in a good way. Nothing else seems to matter as much; all the crap in your life seems a little farther away and less important. Then it wears off. And I think the reason drugs are so easy to get hooked on is on account of you're always lookin' for that feeling again, but you never quite feel it after that first time. Every time you use, even when you take bigger doses, it's never quite the same. Some people realize it'll never be as good as they remember, but people like me, we keep on trying to find that fire again. Well, when Pastor Jon was praying, I felt what I used to feel when I was in the mood to get high, that desire I had to feel something so big and real and different. And somehow I could tell that whatever it was I'd been looking for all those years with drugs was really never in the drugs at all. I asked Pastor Jon if he could teach me how to find it, and he did."

"What did he teach you?" I said.

Joey looked at me, shook his head, and smiled. "That Jesus was what I'd been

missing. I felt abandoned by my dad leaving and my mom dying, and I'd been looking for some way to not feel all that. Pastor Jon taught me that Jesus could fill all
those empty places in my heart and I could be in his family. I can't really explain it
any better, but somehow when I told Jesus I was ready to believe it, I felt that feeling
I'd always been trying to feel. I found it."

"So you became a Christian?"

He nodded. "Yeah. And then Gramma died the next day."

"I'm sorry, Joey," I said.

"It's okay," he said. "She kissed me on the cheek and told me she'd been hanging on a long time waiting on God to get me straight, and now that I was, she could
go on home. She said bye to us, and then she just closed her eyes and stopped
breathing. And for the first time in my life when something bad happened, I didn't
feel like I needed to go out and get high. I was okay, and I know what was different.
I had something real inside me, and I liked it."

"That's amazing," I said.

"I know. It's kind of like a fairy tale, one of those happy-ending stories I never
believed in. Hey, Doc?" Joey said.

"Yes?"

"Not to be a jerk or anything, but I got to get back to work. I got a job workin'
for the county on the road crew. Can we talk about my headaches?"

Just like that, we slipped back into doctor-patient mode, and I heard in the next
few minutes about how Joey's head had started hurting a little more each day, how
the pressure seemed to be building behind his right eye for the past few weeks, how
he'd developed a little numbness in his left hand.

And I knew.

The MRI wouldn't be done until the next day, but I already knew.

GBM is sneaky like that. It waits—until someone's happy, until the baby is on
the way, until the new job starts or the wedding is planned or you're retiring and
finally going to take that trip with your wife—to show up and ruin everything.

Joey had finally gotten his life together, finally seemed to be at peace, and now
he was having headaches. Sure, it could have been anything. Migraines, sinus infection, postcraniotomy syndrome—anything.

But I knew.

I knew in twenty-four hours I'd be telling Joey that he had a malignant brain tumor, that his newly found life would be over in a couple of years, if not sooner. I wondered how his newborn faith would hold up then, since I was about to ruin his fairy-tale happy ending.

Joey's finding his faith and getting his life going in the right direction just in time to have GBM swoop in and kill him was about as logical as Mitch's haiku.

Joey's faith came back;
GBM always does too.
Will it kill his faith?

24

Storm Brewing

"A minuscule cloud, as tiny as the hand of a man, is ascending
from the sea."

Elijah: Go quickly, and give a message to Ahab for me:
"Prepare your chariot, and leave quickly before the rain gets
torrential and keeps you from traveling."

The sky became filled with dark monstrous clouds, the wind
grew wild, the heavy rain fell.

—1 KINGS 18:44–45, Voice

I spent an hour the next afternoon with my friend Sandy Jackson, the radiologist
we kiddingly call the Oracle. We pulled up all Joey's prior images, from the
first night he showed up in the ED after the DEA agent, Keaton, cracked his skull
open with a billy club to the time he cracked open his head again in his car crash.
In between were a few MRI scans that showed the areas he'd damaged and the
cavity I'd created when I took out his blood clot and the intermediate-grade glioma
I'd discovered in the midst of the hematoma.

Then we opened the MRI Joey had completed a few minutes before.

It was like a greatest hits collection of brain trauma and surgery—the metal
plates in his head, scar tissue from old frontal lobe injuries and two surgeries, and
some fluid under the skull flap that young people have only if they've had prior
surgery and lost some brain.

Sequence by sequence appeared, and the Oracle worked through them diligently, reading the different stories told by the numerous ways in which MRI can assess human tissue. I read over his shoulder, like Elijah's servant looking at the over-sea sky, searching for evidence of the storm I knew was brewing in Joey's brain.

Sandy read through all the images and then gave me his opinion, reciting it into his Dictaphone: "I see old skull fractures, surgical hardware in place, subdural hygroma, extensive frontal encephalomalacia consistent with prior trauma and previous craniotomies. Mild white matter swelling, no midline shift or mass effect on the brain, no hydrocephalus, no stroke, no obvious mass lesion, and no hemorrhage."

Sandy turned to me. "Nothing too bad so far. The rest of the images are coming over now."

I nodded. "Wait for it. It'll be there."

There was no reason for Joey to have any swelling in his white matter unless he had active tumor. But many brain tumors aren't visible until after an IV contrast material called gadolinium—"gad"—is given to the patient. The postcontrast pictures would tell the story I was already hearing in my mind.

Sandy hit Refresh on his computer, and a new set of images filled the screen.

And there it was, plain as day, like Elijah's tiny cloud.

An area the size of an almond in the deep frontal lobe on the right side of Joey's brain lit up brightly, standing out like a lighthouse against the dark gray background of the normal brain.

I've seen the end of you, Joey.

Sandy looked at the pictures for a moment and resumed dictating: "Postcontrast imaging reveals a solitary 1.5 centimeter brightly enhancing lesion in the deep white matter of the medial right frontal lobe. Given the patient's history of intermediate-grade glioma, progression of disease to higher-grade astrocytic neoplasm such as anaplastic astrocytoma or glioblastoma multiforme must be suspected. However, this patient has also had two craniotomies and has a history of IV drug abuse, so abscess is also in the differential diagnosis. I do not believe this patient has had radiation treatment before, so radiation necrosis is not considered. Overall, given the amount of cerebral edema and the intensity and pattern of enhancement, tumor is felt to be most likely. Neurosurgeon present at the time of this dictation and aware of the results."

Sandy signed off on his report, the most definitive I'd ever heard him dictate. He turned to me and said, "I think it's tumor."

We chatted for a few minutes about the scan and caught up with each other since I hadn't seen him in a while. His pager went off, and he looked down at its screen.

"Gotta run, Lee. They need me in CT. Good to see you. Sorry about your patient."

We shook hands, and Sandy left.

I reviewed the images again, trying to convince myself I wasn't seeing what I knew I was. After all, Joey was a former—hopefully former—drug addict. Addicts often have immune system deficiencies not seen in "normal" folks, which predispose them to all sorts of infections and other medical problems. After years of exposing their bodies to chemicals manufactured in trailers by high school dropouts, the immune systems of addicts often begin to fail in unusual ways, which results in susceptibility to bizarre and severe infections.

Infections that sometimes migrate into the brain, become abscesses, and cause brain swelling we can see on MRI scans.

I looked at my watch: 3:20 p.m. I was to meet Joey and Louise in my office to go over his MRI scan at 4:00.

I wanted it to be an abscess, and there were a lot of tests I could run to try to determine whether it was. An abscess would mean antibiotics and most likely survival for Joey. The only reasonable alternative was that his intermediate-grade tumor had decided to become malignant and devolve into glioblastoma.

The bright spot on the screen would appear the same, no matter which of those possibilities would prove to be true. And regardless of how many times or for how long I stared at the tiny cloud off in the distance of Joey's brain, the storm it would develop into could be stopped only if I made the right diagnosis and guided him into the proper treatment. If it were a tumor, it would scoff at my attempts and probably kill him anyway. An abscess would not be fun or easy for Joey to manage, but I felt confident I could get him through it.

I didn't want Joey to have a malignant brain tumor. He'd had enough bad news in his life, hadn't he? Much of it self-created. And now, just when things were going well, he had this enhancing mass in his brain. Perfect.

But the problem with neurosurgery—really with life in general—is that it doesn't care what you want or how you feel. It's going to move ahead whether or not you take action. It doesn't wait for you to be okay with it, shore up your faith and believe it's all going to be okay, or find strength for the journey.

I looked at that scan, willing it to be something other than what I knew in my heart it was, praying that God would let Joey have a break for once.

Who's the Oracle now, Lee?

25

The Best Year Ever

I've been snake-bit twenty-seven times, to be exact. Hey,
that's what they do, okay? They're bein' a snake.

—UNCLE SI, *Duck Dynasty*

Here it is." I pointed to the bright almond-shaped area of Joey's scan, and Louise reached out and put her hand on his shoulder. "It's highly suspicious for a malignant brain tumor called glioblastoma, but it could also be an infection in your brain, an abscess."

"It's a tumor, Doc," Joey said.

"You don't know that," Louise said.

"Glee-o-blas . . . ," Joey said. "Hey! Ain't that the one that guy Sam had, the one I was mean to in your office?"

I nodded. "Samuel, yes. Glioblastoma."

"Whatever happened to him? I still feel bad about what I said."

I looked down for a second. "He passed away while you were in the hospital last time."

Joey made a *humph* sound under his breath and looked down for a moment.

"Did you tell him I was sorry that day, after I asked you to?" he said.

"Yes," I said. "He told me to tell you that it was okay, that he knew you didn't mean it. I'm sorry we never talked about that again. I should have told you."

Joey looked past me, focused on his scan for a moment. "Lou, I said it's a tumor because I had that other tumor before and Doc already told us they usually turn into something worse. What are the odds of it bein' in the same place as my other tumor but bein' something else? I don't know much, but I had a little bit of statistics in my math class the other day, and the most likely thing is, it's a tumor. Right, Doc?"

"Yes," I said. "Wait. Did you say you're taking a math class?"

Joey smiled. "Yessir. I'm gettin' my GED. Two more months and I'll be a high school graduate! I ain't never finished nothin' in my life, and I promised Gramma I'd do it."

"He's doing real good too, Doc. I'm so proud of him," Louise said.

"That's great, Joey," I said. "But we need to figure out what's happening inside your head. I'll schedule the tests. If we don't find solid evidence that it's an abscess, we'll have to operate."

Joey looked at me and shook his head slowly. "Doc, we both know what this is. Do what you gotta do, but I'm ready for surgery when you are. I've known since the day I met you it was gonna be cancer someday."

"Joey, have more faith than that!" Louise said.

He smiled. "I do, Sis. When all this first started, I was angry and scared and sure I was gonna die. And Doc told me right up front that most of these low-grade tumors turn into cancers eventually, and I knew with my luck it would happen to me too. Can't blame a tumor for doin' what tumors do, right? The difference is, now that I know the Lord, I ain't scared no more."

Louise looked at the floor. "I think God's gonna heal you."

Joey took her hand. "He might. But it don't matter as much as what he's already done inside me. I feel so much better as a person now, Sis."

I shook my head and smiled. This wasn't the same man I'd been taking care of for so long. "Joey, it's amazing how much you've changed. I'm so glad you're happier. I'll set up the tests for tomorrow."

He nodded. "Great. I gotta go study for school tonight. Much as I'd like for you to find an abscess in there—that's a weird thing to say, ain't it?—I'm ready for you to tell me it's cancer. But hey, Doc? If you gotta go back in my head again, just put in a zipper to make it easier next time."

We all laughed, and I said goodbye to Joey and Louise and walked them out of the office. It was after five, and our staff had gone home. Lisa was picking Kalyn up from show choir practice, and the three of us were the only ones there.

Joey turned before he got on the elevator. "Say hi to Miss Lisa for me. And good luck lookin' for that pus that ain't there in my head."

The elevator doors closed, and I locked up the office. Joey had become a completely different person from the man I met that night in the ED. Getting his GED? Not afraid or angry anymore?

Install a zipper in his head?

That was hilarious.

"Good luck lookin' for that pus that ain't there."

Not hilarious.

But probably true, I admitted to myself.

We'll find out tomorrow.

———

That night we sat down to dinner at home. The kids were off doing other things, so Lisa and I had a quiet night with just the two of us. Lisa set the plate in front of me, a piece of grilled chicken with salad and some vegetables.

I took a bite of the meat, and my mouth was rewarded with a burst of flavor. The meat was moist, had hints of aromatic herbs like rosemary and thyme, and overall had a robust and hearty taste unlike any chicken I'd had before. It was perfect.

"Honey," I said, "that's delicious. How'd you make it?"

She smiled. "The magic's in the marinade. There's an art to making a marinade so it complements the meat but doesn't overwhelm it—and a science behind how long you let it soak."

We had a great conversation, and I went to bed that night with my belly full of Lisa's chicken, my heart full of love for a woman who can do anything, and my mind for once not worrying about what Joey's tests would show the next day.

———

Of course, it wasn't an abscess.

Despite my desire to tell Joey it was something—anything—other than GBM, my best Oracle imitation couldn't make it so. Every lab test we ran the next morning pointed away from infection and toward tumor.

I was out of hope and out of options.

Joey was going back to surgery.

———————

In the end Joey's surgery and the events surrounding it were so routine, so uneventful, so much like the many times I'd obtained consent and taken someone to surgery, performed uncomplicated tumor removals, spoken on the phone to Grossman and heard him say, "High-grade astrocytic neoplasm, necrotic tissue, multiple mitotic figures, increased vascularity consistent with glioblastoma multiforme. Sorry, buddy," and had *the conversation* with the family.

But it was so very different from my previous surgeries with Joey.

Before, he'd been dirty, inebriated, hostile, snarling, sedated, bloody, violent, hateful, scared, acting out. When he woke up in the recovery room on previous occasions, he was sullen and vulgar.

Now he was clean, sober, and peaceful. He smiled, prayed for me before we went to the OR, and awoke with the words *thank you.*

Louise was stoic when I told her. Her lip quivered a bit, but she shed no tears. She held on to Zane's hand—Joey was right about his incredibly red hair—and nodded while I said, "It is a cancer, glioblastoma, like we thought. The surgery went very well, and I removed the entire tumor, but Joey will require chemotherapy and radiation."

In the ICU I found Joey sitting up in his bed like so many days before, but instead of wrist restraints confining him and sedatives dripping into his veins, he looked content, and his nurse stood at his bedside, having a pleasant conversation with him.

He smiled when he saw me, his eyes still a little cloudy, his half-shaved head wrapped in bandages, a goofy-looking kid in a grown man's ridden-hard body.

"How'd it go, Doc?" he said.

I put my hand on his shoulder. "The surgery went well. I removed most of your right frontal lobe and all the obvious tumor. It is a glioblastoma—"

"Told you so!" Joey said, still smiling.

"You were right," I said. "It's not an infection. And now we have to get the medical and radiation doctors involved."

"The cancer doctors," Joey said.

"Right. We'll let the wound heal for a couple of weeks, but then we'll treat this very aggressively."

"I'm ready," he said. "Whatever we need to do. I'm all in. Did Lou tell you the good news?"

I shook my head. "No, what?"

He smiled, and there was less drug in it now than real joy. "I got accepted to a community college. I start in the fall."

"College? That's great."

He nodded. "I know. Nobody in my family has ever been to college before. If I graduate . . ." He looked away for a moment, thinking about something. "Hey, Doc—how long do I have?"

"Let's not focus on that right now. The final pathology report will take a few days. We'll know more then."

Joey's eyes narrowed, and he sniffed. "Doc, we've been through a lot together. You don't gotta blow smoke at me. How long?"

"The average is about fifteen months," I said.

"Okay," he said under his breath. "That gets me through my freshman year anyway. Who knows? Maybe you'll find some cure for me by then."

"Maybe," I said. "There's a lot of research going on. I'll try to find a study you can be in if you want."

He looked at me for a second. "Yeah. Somebody oughta study my goofy brain anyway."

He picked up the remote and switched on his television.

"More reality TV?" I said.

"Yep. I got a new favorite, *Duck Dynasty*. You seen it?"

"A couple of episodes," I said. "Reminds me of some people I grew up around."

Joey's face brightened as the sound of Louisiana accents came from the television. "Found it! Man, I love how their whole family sits around and prays together at the end. Reminds me of Gramma's house when I was a kid." His eyes glistened. "I really miss her, Doc."

"She was a good woman," I said. "I've gotta run now, Joey. Get some rest, okay?"

He nodded. "I will. But hey, Doc?"

"Yes?"

"Did you put in the zipper?"

I laughed. "No, I did not. Sorry."

"Dang. That would have been cool."

Three months later Joey had completed radiation therapy and several rounds of chemo with temozolomide—his tumor markers were all favorable—and he'd been approved for a new treatment called Tumor Treating Fields, or TTF. The funny thing was, TTF is a direct descendant of the goofy helmet Robert Andrews's wife had made him wear, the Glio-Wave 6000. I'd been highly skeptical and had even made fun of that helmet, but studies had shown that people lived longer and with higher quality of life when TTF was added to standard treatment regimens for glioblastoma.

Another thing I thought I knew.

So when Joey came to the office with Louise and Zane for his recheck, he wore his helmet and the backpack that its battery and controls were housed in, along with a T-shirt that said HAPPY HAPPY HAPPY, the motto of *Duck Dynasty*'s patriarch, Phil Robertson.

He also had a bandage on the left side of his neck.

"What's that?" I said, pointing to the gauze and tape.

"I'm havin' my tattoos removed. The nekkid girl was really offensive, and I don't wanna make people think I'm that kind of person anymore."

I stole a glance at the back of his right hand. He caught me looking at the swastika that was still there.

"I'm keeping that one," he said, "to remind me of who I used to be. I've noticed that people sometimes get pretty full of themselves when they get saved, like they had somethin' to do with it. I want to remember how far God's brought me, how I was about as bad a person as you can be, and thanks to Gramma and Pastor Jon and God, I'm not that way no more. This gives me a way to show people who I was and who I am now."

"Joey, you never stop surprising me," I said. "Let's look at your MRI."

There was no tumor. No swelling, no bleeding, nothing but a cavity where I'd resected his glioblastoma and a lot of artifact from all the plates and screws in Joey's head.

"It's clean," I said. "We need to do another one in three more months."

"Awesome," he said. "Hey, let me show you something."

He pulled a phone out of his pocket and opened his photos. There was a smiling Joey standing in front of the local community college, wearing a cap and gown, holding up his GED diploma, flanked by Louise and a young lady I didn't recognize.

"You did it! You got your GED," I said. "Congratulations, Joey. I'm proud of you."

He smiled bigger than I'd ever seen him smile. "Thanks, but that's not the best part. You see that girl? That, Doc, is Sharon Jean. My new girlfriend. Met her at church."

"She's very pretty," I said. "I'm happy for you."

"Me too." He pointed at his TTF helmet. "And she likes this. Says I look like Iron Man."

I laughed. "So are you starting college soon?"

He nodded. "Yeah, but changed my mind. I'm going to Bible college. I spent my whole life running from God. Now that I might be dying, I want to know as much about him as I can before I meet him."

⸺

We had similar visits at six and nine months. His interval MRI scans showed no evidence of tumor recurrence. Joey would give us updates on how Bible college was going, and Lisa and I got to meet Sharon Jean. Joey seemed to be getting stronger over time, happier, and he had on a new *Duck Dynasty* T-shirt every time I saw him.

Eleven months after surgery Joey stood up in class at Bible college one day, then fell to the floor and had a generalized seizure for several minutes. I ran into the ED when Stinson called me and found Louise, Zane, and Sharon Jean standing around Joey's bed. He looked up at me, eyes unfocused and glazed, and said, "Hey, Doc," his face drooping.

The MRI, which had looked so pristine two months before, showed a massive recurrence of tumor and severe swelling of Joey's brain. The tumor had invaded his brain stem and was now in both sides of his brain.

Within days Joey was paralyzed on the left side of his body and could no longer swallow safely without choking.

The last time I spoke with him, he looked up and said, "Doc, thanks for all you've done for me. I still wish you'd have put in that zipper though."

"I wish I could do more," I said.

He smiled with the half of his face that could still move. "Nah. I'm good. Everybody dies sometime, right? At least I got to see it coming and do something about it. This has been the best year ever."

"How so?" I asked.

He said, "You know, I never even let myself think about seeing my mom again after she died. But Pastor Jon gave me hope for that again. I helped a lot of people get hooked on drugs—including my baby sister—but I never helped one person in this life feel anything good until this year. I stole, I cheated, I hurt people, all because of how hurt I was on the inside, but now I know I'm forgiven for all that. And I believe it, Doc. I'm gonna see my mom and my gramma again. I'm gonna be okay again, I know it. It's been a great year."

He slipped into a coma the next day, Cheyne-Stokes respirations started soon after, and he died in less than a week.

The day he died, Pastor Jon and Louise were there with Zane and Sharon Jean at his bedside. He looked peaceful. *Duck Dynasty* was on the television, and Jackie and Carl and all the other nurses in the ICU came to say how much they'd grown to care about Joey. Louise said Joey had apologized to her for all the pain he'd brought into her life with drugs, and she'd told him she forgave him and was proud of him.

Then she gave me more news.

She put her hands on her belly and said, "Doc, me and Zane are having a baby. A boy. We're gonna name him Joey, and we hope he grows up to be the kind of man my brother became over the last year. He was so happy, so full of faith and hope, so kind and loving. It's like he was a totally new person."

Later that day, after they'd taken Joey's body to the morgue, Lisa and I sat at home and recounted our experience with the surprising Joey Wallace and how he'd touched our lives. We talked about all that Joey had been through even before he was sick. Abandoned, orphaned, addicted, assaulted, arrested . . . no wonder he'd been so bitter and angry when we met.

And would it have been surprising if he'd been even angrier when he died? After the pain of his earlier life, he'd encountered one of humankind's most malignant cancers, a losing battle from the start. Even after Joey became a Christian, he'd had reason to be angry, at least according to the math most of us use to assess such matters. He'd given his life to the Lord, trusted in him, prayed for a cure. He'd been faithful and done what he was supposed to do, but glioblastoma ravaged him anyway, just as he finally found love and a path to a good life.

But despite all that, Joey hadn't been angrier. Instead, he was transformed by his faith into a different person, refined and somehow improved by the experience of dying.

And something changed inside me as Lisa and I discussed it—a fundamental shift in my thinking. It probably started with Samuel and developed further when I met Rupert Chang. I realized what Pastor Jon had meant in the chapel that first day when he'd challenged my view of prayer with his statement *"You think your prayers are only valid if the outcome is what you want."*

And there it was: Joey's "best year ever" was the same year in which he deteriorated and died from brain cancer. But to him it was the year he was delivered from the pain of a rough childhood, from the notion that he was unlovable, a perpetual failure, a screwup. Joey found redemption, love, peace, and even happiness while he was getting sicker and dying, which makes no sense to me outside the context of faith.

His gramma's prayers surely were not just that Joey would live a long life but rather that he would discover and claim the things that make a life of any length worth living.

And he had.

The prayers, even mine, for Joey to be cured of his cancer were answered no.

For my entire career I had focused on trying to be the yes to prayers like this. Indeed, I had been in many cases—in the war, in countless trauma bays and ORs in Pittsburgh, San Antonio, Iraq, Germany, and Alabama. But I'd made the mistake, when those prayers were answered no, of letting it affect my faith, to the extent that I had sometimes doubted whether God was really there at all.

Joey had shown me a different—a better—way.

His faith grew stronger even though his prayers for a cure went unanswered or were turned down. Somehow, I thought, Joey's immersion into disease and suffering had improved him, when so often it scars and overshadows people's entire lives. I remembered what Lisa had said about her cooking—that the magic was in the marinade. A bag full of stuff you wouldn't want to drink or eat on its own—Joey's life of painful events—still managed to make him a better person.

Joey's best year ever taught me the most important faith lesson of all: although Joey was not cured, he was surely healed.

26

Work in Progress

Do not despise these small beginnings, for the LORD rejoices to
see the work begin, to see the plumb line in Zerubbabel's hand.

—ZECHARIAH 4:10, NLT

It's nonsurvivable," I said to everyone. We were huddled around the monitor in
radiology, watching the CT scan images scroll across the screen, pictures of the
brain of another self-inflicted gunshot to the head. She was middle aged and healthy,
but somehow the wrong guy and too much alcohol and a day that must have
seemed more hopeless than all the others had led her on this night to decide it was
time to quit.

The path of the slug through her brain crossed so many vital structures that I
knew there was nothing I could do to save her.

"I'll go clean up her face and try to close her scalp so her family can see her," I
said. One of the fundamental parts of trauma surgery is the occasional need to
perform cosmetic procedures to make patients more presentable for their families—
operations designed to help the living even though the dying do not benefit from
them at all.

The bullet from her .45-caliber handgun had destroyed most of her left frontal
bone and scalp and left a six-inch-wide hole in her head. Two pieces of skull were
flapped outward, like saloon doors stuck open. As I tried to find enough skin to
suture so I could bandage her head, my hand brushed against the edge of one of the

bone fragments. "That's really sharp," I said. "Someone could cut their hand on it. Anyone have scissors?" A nurse handed me a pair of bandage scissors, and I cut the muscle and hair to separate the bone from them. "That's better," I said.

I heard a groan to my left, and I glanced over to see one of my colleagues, a medical doctor who was working the ED that night, with a horrified look on his face. "How can you do that?" he asked. "It's gruesome. Her whole face is blown off. How do you deal with it emotionally? It's horrifying."

"You just focus on the problem at hand," I said. "You don't think about anything but the piece of bone that's too sharp to leave, the hole that needs to be closed—whatever it is that has to be done right now."

"I couldn't do it," he said. "I guess that's why I'm not a surgeon."

Later that night, lying next to Lisa and trying to sleep, the woman with the shot-off face revisited me, as trauma patients often do. I recalled the conversation with my friend and wondered how I became a person who can cut skull fragments from someone's head without a hint of nausea or repulsion. Me, the kid from Oklahoma who fainted the first time I saw blood.

I thought about a woman so crushed by life that she decided a bullet to her brain was more tolerable than another day in this world. She'd been pretty—her nails were manicured, her breasts augmented, her abdomen flat, and her muscles toned. She had obviously spent a lot of time working to present to the world a picture of herself she didn't see with her own eyes. And despite her efforts to look a certain way, she obviously could not *feel* whatever it was she thought she needed. I thought about how in the ED I'd been able to notice all those things but still step up to the table and cut pieces of her skull away and wrap her head in gauze so her family could remember the image she'd worked so hard to give them and not see the horrible gaping hole in her skull.

Joey had been dead about a year, and I'd spent a lot of time thinking about how his illness had in some ways redeemed him. Now the suicide of this woman and my friend's question came together in a way that might not have seemed as clear to me if I hadn't been so exhausted.

Early on in surgical training, they teach you to zoom in on the problem at hand. When a patient rolls into the trauma bay, interns are not capable at first of understanding and managing everything wrong with the patient. Our heads spin and our hearts race with the enormity of the emergency. We don't yet have the training and experience necessary to calmly assess the situation and break it down into the steps needed to save the patient. So, in their great wisdom, the teachers of would-be surgeons give us little things to do.

"You, Warren," the chief resident would say, "check his sphincter."

In the assessment and care of a patient with multiple injuries, one of the less glamorous but vital tasks is for someone—always the most junior person—to insert his finger into the patient's anus to assess the tone of the anal sphincter. Sphincter tone is a reliable indicator of spinal cord integrity. If the sphincter is loose, the cord is probably injured, but if it's strong and puckered, the cord is probably okay.

"Good tone," I would say, looking for the "Attaboy" from the chief.

Over time you get promoted from sphincter duties to slightly less disgusting tasks. Cut off the clothes, start the IV, scan for other injuries, or insert the breathing tube, nasogastric tube, or chest tube.

And what you learn is the art of finding calm during chaos. Despite someone trying her best to bleed out, you must zoom in and check that sphincter, start that line, insert that tube. You have a job, and it must be done.

As time passes and more trauma patients present themselves to be thus managed, young surgeons-to-be find they can focus on more than one thing at a time—and eventually on all of them. *Yes, the tube must be inserted, but I also need to keep an eye on the blood pressure. Of course I'll cut off that dead skin; however, her coloration makes me think she's not breathing well. Better check her oxygen level.*

The goal of this type of training is to produce doctors who can take patients through complex operations or resuscitate them from multiple injuries and have the patients survive. But on a higher level, the training teaches surgeons how to zoom in to handle immediately threatening scary things, like the unplanned rupture of an aneurysm or a leaking heart valve, *and* maintain perspective on the rest of their patients' situations.

Some surgeons are never able to master this skill. They can manage an operation quite well until something unexpected happens. An artery pops, and they're swearing like drunken soldiers, throwing instruments, sweating, berating staff members, and generally losing their grip. These surgeons are dangerous because unplanned events are common in trauma situations, and people can die or have unnecessary complications if there is a poor response to those intraoperative catastrophes.

Equally dangerous are surgeons who zoom in well but forget there is a whole patient while they're focused on a small thing—a very real threat in my specialty. Neurosurgeons spend most of our careers operating through a high-powered surgical microscope. This is a great tool because it enables us to see tiny structures with great clarity and focus, brightly lit and crystal clear. But the higher the magnification, the narrower the field of view. The more you zoom in, the fuzzier and darker the edges become. When you look through the scope with both eyes, your worldview becomes very small, which requires you to assess what's happening outside the field of view frequently if you don't want to miss something important.

Once when I was too junior to fully comprehend what was happening and too timid to speak up about it, I watched a surgeon who was so focused on trying to remove a tumor that he failed to notice that his patient was practically bleeding to death from several open veins a few millimeters away from the mass. He focused the microscope so tightly that he couldn't see anything but the tumor, and every time blood would creep into his visual field, he would just shove a little cotton patty over the tumor and wipe away the blood.

Only when the patient's pressure tanked did the anesthesiologist notice the amount of blood the patient had lost, and then only because the patient's heart suddenly went into an abnormal rhythm and she coded on the table. Intraoperative CPR and a massive effort from the code team brought her back, but it nearly turned into an intraoperative death, all because the surgeon had lost sight of the big picture. Keeping the blood out of your line of sight by wiping it away with cotton patties does not mean your patient has stopped bleeding any more than me wrapping the lady's head with beautiful white gauze eliminated the gaping hole in her skull. Problems unseen are still problems.

Our response to this need to zoom in while still being able to zoom out, maintain perspective, and handle multiple issues at once in some ways leads us to the type of work we are comfortable doing. Those of us who are wired to thrive on chaos become trauma surgeons, vascular surgeons, neurosurgeons.

In life outside the operating room, we surgeons sometimes struggle because despite how good we are at managing life-threatening situations in surgery, we can't have a conversation with our teenagers or our spouses. We can handle incredibly complex and difficult issues under the surgical microscope, but can we zoom out and notice that our wives need a hug? How many piercings, tattoos, hair color changes, or sketchy boyfriends do our daughters have to have before we notice they're trying to get our attention?

Lying there that night with Lisa, I realized that Joey and my newest patient illustrated both sides of what I was trying to learn in my struggle between knowledge and faith.

Joey had learned to zoom in and address the current problem—have the craniotomy, go through the radiation and chemotherapy, come to grips with his cancer and his imminent death—but he also zoomed out to look at the rest of his life. He'd seen that changes were needed, found his way, reconciled with his family, fallen in love, encountered joy, met and embraced his God.

Prior to cancer, Joey's life had been a series of crises, disappointments, and troubles. He had stayed zoomed in so long that he'd never recognized all the possibilities and people out there offering him a wider and better experience. Yet in the worst moment of his life, he finally gained the ability to take the larger view, and it saved him. Not from physical death but from the death his heart had suffered since he was old enough to realize his dad had left and his mom was dead.

My suicide patient never figured it out. She stayed focused on the problems, zoomed so far in to the issues that she was unable to look a little to the left or right to find hope elsewhere. Her life, in her mind, was uniformly malignant, and she diagnosed herself as terminally hopeless.

The contrast between Joey and this other patient spun my thinking about patient care on its axis. As the months passed, I began to rethink my role in the spectrum of patient care. I felt very much like an intern again, a work in progress.

I stopped thinking of health care as the battle between life and death; rather, I now saw it as the opportunity to help people live life fully while they have it and to help them approach death bravely when they must. Because length of life, I so clearly now saw, is not as important as quality of life. I'd seen old people die, fighting with every breath to hang on a little longer, terrified of what was to come, not wanting to let go of the now to experience the next. And Joey, too young and dying too fast, had been transformed entirely by the experience.

I remembered again something my first chief resident always said: *"There are some things worse than being dead."* I understood that he meant it as a semi-joke about how coma and stupor and disability are in some ways more difficult for families to manage than death itself. But over the years I've learned that Jed was right:

I've seen people who were so upset about their illness, so alarmed by the notion of meeting an early death, that their every living moment was spent shackled by fear. Their lives became prisons of anger that ruined relationships and left behind questions their loved ones would never be able to answer.

This is a patient-caused cancer not easily cured because the survivors are the victims.

My other patient, the sad lady who took her life with her own gun, appeared to have agreed with my old chief's adage. Living was worse than dying to her, even though the disease from which she suffered was one of emotion, neurotransmitters, and negative outlook, rather than necrosis, mitotic figures, and hypercellularity. It was her own trifecta of terminality, as my pathologist friend Grossman would say, every bit as deadly as Joey's.

I'd read some recent reports in neurosurgery journals about long survivals, even possible cures, of glioblastoma in rare cases. New research out of Duke University and other places reported using viruses to attack the tumor as if it were an immune problem, and the data were encouraging.

I thought about Eli Bailey, my GBM patient with the clean margins, who was due to see me the next day in the clinic and had so far, through more than three years of frequent surveillance MRI scans, remained cancer-free. The next day I would see his latest scan and tell him whether he was still a statistical outlier who was proving that not everyone dies from glioblastoma.

I wanted it to be true for him, and I prayed for it to be so.

It was beginning to look as if glioblastoma multiforme might not, in fact, be uniformly fatal.

But as my suicide victim had discovered, hopelessness certainly is.

27

Writing My Own Story

In order to find our way in this chaos, we seek stories that give us hope and faith that we can persevere.

—SHAWN COYNE, *The Story Grid*

The MRI is clean, Eli," I said. "You're now officially my longest disease-free glioblastoma patient. Other than the postsurgical changes, I can't tell you ever had a tumor."

"That's great news, Doc. And with the tail kicking Bama gave Auburn last week, it makes for a pretty good month for me."

Eli was still using metaphors.

"I'm really happy for you, Eli. Keep it up. I'll see you in six months for a new MRI."

All that day after Eli left the office, I was reminded of how I'd been wrong when I first saw his initial MRI and thought, *I've seen the end of you.* Here we were, more than three years later, and none of the things I'd been sure I knew had come true. He was fine, still working, healthy, and happy. I'd prophesied disability and death over him based on his tumor and other patients and the entire body of neurosurgical literature going back to Harvey Cushing, but I was wrong.

At least so far.

And then I checked myself. Why do I always add that back-end thought to my own ponderings of things that seem to be answered prayers? After all I'd seen, I was still the guy who said, "I do believe; help me overcome my unbelief!"[37]

In my early-morning hours during the months in which Joey had been dying, I'd been writing. But not this book. A few months after *Called Out* was released, I'd run across an essay on Philip Yancey's website about the Iraq War. He'd been very kind to correspond with me several times regarding my struggles in understanding faith and doubt in the context of patients with brain tumors and their seemingly hopeless prognosis. And it had been Philip Yancey who'd said, "Write about it."

Yet instead of writing about it, I'd written an entirely different book. Somehow, every time I sat down to tease out my understanding of the "I've seen the end of you" problem, wherein I assume I *know* something instead of approaching it with faith, I'd end up writing about Iraq instead.

When I saw Philip's article about Iraq, I sent him a copy of *Called Out*. He called me a few days later. It was the first time we spoke on the phone. "Lee, your story deserves a wider audience," he said.

I was flattered. I thought he was about to say my book was destined to be a bestseller, but I was wrong.

"It's a great story," he said, "but it's not well written. I think you need a ghostwriter to help turn it into what it could be."

That conversation and Philip Yancey's kind yet honest assessment of my writing skills led him to introduce me to an agent and a potential ghostwriter.

Months later Lisa and I had met with two potential writers and had formed a relationship with Philip's agent, Kathy Helmers of Creative Trust in Nashville. The problem was, I couldn't come to peace with the notion of letting someone else write my book.

We had another meeting, and I asked Kathy, "Do you think I could write it myself if I worked hard enough?"

She thought for a moment. "I don't know. Do you think I could teach myself to be a brain surgeon if I really tried?"

I got it. Professional writers take offense when amateurs think they can sit down and immediately become quality writers themselves.

Then Kathy came up with the idea of hiring an editor to coach me through writing my book, and I started studying the craft of writing as hard as I'd ever studied anything in my life.

My editor, Dave Lambert, wouldn't let me get away with anything less than the story deserved, and over time I learned how to write. Zondervan purchased the manuscript of *No Place to Hide,* and the book was to be published around the time Eli's next MRI would be done.

Lisa and I believed my story could help people who had been through hard things, wars real and metaphorical. It seemed as if God had opened a door into the publishing world for us, all because of Philip Yancey's graciousness and his urging me to write.

I knew that *No Place* wasn't the only book I was supposed to write, and after the edits for it were all done and we had nothing to do but wait for the publication date, it was time to start writing this one. My experiences with glioblastoma and trauma patients had taken me on a faith journey I'd never anticipated, and I knew people would benefit from walking that path with me. I felt I was supposed to share how I used to think I knew everything about brain cancer but how I had learned so much more. It was going to be a great book in which I would dispense wisdom I'd gleaned from watching patients like Samuel, Rupert, and Joey grapple with human-kind's deadliest cancer.

I was now ready to write the definitive book about faith and doubt because I'd seen so many people struggle with both. I believed God had led me to write *No Place* first because the story needed to be told but also to prepare me to write this one. I was ready, I thought, because I was an expert observer of other people's troubles, and now I knew how to write.

And then my son died.

PART TWO

During

Fragmented, my self knows no peace.
  I cannot remember what it's like to be happy.
"Failed," I say to myself. "My hope fails."

—LAMENTATIONS 3:17–18, Voice

28

The Difficult Dark

Einstein is loved because he is gentle, respected because he is wise. Relativity being not for most of us, we elevate its author to a position somewhere between Edison, who gave us a tangible gleam, and God, who gave us the difficult dark and the hope of penetrating it.

—E. B. White

Mitch's last few years at home had been difficult. He had become increasingly anxious and begun associating with kids who made him feel safe: musicians, theater people, stoners. He got into trouble twice with marijuana when he lived with his mother, both times with the same group of kids. I insisted he come to live in Auburn with us, and in the three years he lived there, I tested him every week for drugs as a condition of allowing him to have a car. He never had a positive drug test while he lived in our house.

Everything we did to try to help him failed, as he, like millions of adolescents before him, was convinced we wanted to control him and not protect him.

Then came college. Attending Auburn proved to be too much freedom for him. He made poor choices and ultimately left school and went back to old friends and old habits. For nearly a year he had little to do with us. Lisa and I texted and called him every day. He rarely answered, and we poured out our broken hearts in voice mails and texts so many times that I began to wonder whether we would ever reconnect. We prayed countless times that God would soften his heart toward us and that he would restore our family.

And then, on the morning of August 19, 2013, my phone rang. I looked at the screen and saw *Mitch*.

"Hey, Mitch!" I said.

"Dad. I want to come home."

Few moments in my lifetime have affected me as deeply as hearing my nineteen-year-old son say those words. We talked for an hour, and he told me that he realized how much we'd tried to help him and that he felt ashamed of himself for not listening, for leaving school, for using drugs. He wanted to go back to Auburn, finish his degree, get his life back on track. He was coming home in three days.

"I love you, Mitch, and I'm so proud of you," I said.

"I'll see you Thursday. I love you, Dad," he said, the last words I ever heard him say.

The next morning Lisa and I tuned in online to our church's 6:00 a.m. prayer service, which was part of an annual Twenty-One Days of Prayer event. The speaker was the youth pastor, and the prayer at the end had us weeping as we solicited God to protect our kids and thanked him for our reunion with Mitch.

We were filled with great hope.

We all make certain assumptions about how our lives will play out. One of them, to which I had never given two seconds' thought before a Tuesday night that August, is that our children will outlive us.

It's not clear to me now why I believed this was a given, since I work in a world in which tragedy and early deaths are common. And even in my own extended family, we had experienced profound grief when my brother's son died young.

But somehow, despite knowing the realities of disease and death, I never thought it could happen to me, to us, to our nuclear family.

In retrospect I suppose it was unrealistic for me to keep falling back on my "it's gonna be okay" paradigm. After all, I had been through hard things: divorce, the Iraq War, posttraumatic stress. My own history had given me no reason to suspect that my family or I would be immune to great trials or heartache.

Yet, as people do, I allowed myself to live with the notion that good parenting and God's protection would keep my kids safe.

Lisa and I prayed for all five of them every day, and we had specific concerns about each of their lives and their futures. Even on the morning of the day it happened, we had been in deep prayer for an hour, naming each of our children and lifting our worries and dreams for them to God.

And even when the phone rang that evening, when I saw my ex-wife's number on the screen, even when the thought flashed through my mind of how unusual it was for her to call me anytime, let alone at night, I never anticipated the news I was about to receive. If I had been asked in that moment to write down the one hundred most likely reasons for her to be calling me then, the actual reason would not have been on the list.

I can, as I type these words, hear her sobbing, desperate voice. "Mitchell is dead."

In that moment I went from being an observer of other people's troubles, a coach in their hard times, a counselor in their distress, a person who intervenes in life-threatening situations and then goes home at night to his own safe world, to being center stage in my own worst nightmare.

I would give anything to be able to explain what happened. But that would require my understanding it or being confident of the details. Even years later the only thing we know for certain is that our son and another nineteen-year-old boy he'd been best friends with since elementary school were dead, both from knife wounds. Two bloody knives were found in the house. Mitch had wounds from both. The police report details a scene so different from our experience with our gentle son that it remains impossible for us to fathom; he was not a person who would attack someone else or harm himself, and his spirit was so kind and loving that as far as we knew, no one had ever been physically violent toward him in his life. The coroner's report did nothing but add to our confusion, as Mitch had no drugs or alcohol in his system when he died.

Two days later we stood in a funeral home and touched his body. He was cold, and in my too-informed clinical mind, I realized he had been in a refrigerator before we arrived. I found myself looking for a blanket to cover him, keep him warm. I leaned down to kiss him and noticed he smelled fresh and clean, but he did not smell like himself. Someone else had bathed him, using different soap and shampoo than he used.

I noticed the makeup on his neck, covering the injuries that had killed him and the rough, hastily repaired incisions from the coroner's knife used in the autopsy, and I thought, *I would have been more precise, used more care, made them look better.*

All those thoughts swirled through my mind, probably to keep me from having to process what was really happening. My beautiful, brilliant, hilarious son was dead at nineteen. The next day I wrote a eulogy for him. These words still seem impossible as I type them now.

> Mitchell loved—loudly, freely, everyone.
> He made the world smile, even when he wasn't smiling inside.
> He had a brilliant mind, even though it sometimes tormented him.
> He had limitless potential, which has left an unfillable hole in the
>   universe.
>
> Mitchell saw humor and made us see it too, in everything.
> He reminded us to laugh, and he wants us to remember that now.
> He carried everything inside himself, but he doesn't have to anymore.
> He's smiling again.
>
> Mitchell was a good son, a good brother.
> He was an amazing friend.
> He was a gentle soul.
> He is not defined by this; Mitchell loved.
>
> Mitchell thought he needed something, something more.
> He needed to feel something, something calmer than his mind.
> He searched for that in all the wrong ways and places, but
> He finally found it, and now he has everything.

Mitchell knew the Lord and pronounced his name "Gee-Zus"
    every time.
He lost his way but made it home.
He learned how to say *Jesus* when he met him.
He's laughing about that now, with us.

And then we had a funeral, where I listened and nodded and sometimes seethed as well-meaning people uttered platitudes that were alternately mildly comforting and downright offensive. I processed the thought that I'd done the same countless times to families and patients and even relatives, as we all try to be helpful while saying things suffering people cannot believe in that moment—things like "He's in a better place now," "God must have needed him more than you did," "All things work together for good," or "Everything happens for a reason."

One morning I went into Mitch's room and opened his closet. I could still smell him on his clothes, and I buried my face in one of his shirts to try to remember what it felt like to hold him. When I turned around, there was his bass guitar on its stand in the corner. The last Christmas we had together, Lisa and I surprised him with a midnight-blue Rickenbacker model 4003 bass, his dream guitar. He'd become very skilled at bass and was playing in a band and even occasionally on the worship team at church. But now his bass sat untouched in his room, and he was gone.

I took the bass to the church and asked the worship leader if they would use it so the beautiful instrument could still be of service and so some part of my son would live on every Sunday. I'm not sure why that gave me some comfort, but it did. Each week when we went to church, I would wonder whether Mitch could see and enjoy hearing his bass from his vantage point in heaven's worship band, and then I would secretly feel ashamed that I would rather have him here even though Christians are supposed to think it's better to be in heaven.

People started giving us books about grief, a section of the library I'd previously skipped. I think I read all of them over the following year: C. S. Lewis's *A Grief Observed,* Nicholas Wolterstorff's *Lament for a Son,* and Gordon Livingston's *Only Spring* and *Too Soon Old, Too Late Smart* were among the most helpful.

Probably the most important thing I can say as a person living through the loss of a child is this. Dr. Elisabeth Kübler-Ross's famous five stages of grief were outlined to explain how people cope with the news that they are dying. The stages were not defined within the context of how people handle great loss in their lives, although they are commonly used in that way. God forbid you ever have to face such a time, but if you do, do not look for sense or order in the process, because none shall be found.

The grief one feels over losing a spouse, sibling, or child is a loose mold filled with wet cement, runny and slow to set. It is ill defined, poorly explained, and different for everyone encountering it. And although you will inevitably pass through the denial, anger, bargaining, depression, and acceptance phases, as soon as you think you've moved from one to another, you'll find yourself hopelessly lost in the labyrinth of a prior stage and wondering whether you'll ever get out.

I've often thought that it would have been easier for us to process losing Mitch if he had died in a different way: a car accident, a sudden illness, anything "normal" we could have wrapped our heads around. And I've almost envied the people whose children die of prolonged illnesses, as I made myself believe that knowing it was coming would have allowed us to prepare, make amends, spend more time with him. But after living through it and observing other families over the years, I now know that understanding *how* you lost someone does not replace the mystery of *why* you lost that person, why God allows such things to happen at all. And I've come to know that grief is not relative. Whether your child dies of cancer or a car wreck or with a knife plunged into his beautiful neck, you'll hurt just as badly and will not see someone else's loss as worse than yours.

Your grief will feel worse to you.

We in our family were given a death we could not and cannot explain or understand, one so different from the kinds of things that happen to us that none of us could even process it. Our task was to learn to live again anyway, despite the huge loss and the unknowable whats and whys.

Before Mitch died, I was preparing to write a book about how to have faith even when life makes you doubt the things you think you know—this book. I planned to write it as an observer of other people's troubles, but now I am writing it as a fellow sufferer of grief, loss, and pain. The Greek philosopher Thales, when asked what was easy, said, "To advise another." When asked what was difficult, he said, "To know one's self."[38] So here I was, trying to write a book about how to hold on to your faith during the storms of life while I was struggling with my own.

Our family's loss has been devastating and life changing, but I am confident that other people's losses are as great to them. Thus, the point of sharing it now is not to gain sympathy for our tragic circumstance but rather to share the lessons it has taught us and hopefully make the path a little easier for others to travel when it is their turn to face such a thing.

This is a book about faith, doubt, and the things we think we know.

And just at the time I thought I was ready to begin writing it, when I thought I understood how people go through their darkest hours and still hold on to their faith, I was thrust into mine and had no idea how I was ever going to survive it.

For me it was even harder to face my son's death *with* faith, because it felt as if the whole thing were a dirty trick by God. After months of trying with all our might to reconnect with Mitch, he had called and we talked and everything seemed as if it were going to be okay, right up to the moment it wasn't.

Too soon after we lost Mitch, Lisa and I found our grieving interrupted by the reality of owning our own business. We had to go back to work. Our employees' salaries and our overhead were not going to pay themselves, and our referring physicians, who fed us patients, keeping us in business, were not going to magically wait until we were healed of our grief; if we did not go back to work, other surgeons would capitalize on my absence, and our business would be in trouble. Time, as they say, waits for no man. Neither do hurting patients, growing tumors, or impatient referring physicians.

After we returned to work, I found myself tying my tie and wearing my suit to the office as always. I made good decisions in the operating room, same as usual. But things were different. I had no capacity for small talk. I became all business, all the time, with patients and colleagues alike. I moved through my days just as I had during mortar attacks in Iraq: do what you have to do, wait for the all clear to sound, go to your room. On my surgery days it was go to work, do your job, get home to Lisa and Kalyn as soon as you can. On office days Lisa and I waded through the work set before us and then drove home together, holding hands, often not talking, wiping away the tears we'd held in during normal business hours. Only in the house, with my eyes and hands on my wife and daughter, did I hear the all clear.

We had a strong sense of the importance of helping Kalyn get through her junior year of high school with as little disruption as possible. Kimber was a senior at Auburn University at the time, Josh was in San Antonio working, and Caity had just delivered our first granddaughter, Scarlett. Just as with our work, there was no option for any of our kids to pause their lives so they could deal with their grief over losing their brother. Death is not a gentleman.

The effects of grief and stress on my body were obvious. I had an attack of shingles on my back, among the more painful physical ailments I have ever experienced. A few days later I woke up one morning to find that a large patch of hair on the left side of my head had turned from sandy blond to gray overnight. Gastric distress, diarrhea, headaches, and fatigue plagued me. I felt like the biblical Job, grieved, afflicted, pained, in spirit and body.

Grief ravages the spirit and the body as surely as cancer or heart disease, but there is no tumor or clogged artery to cut out, stent open, or otherwise repair. The patient is at the mercy of the disease, for no cure exists. I realized that even if time somehow could make it not hurt so much, my son would still be dead. And just as patients sometimes become angry with me when I cannot cure them, transferring their emotion from the disease they cannot see to the physician in front of them, I was angry at God, the so-called great physician, because I knew in my heart he was the only chance I had to heal, but I also blamed him for allowing this awful tragedy into our lives in the first place.

Throughout those terrible first few months, I came to realize a few things about myself. I could work with great stamina, but as soon as I was home, I was entirely depleted of any sort of energy or drive. I stopped exercising, and since I couldn't close my eyes at night without seeing the awful and traumatic death of my gentle son, I sought other ways to block those images from my mind. But I learned that sleep aids, brain-wave-aligning soundtracks, and falling asleep to *SportsCenter* only push the dreams and thoughts into the daylight; they do not eliminate them.

Lisa and I clung to each other, and I could not have survived without her. But she was in the difficult dark with me. Two people can huddle together in the blackness, but in the absence of light, they both remain lost. Somehow I knew it was my job to lead the kids and my wife through it, to try to protect them, to support them and help guide them through the jungle even though it was new territory for me as well. And I knew, from my parents' wise example and my time in real and figurative wars, that the path forward was to cling to God.

I found Psalm 34 incredibly comforting: "When someone is hurting or broken-hearted, the Eternal moves in close and revives him in his pain."[39] I could read those words, and even on the days when intellectually I wanted to shake my fist and declare my hatred for a God who would let my son die, in my spirit I knew the verse was true.

My morning writing time became time spent reading the Bible and noting the disconnect between what I read and believed and how I felt. Every day I would email the kids some scriptural rung on the ladder I hoped would help them climb out of the hole, and then I would go to work and no longer pray with my patients. Before, I almost always offered to pray with people before they went to surgery. But after we lost Mitch, I somehow lost the belief that it made any difference.

I was caught in a quandary: I *knew* that holding on to God was the path forward for my kids and even for Lisa and me. But I didn't *believe* it. Maybe it worked for Joey, who found hope in his faith toward the end of his life. But for me it was an intellectual issue I still do not fully understand: I believed and I doubted and I actively disbelieved *at the same time.*

"Believing is not the same as knowing," my old professor had said. *"Seeing is knowing."* Like Thomas, I believed, but I needed to see through the difficult darkness.

Most of the time it seemed impenetrable, impossible, opaque.

Zondervan graciously delayed the release date for my book *No Place to Hide.* Everyone there was incredibly sensitive to the fact that I could not have gone on a book signing tour or done marketing events in those early days. Their tenderness and kindness in putting my needs above their business interests were unbelievable. Kathy Helmers and Philip Yancey and Max Lucado reached out over and over, pastored and prayed for and mentored and loved on us, as did hundreds of other people who took the time to try to minister to us, and it helped. Pastor Jon kept showing up at just the right moment, offering support, a hug, or a prayer. Knowing we were not alone was a powerful salve on our wounds of despair.

But as time marched forward and our days began to look more "normal," it became apparent that there *was* no more normal, because at every turn there was someone missing, an empty seat at the table, a missing form in the pictures, a speed dial number no one was there to answer anymore, an empty bedroom in the house.

And as I moved through my work among the sick and broken, I realized something else that was new: I could see dead people.

In M. Night Shyamalan's brilliant movie *The Sixth Sense,* a young boy named Cole (played by Haley Joel Osment) seeks the help of child psychologist Dr. Malcolm Crowe (played by Bruce Willis). Cole's problem is that he can see dead people—but only dead people who don't know they are dead. Of course, Shyamalan's films almost always contain incredible twists (please skip the rest of this paragraph if you haven't seen the movie): the reason Cole is meeting with Dr. Crowe is that Dr. Crowe is actually dead but doesn't know it.[40]

I developed a sixth sense, an ability to see clearly into people who were dead inside: going through hard things, facing terrible loss, or dying in their bodies but already buried in their spirits.

For a time I noted these living ghosts around me, but I made no effort to engage them. I did not have the reserve to deal with my own pain and interact with them also.

And then I came to the shocking realization that I wasn't Cole in the story; I was Dr. Crowe.

I was dead too.

And if I were ever to live again, I had to find the light somewhere.

The dark was too difficult to penetrate alone, even with Lisa at my side peering into it also.

My heart knew that God held the answers, but my brain kept telling me he wasn't real or didn't care, at least about me.

Something had to give, because when I looked in the mirror in the morning, I said to myself, *I've seen the end of you.*

29

All or None

It is impossible for God to lie.

—Hebrews 6:18

I saw Eli again six months after Mitch died. He looked great, had been promoted at work, and had another completely clean MRI. He wore, as usual, khaki pants, boat shoes, and a Southern Tide button-down long-sleeve oxford shirt with the little script *A* on his lapel. He looked healthy and happy and perfect.

"I'm getting married, Doc," he said with a big smile. "We've been dating about a year. I figured if a girl will go out with you when you're still bald from radiation therapy, she will stick with you forever."

"Congratulations," I said, still believing in the back of my mind he would have a recurrence someday and leave her widowed. "I'm happy for you." That was true, even with my reservations.

He looked down for a second. "We'll have a long engagement. I'm realistic about my disease, but after all this time I'm starting to believe I'm going to make it. If I'm still cancer-free next year, we'll tie the knot."

"Tie the knot?" I said. "Do you remember when we first met, you couldn't understand metaphor?"

He smiled. "Yes, but losing my math skills was a much bigger fear for me. I can't thank you enough for your help."

I nodded. "That's why I'm here. You're doing great. I'll see you in six months."

He shook my hand and stood. Then his eyes fell, and he said softly, "Doc, I heard about your son. We've been praying for you."

I thanked him. "It's been hard, but we're doing okay."

"I don't know if I could survive it, losing a child. Your strength is amazing to me. Do you think you could do me a favor?"

"Of course," I said. "What?"

He sighed deeply. "My sister just lost her five-year-old son, Robbie, to liver failure. Her husband is a believer, but this has just destroyed him. He's having a hard time. Do you think you could talk to him, try to help him?"

"I'm so sorry," I said. "I'll be praying for them. But how do you think I could help?"

He reached into his pocket and pulled out a business card. It read "Jack Phillips, Vice President, MidSouth Bank." Handwritten below his name was a phone number. Eli said, "That's Jack's cell phone. Maybe you can call him? If just to show him that in six months he'll still be breathing, that he can make it. You're handling it so well I thought maybe you could just tell him how you do it."

I didn't know what to say. Eli was wrong; I was *not* handling it well. How could I help another grieving dad?

———

Lisa and I sat in our office that afternoon and held hands while we looked out the window. Jack Phillips's card sat on my desk.

"You have to call him," Lisa said.

"I don't know what to say. He's going to ask me how we're making it, and the truth is, I have no idea."

Lisa stroked the back of my hand and looked into my face. Her hazel eyes glistened and a single tear hung on her lashes. "Honey, do what you do with your patients. Tell him the truth about what to expect. Tell him what's coming, and he'll know he can make it because you have. Tell him how you talk to the kids and to me so he'll know he can lead his family through it too. And tell him how God's been there so he'll know where to look to find him too."

———

The next morning I was up at three, holding a cup of coffee and sitting in front of my computer. I started a document to help me frame my thoughts before I called Jack later. I titled it "Things I've Learned Since My Son Died."

Jack was a few days into the journey I'd been on for six months. I tried to remember those early days, but all I could recall was the bitter pain and the darkness. No one could really help other than to just be there.

As I let my mind slip into the memory of those first days after we lost Mitch, my body began to remind me—just as it is doing now as I type these words—that grief is a physical ailment. The bitter taste of acid rose in my throat, I felt a subtle ache in my right shoulder blade where the shingles had been, and I felt pain in my jaw from grinding my teeth all night. (That was another gift that grief gave me: while sleeping, I ground one of my molars so hard it split in two.)

I remembered the things that made the pain worse, such as ill-received Christian platitudes. Even more hurtful were people who would avoid the topic altogether or even turn and walk away when they saw me coming, obviously dreading having to say something to me. I knew Jack must be experiencing the same things.

And then I remembered one of the most unlikely kindnesses I received during that time. Another surgeon, a man I had hardly ever spoken to, walked up to me on the first day I went back to the hospital. He put his hands on both my shoulders, leaned his face close to mine, and said, "Lee, I don't have any idea what to say to you, but I just want you to know I care."

His acknowledgment that there really isn't anything you *can* say meant the world to me right then. We were not friends—are not friends now—but he addressed me sincerely, and it helped.

All those memories swirled around with the coffee in my waking brain, and I remembered a scripture from Psalm 144 that had meant a lot to me during the bloodiest moments in Iraq: "Blessed be the Eternal, my rock. He trains my hands for war, gives me the skills I need for battle."[41]

When I read it during the war, this psalm startled me with its truth. I landed in Iraq terrified of what would happen and doubting whether I could handle it professionally or personally. Even now I can clearly recall how amazed I was that during the mass casualties and the mortar attacks and the horrible human tragedy we saw every day, the promise of Psalm 144 was valid: I *was* prepared. I never freaked out when things went crazy, which they did almost daily. And I had no reason to credit that steadiness under fire to my own strength. Credit was due solely to God, who had kept his promise and prepared my hands for war.

Then I remembered that every day after Mitch died, I woke up certain of two things: I had no idea how to survive the day, yet I somehow had to find the words to help lead my family through the war life had brought to them.

And during those awful days, my heart and my mind recognized that God was keeping his promise: "When someone is hurting or brokenhearted, the Eternal moves in close and revives him in his pain."[42]

Each day started so hopelessly then. In the first few weeks, all I could think about was loss: Mitch was missing in the present, and in the future we had no hope of seeing him grow into manhood, fall in love, and have children or of having him there when it was our turn to be old and sick. And every morning as I sat in the dark in front of my computer, trying to find the words to send to my family to give them something to hold on to even as I was free-falling into the abyss, there would be something to help me.

Perhaps it would be an email from a friend saying, "You're on my mind this morning," or a text from Pastor Jon encouraging me, "Remember today that you are loved," or the verse of the day from biblegateway.com pointing to a scripture about peace or hope. Every time I opened my eyes to the darkness of predawn and felt that the gravity crushing me into bed was too strong for my feeble bones to overcome, I managed to get a foot on the floor and stumble into the kitchen.

Often there were already tears in my eyes when I first opened them, from crying in my sleep. But once on my feet, even as the first cup of coffee was brewing, I felt God there. I would pray and cry and tell him I hated him and didn't understand why he'd done this, and then in the next moment, I would ask him to make it go away or at least make the pain a little less so I could breathe.

And he was there.

This might sound crazy to you if you don't believe in God, but I can tell you unequivocally that in the deepest crevasse of pain, with no one there to belay or assist me in climbing back to safety because all my people were in that crevasse with me, the scripture proved true.

He moved in close and revived me in my pain.

Every day I managed to pray through it, to get to a place where I'd said my piece to God and he, like a gentleman, allowed me to do so and then reminded me of his presence through his Word or an email or a text or Lisa waking up just when I thought I couldn't bear it alone for another minute and saying, "Good morning, honey. I love you."

And in my search for words to use as medicine for my hurting children, every day he would give me something. Sometimes when I told them that God would use this pain and redeem it so they could help others or that Mitch was at peace and safe now, I didn't really believe it. But then one of my kids would write back and say, "Dad, that was exactly what I needed to get through today."

Jack, I knew, was wondering how he could help his family through this dark place even while he was struggling in it himself. And I remembered a paradigm shift that happened in my heart one day when I found a verse, Hebrews 6:18, that says, "It is impossible for God to lie." With shock I realized then that if this verse was true, all the other promises in the Bible had to be true as well. And that was vitally important because for me to keep going, I have to know I'll get to see Mitch again someday, which is the only sustaining hope a grieving parent has. I need it to be true that there is a resurrection after we die and that we get to live forever.

And if it is true that God cannot tell a lie, then even when it seems impossible, it must also be true that God can use everything for good.[43] Jack needed to know that because it was one of the key mental shifts that kept me alive after Mitch died.

That realization about Hebrews 6:18 was a subtle bit of grace I wasn't fully able to appreciate at the time, but I could feel its weight and somehow knew it was the rope I'd been looking for that would pull me out of the hole: all God's promises are true, or none of them are. Said another way, if God cannot tell a lie, then all his promises are true. Even when it doesn't feel like it. Even when you're going through the hardest thing you can imagine.

When the worst things happen, when your son dies or your doctor says it's cancer, when your husband strays or the bank forecloses, Romans 12:12 seems ridiculous on its face: "Do not forget to rejoice, for hope is always just around the corner" (Voice). This is ludicrous when your life is falling apart, unless it is actually true.

But if these words are lies, then we, as the apostle Paul put it, are "of all people most to be pitied."[44]

While I sipped my fourth cup of coffee that morning, I had to make a choice:

Did I really believe all these words were true, or did I just use them, as Karl Marx said, as metaphorical morphine to dull the pain caused by life's troubles?[45]

I realized that what I'd originally asked Philip Yancey was the wrong question. I'd asked, "How can I pray for my patients when I already know how God is going to answer?" But the real question is "How can I help people (including myself) hold on to their faith when life is hard, no matter how God answers their prayers?"

And with that realization, suddenly I had context for the painful parts of my life and those of my patients.

Most of us—probably all of us if we're honest—approach life expecting everything to be good all the time. And then when life is difficult and bad things happen, we wonder where God is and doubt our faith or abandon it altogether. We pray for one thing and get another, and we respond by deciding that God can't be real, because he's not behaving as we want him to.

But my experience with all the tumor patients, trauma victims, and personal tragedy I'd faced had shown me something else. Something I'd missed before.

Life is a Hobson's choice.[46]

You get good stuff mixed in with a lot of pain, or you get nothing.

It's your choice, and the choice is to take it or leave it.

The trick is to be able to live happily and with purpose even during those tough times. I'd seen it in Samuel and Rupert and Joey, and now I had to try to find my way to the same choice despite losing my son. Because the alternative was what people like my depressed patient did when she couldn't swallow Hobson's choice. Faced with the hard reality that she could have life *and* pain or have nothing at all, she put a bullet in her brain.

But although I was at the very edge of the most important discovery I'd made in my faith journey, I couldn't afford to keep pursuing it any more that morning.

It was time to call Jack Phillips.

30

Impossible

I sat there in despair, my spirit draining away,
my heart heavy, like lead.

—PSALM 143:4, MSG

The call went to voice mail. I left a short message: "Hi, Jack. This is Lee Warren, a friend of Eli's. He told me about your son. I'm so sorry, and I want you to know I'm praying for you. We don't know each other, but we've both lost sons, so I know something about the pain you're in right now. If you need someone to talk to, I'm here for you."

And then I went to the office.

Later that morning Stinson called me on my cell phone from the ED. I knew it was important, since he usually paged me.

"Got another bad one for you, Lee," he said. "Better get over here."

"What's going on?" I said.

"Young lady with a big brain hemorrhage. Right pupil is blown; she's posturing. I intubated her and gave her mannitol, but the scan looks terrible."

"On my way," I said.

Lisa canceled the rest of our clinic appointments, and I drove to the ED.

As I ran in, Claudette directed me to trauma bay 2. Stinson stood next to a stretcher where a thin young woman lay motionless except for the rise and fall of her chest from the mechanical ventilator. A young man stood at her bedside.

Stinson said, "Dr. Warren, this is Artie McBride."

We shook hands.

Stinson added, "Artie is the patient's husband. Teresa is twenty-eight, previously healthy with no past medical history. Collapsed at home while she and Artie were having breakfast. CT scan is up on the monitor."

The scan showed a large hemorrhage in her right temporal lobe, which was shifting her brain severely from right to left. Her ventricle, the space where cerebrospinal fluid is made and stored, was trapped and significantly enlarged—obstructive hydrocephalus. This problem alone would kill her in minutes. The hemorrhage and brain shift would take a few hours to do her in, but hydrocephalus is a much more efficient assassin.

"Sir," I said to Artie, "this is very serious."

I showed him the scan and explained it.

"I have to take her to surgery right now," I said, "or she won't survive."

He shook his head. "What happened?"

"I don't know yet," I said. "It could be an aneurysm or some kind of vascular malformation, but the CT doesn't show anything clearly. We don't have time to do an angiogram because the fluid buildup and pressure would kill her before we could get it done. After I decompress her brain, we can work to determine the cause and make sure it doesn't happen again, but for now we need to go save her life."

He nodded. "Go, then. Please save her, Doctor. She's twelve weeks pregnant with our first child."

I looked at Stinson, who slightly shrugged his shoulders. He hadn't known that either.

"We're going to try," I said. "But we've got to go now."

The OR nurse came in, and I gave her a few orders. Then I turned to leave. Artie grabbed my arm. "Doc, please—I can't live without her."

I choked down the truth I knew I couldn't tell him: *She's in serious trouble, and I don't think she's going to make it.* I nodded. "I'll do my best. I promise."

I was halfway up the stairs to the OR when my cell phone rang. I looked at the screen. Jack Phillips.

I didn't have time to talk to him, so I let the call go to voice mail.

Fifteen minutes later I had shaved Teresa McBride's head and prepped her scalp with DuraPrep, the yellow-orange iodine solution we use to clean the skin before surgery. I made a small incision and drilled a little hole with a hand drill. Then I inserted a ventriculostomy catheter about six centimeters into her head and felt the comforting pop of the catheter entering her lateral ventricle. Cerebrospinal fluid shot out of the catheter and hit the ceiling above my head. Her intracranial pressure (ICP) was about sixty—six times normal.

"That will give us a few more minutes to get the clot out," I said. Controlling the ICP would relax Teresa's brain enough that she would not die while I was getting the bone off to access her blood clot.

Minutes later I ran the drill around her skull and removed a hand-sized circle of her right temporal and frontal bones. The dura mater underneath was taut, bulging, and purple. I took a scalpel and incised the dura. Blood gushed out. I extended the dural opening and began to suck out the clot, which had ruptured through the brain surface and was now moving toward the outside of the head and away from her brain stem. The temporal lobe began to pulsate and move back toward the dural opening. It looked much more relaxed with every ounce of blood I removed.

We'd gotten her to the OR in time, most likely.

The problem was, it wasn't just blood.

The clot was thick and black and came out in chunks. I'd seen it a few times before in my career, and when I rolled one of the chunks around in my hand, I knew.

It was melanoma.

Grossman wasn't working that day, so we could not get a frozen section. I sent the specimens to the lab and told Artie in the waiting room that the clot was out but that it looked very suspicious. We would know more the next day.

In the ICU post-op, Teresa woke up within a few minutes. She was groggy but lucid, and when she saw Artie walk in, she smiled around her breathing tube. Her ICP reading was normal, and her pupils were now reactive and small, as they should be.

She was going to survive her hemorrhage.

Just not her cancer.

———

The next morning when I came into the ICU, Teresa looked great. Artie was in a chair by her bed. Grossman had called me on my way to work and confirmed that the mass was, in fact, malignant melanoma.

Artie held her hand and kissed her forehead and told her how much he loved her. And while the nurse removed the breathing tube at my request since she was awake enough to protect her airway, Artie gave me a hug and thanked me over and over. The whole time I was trying to find the words to tell them both that the hemorrhage was just her cancer's way of announcing itself. Yesterday's seeming victory was just the beginning.

I was about to take away their joy and give them a horrible dilemma instead. There was no outcome that would be happy for both Teresa and her baby. While the McBrides had thought a happy family life was gestating inside Teresa's womb, she had instead been growing a cancer that would fragment their lives, rob them of their peace of mind, and destroy mother or child—or both.

I'd seen the end of Teresa McBride, and it was black, vile, malignant, and ruthless.

I decided to give Teresa and Artie a few minutes more of naive peace before we had the conversation.

I needed to go to the chapel.

<hr />

Pastor Jon was there, restocking a rack of church brochures and pamphlets. He smiled when I entered. "Hey, Doc, how's your day going?"

"Not good," I said. "Another brain tumor patient, and she's pregnant."

He motioned for us to sit, and he turned in his chair to face me. There we were again, with the Last Supper's participants staring us down.

I told him the story and what I was about to have to do.

He shook his head. "Poor people. Sometimes this life . . ." His voice trailed off. "How are you holding up, by the way? We haven't talked a lot since you lost your son."

Just like Pastor Jon: ministering to me instead of offering advice.

My phone beeped in my pocket, reminding me I had a voice mail from Jack Phillips.

I told Pastor Jon about him too. "How do I talk to this guy, this poor guy who lost a son, when I still don't even know half the time how to talk to myself about it?"

"It's the senior-freshman conversation," he said.

"What?"

He smiled softly. "Look, when you're a freshman on your first day of high school, everything seems so big and scary and impossible. You're lost, and you don't know what to do. Then some senior comes along and gives you a pointer or two. He seems so confident, so strong, and so smart, and it makes you feel better. But when he was a freshman, he felt the same as you. The only thing that qualifies him as a person worthy to guide you is that he made it through. He's a senior because he kept going. That's all Jack needs to know from you. He can make it if he just keeps going."

"But I'm not a senior. I'm still wandering around in this too."

He put his hand on my shoulder. "So you're a sophomore. You're still more informed than he is about how this plays out. A few months after my daughter died, my sister lost her son in a car wreck. And all I could tell her was to keep waking up in the mornings and praying that God would give her enough grace to get through that day. He did, and she survived it. But at that time it was all I could give. Because it was what I was still doing."

My phone rang, shattering the quiet calm of the chapel. It was the ICU.

"Sorry, Pastor, but I've got to get back to work," I said.

He hugged me. "No problem. I'm praying for you, Lee."

I walked out of the chapel and answered the call.

"Mr. McBride wants to talk to you," the ICU nurse said.

On my way I listened to Jack Phillips's message.

"Dr. Warren, thank you for calling. I don't really feel like meeting anyone right now, but I appreciate the offer. My wife thinks I should pray with you, but I think I used up all my prayers before my son died. Those didn't do any good, so I'm not sure how saying more now will help."

The elevator opened on the third floor just as Jack's message ended. I stepped out into the hall and put my phone back in my pocket. Jack's words played over in my mind, and the thing that bothered me the most was that I agreed with him completely.

31

A Bag Full of Pictures

The sort of general malaise that only the genius possess
and the insane lament.

—Dr. Evil, *Austin Powers*

Artie stood at his wife's bedside, holding her hand with its IVs and pulse oximeter. She still looked groggy with her head wrapped in white gauze and the postanesthetic glaze in her eyes, but she was awake, and she looked at me when I walked in.

"Hi, Teresa," I said. "I'm Dr. Warren, your surgeon."

"Artie told me you saved my life." She put her other hand on her belly and looked down. "Our lives."

Saved, yes, I thought. *But for how long?*

"Are you comfortable?" I asked.

She nodded.

"I need to talk to you both about what we found in surgery."

Artie squeezed her hand a little tighter, and they both looked at me.

"The reason you bled into your brain is that you have a cancer called melanoma. It grows so fast that it frequently causes arteries to form that are too weak to handle your blood pressure, and they rupture and cause hemorrhages like yours."

"Melanoma?" Artie said. "I thought that was a skin cancer."

"It is," I said. "But it often spreads to other parts of the body."

Teresa coughed, cleared her throat, and asked, "What about our baby?"

"We will have your OB doctor come see you, but there's no reason so far to think that anything happened to the baby. We do need to talk about the risks involved in treating your cancer."

"I'm not having any treatment that could harm the baby," Teresa said.

"Honey," Artie said, "let's just hear what the doctor says."

She flashed her eyes at Artie. "It took us years, and we went through so many tests and treatments to get pregnant. I'm not going to hurt the baby."

Artie's eyes filled with tears. He rubbed the side of her face with his hand. "I know. It's just . . ."

"I'll have the oncology doctor come see you tomorrow," I said, "and she'll give you all the information and answer any questions. For now you should get some rest."

I walked out of the ICU, past the room where Samuel had died. I heard someone moaning in pain from another room, the sound my heart was making right then.

———

Dr. Grimes examined Teresa the next day and found a small black mole behind her right ear, the likely source of the metastatic melanoma that had nearly killed her two days before and almost certainly would eventually.

She ordered a PET scan to see where else the melanoma had spread, and the results were not good: the cancer had spread to her liver, lungs, both femurs, and multiple lymph nodes in her abdomen and pelvis.

I was there when she told Artie and Teresa that the chemotherapy and radiation needed to give Teresa a chance to survive would kill the baby and that she recommended a therapeutic abortion if Teresa wanted a chance to live.

"And even if you don't have the treatments, it's very likely that the baby won't survive anyway because this cancer often spreads to the fetus," Dr. Grimes said. "I highly recommend you choose to fight for your life."

Teresa's eyes were red, and she clenched her fists. "I am not doing that to my baby."

Artie turned away and looked out the window but said nothing.

Four days later Teresa still had not changed her mind. But she had recovered enough to go home from the hospital. On the day I discharged her, I walked into her room on the fifth floor of the hospital, and my sixth sense was fully functioning when I saw Artie's face. He looked terrible, a dead man walking, as if he hadn't slept since all this fell from nowhere into his life. He'd gone from joy three months ago when Teresa finally got pregnant, to sheer terror when she nearly died, back to joy when I saved her, only to be crushed by my news that the hemorrhage was caused by an almost uniformly fatal cancer.

He motioned with his head for me to step out into the hall. Teresa was in the restroom, and Artie had something to say to me.

"Doc, you gotta talk to her," he said. "She's willing to die to save the baby, but I can't sign off on that." Tears rolled down his face. "I don't even know this child yet, and I sure don't know how to raise it alone. But Teresa's been my best friend since junior high. And now we're fighting over whether I should want to save my wife or my baby! Why does God do things like this?"

I didn't know exactly what to say, but I knew more than I had before I lost Mitch.

"I don't think he does," I said.

"What?"

"I just know that the Bible says that when God lost his Son, he ripped the temple veil and caused earthquakes and all kinds of havoc. There was darkness on the whole earth.[47] I understand that kind of pain. I don't think God wants us to feel it, and I definitely don't think he actively does it to us."

"Then why does it happen?" Artie asked.

"I don't know," I said, "but I do know God cares about you and Teresa and your baby, and he cares about your pain. I promise that if you hang on to your faith through this time, he will help you make it through."

Artie looked at me for a long time. We heard Teresa call from the room, "Artie, I'm ready. We can go."

He shook his head. "Doc, I want to believe what you said, but I just can't see it right now. If God loved us and cared about us, this kind of thing couldn't happen."

"It's been six months since I lost my son," I said. "And most days I can't see it either. But believing that I will see it someday, that I will see him again someday, is the only thing that keeps me going."

Artie let out his breath. He looked empty, colorless. I can still see his pale, grieving face. He was crushed by one and possibly two horrible losses that hadn't even happened yet—and also by the impossible choice his family was being forced to make. "Look, I appreciate what you've done for us, and I'm sorry about your son. But what kind of God makes a man choose between his wife and his baby? I don't want to know that God right now."

They left the hospital, and while I was making rounds, I sent a text to Jack Phillips:

Got your message. Here for you if you want to talk. Lee

I saw Teresa to remove her staples two weeks later, but Artie didn't come to the appointment with her. She rode with her mother.

"How are you feeling?" I said.

Teresa slowly nodded. "Pretty good. I think bald looks good on me, by the way. My head's a little sore, and my legs both hurt—I guess from the bone tumors. But I'm okay. Artie's still mad at me, mad at God. He had to work today since he missed so much while I was in the hospital."

"Have you reconsidered what Dr. Grimes said? Your wound is healed now if you decide to go ahead with radiation and chemotherapy."

She shook her head. "No, sir. Artie says the baby hasn't earned the right to take my life, but I told him my mother didn't make me earn it, and I'm not going to do that to our little girl either."

"Girl?" I said as I started removing Teresa's staples.

She smiled softly. "Yes. Just had the ultrasound."

"Congratulations," I said. "Please tell Artie I said hello."

"I will. He's going to be okay, Doc. He's a good man, but this has been really hard on him. He just can't understand how God could let all of this—any of this—happen. I told him the Bible never promised us an easy life, just an eternal one if we keep the faith. That's what's keeping me going."

"How can you be so strong?" I said.

"I'm not strong. I'm terrified. And I'm angry I won't be around to see my little girl grow up or to enjoy retirement with my husband. But every time it all gets so heavy I can't carry it anymore, I ask God to lift it for me, and somehow I get through that moment. I don't know what I'd do if he wasn't there, especially while Artie's struggling so."

As Teresa was leaving the office, she turned and said, "Oh, I forgot to tell you we're moving to Birmingham. Artie's job transferred him, and it's perfect because both our parents live there, so he'll have a lot of help with the baby when"—she cleared her throat—"if I don't make it."

I never saw her again.

———

Three days later my cell phone rang.

"Hello," I said.

"Lee, it's Jack Phillips." His voice was quiet, strained.

He asked whether we could meet for coffee, and the next morning I walked into Mama Mocha's in Auburn and saw a man who looked as if he'd just crawled out of a gutter.

"Jack?" I said.

He nodded. "Hi. Thanks for meeting me."

His white business shirt was wrinkled, his tie was crooked, he had a few days' growth of beard, and his hair was a mess.

We ordered coffee and sat down.

"I have to go back to work today," he said.

"That's hard," I said. "How's your wife?"

He sniffed. "Cindy's starting back at her job today too. It's funny. They give you eight weeks if you have a baby but no time if you lose one. Adjusting to not having a kid to take care of is a lot harder than learning how to change diapers."

How true. Mitch's death had become a lodestone for all of us in my family. Every family event—graduation, birthday, holiday—deflected in some way to the magnetic force of his absence or his memory: *"Mitch would have loved this." "We sure wish Mitch were here." "Mitch would have been twenty today."*

"You're right about that," I said. "It changes everything about how your family works, doesn't it?"

Jack nodded. "Yeah, and half the time I feel like I'm going crazy because I come home and fully expect Robbie to be there. The other day I'm pretty sure I saw him walking through the house. But I don't believe in ghosts. I feel pain in my throat all the time, even when I haven't been crying." He looked out the window for a moment. "And the worst part is that Cindy and her family keep telling me God has a plan in all of this, that it will all work out somehow, that I need to hold on to my faith. But to be honest, I wasn't really sure how much of that I believed before Robbie died, and I definitely don't believe it now. Look around the world, Doc. We're on our own. God's not out there making things happy for any of us. Robbie was a good kid. He didn't deserve being born with a bad liver and all he had to go through. It's not right. And even if God's real, I'm not letting him off the hook for taking my boy by saying it's part of some plan. If that's the plan, then I don't agree with it."

I wished I had some profound words for Jack to help him swallow the horrible poison I could tell was building up in him, but I had nothing because I didn't disagree with him. Jack experienced grief the same way I did. It wasn't some vague sense of sadness but rather physical pain. I still have a dull ache in my back and side where the shingles attack happened, and my broken molar came from such severe nocturnal teeth grinding that my masseter muscles still hurt most of the time. At any moment a funk, a general malaise not understandable to those outside the lost-sons club, can descend on us and try to take us out of any momentary escape we've found, drag us back to the moment we learned of our great loss, and threaten to keep us there forever.

But the bodily manifestations of our grief do not eclipse the spiritual ones brought on by platitude-wielding Christians. It is a terrible thing to lose a son and have people tell you it's all for some higher purpose.

The closest I've come to punching a person since I was an adult was a few days after we lost Mitch, when a well-meaning but insensitive man said that everything happens for a reason, even kids dying, and that God expected us to give him thanks in advance for the good that would come of it.

And here was my problem: I could sit in the stillness of the morning with my worship music and my writing and work myself into seeing that God was there, ministering to us, helping us deal with this terrible malady called grief. And intellectually I could align myself with the notion that life is hard but that our faith can equip us to deal with it anyway. When I was alone and quiet, I could almost hear God saying, *Lee, you have to move past emotion and into a place where earthly troubles can't shake your belief in the long-term triumph I'm preparing for you. Don't let feelings become facts for you.*

But in the real world, standing with Artie or drinking coffee with Jack, I couldn't find the words to explain why seeing the end of someone shouldn't make us ball up our faith and toss it out with the rest of the day's garbage.

There were things I believed: I believed in God; I believed he's good; I believed he can heal people, solve problems, work miracles, and give us strength to go through difficult times. Because I'd seen it in Samuel and Joey and so many others.

There were things I doubted: I doubted I would ever heal from losing my son; I doubted my words could offer any real comfort to another grieving dad; I doubted that tomorrow would seem any more hopeful to Jack—or to me—than today.

And there were things I thought I knew: I knew that GBM kills everybody, that metastatic melanoma is not survivable, that losing a child is the most malignant disease I've ever encountered in my own life.

The most important surgery I would ever perform would be the stitching together of my faith, my doubt, and the things I thought I knew. But at that moment I had neither the training nor the instruments to pull it off.

Jack's words—*"Even if God's real, I'm not letting him off the hook for taking my boy by saying it's part of some plan. If that's the plan, then I don't agree with it"*—still wafted through the air along with the steam from his mocha latte.

"I don't agree with it either, Jack," I said. "But somehow I still believe he cares and he'll get you through it."

He looked at me for a long time. Then he slowly shook his head. "He might care. But I'm not sure if I care whether he does or not. Tomorrow's my birthday. I'll turn another year older. But I realized this morning that I'll get older every year, but Robbie will always be five. That's going to happen to you too, Doc. Someday you'll be an old man, but your boy will still just be nineteen. You tell me how we can reconcile that with God caring about us, and maybe we can talk again. But now I have to go to work."

I sat there in Mama Mocha's for a few more minutes, trying to finish my coffee. Jack was right about our sons being frozen in time, and I'd had a similar discovery the day before. A package had arrived from my ex-wife containing several gallon-sized Ziploc bags full of copied pictures from before the digital camera days: Mitch as a newborn and an infant, on his first day of kindergarten, with my now-dead grandfather, at my medical school graduation, holding his baby sister, Kalyn, who was now sixteen. As much as I treasured those pictures and was grateful to have them, they also broke me open again when I realized what they were: my son's life in toto. There would never be a new photograph.

A loving God, nonsurvivable cancers, dying children. Can such things be reconciled?

I remembered what Teresa McBride had said: *"The Bible never promised us an easy life, just an eternal one if we keep the faith. That's what's keeping me going."*

The waitress interrupted my thoughts. "Let me top you off, Doc."

She poured more coffee into my cup, and the foam in the bottom rose to the top and swirled around. Black coffee and cream mingled in an arc across the cup.

On the heels of the echo of Teresa's words came the echo of Jack's: *"Someday you'll be an old man, but your boy will still just be nineteen. You tell me how we can reconcile that with God caring about us, and maybe we can talk again."*

Teresa had figured out a way to navigate something I'd never been able to reconcile: the tension between losing your faith when bad things happen and having your faith support you during those times. *"How can you be so strong?"* I'd asked her.

"I'm not strong. I'm terrified. And I'm angry. . . . But every time it all gets so heavy I can't carry it anymore, I ask God to lift it for me, and somehow I get through that moment. I don't know what I'd do if he wasn't there."

Tightrope walkers depend on the tension in the rope to keep them up. Too much slack and there's nothing solid under their feet. Jack and I had both lost sons, and Teresa was ready to die to keep her child alive. But somehow she was walking the rope better than either of us. I finished my coffee and hoped that if Jack fell off the rope, the safety net of faith would catch him.

The next morning I woke up in a sweat with Lisa calling out to me, "Honey, are you okay? You were having a bad dream."

I opened my eyes and sat up. The whole thing was right there in front of me, fresh, as if I'd just lived it in the real world. "Yeah, a bad dream," I said.

She held my hands. "Iraq?" She's had to wake me from many of those dreams over the years.

I shook my head. "No. It was about our patient Teresa. She was walking into the sunset, and her family was a few steps in front of her. She looked back over her shoulder into the darkness behind her, and half her face was blacked out. Somehow I knew she was dying and the darkness behind her was cancer. Her family had to keep moving though. They couldn't stay there with her."

We talked for a while about Teresa and Artie and Jack and the balance between faith and doubt. While I got ready for work that day, my mind was a swirl of tension and tightropes, mingling like the coffee and foam in my cup the day before. Teresa seemed to understand it much better than I did.

But it wasn't me in the dream, stuck in the darkness while my family moved on.

PART THREE

After

Faith is a footbridge that you don't know
will hold you up over the chasm until
you're forced to walk out onto it.

—Nicholas Wolterstorff, *Lament for a Son*

32

Hacking My Way Through

When I begin a book, I take up a machete and start hacking
my way through the jungle, not to clear a trail for others,
rather to find a path through for myself.

—Philip Yancey, *Reaching for the Invisible God*

I have refined you, but not in the way silver is refined.
Instead, I try you in the furnace of suffering.

—Isaiah 48:10, Voice

Time passed. My book would be released in May 2014, whether I was ready
or not. My publisher asked me to begin working on platform development,
hoping that would help in launching a new and unknown author. I reread the email
I'd received a few months before on the topic, learned how to build a website, and
started a weekly newsletter and blog. "You are more than one story," the email had
said, and I realized how easy it would be to have my life become about one story.
The internet is full of blogs and websites from people who had a singular experience
that went on to become their defining moment: divorce, loss, triumph, and so forth.
The challenge for me was to find a voice for my stories that would resonate *beyond*
any one of the things I'd been through and help people no matter what they were
facing.

My book was about war and how it affected me. But in trying to develop a platform to help the book succeed, I realized the natural audience for such a book—people interested in the military, in medical stories, in neurosurgery—was smaller than the audience of people who had faced or would face great trials in their lives and need some help navigating them. I desperately wanted to reach that larger audience.

While I wrote *No Place to Hide,* I'd had a sense that the story was more powerful as a metaphor for life and learning to let God be in control during the hard times than it ever would be as a simple war story. So when I started thinking about the group of people who might be drawn to my writing and see me as someone who could help them, I realized the things I knew about and had been through—the brain, neuroscience, war, stress, divorce, the loss of a child, grief—could each have easily become the *one story* my life told.

In those early-morning hours of trying to write my blog and build my website, to do my duty as a budding author and help my publisher make good on their investment in my story, I struggled with a sense of legitimacy: Who was I to try to write to anyone about how to have enough faith to get through life? The truth was, I was still unsure half the time where I was with my faith. Did I even still have it? I was, as Philip Yancey wrote, hacking my way through the jungle of pain and doubt, hoping to crest a hill at some point and find a clear path to peace.[48]

After I met Jack for coffee that morning, he stopped answering my calls and texts. We never met face to face again, and I prayed that someone else in his world would be able to help him find his way, since obviously I had not been able to do so. Months went by, and I heard from Eli at his next appointment that Jack was struggling, drinking too much, and not going to church and that Jack and Cindy were having a hard time.

I felt powerless to help him and knew that the path he was on could easily have been my own. Yet somehow Lisa and I had gotten stronger and grown closer through the experience of losing Mitch. It was not lost on me that having been through my posttraumatic stress events after the war and healing from that through writing *No Place to Hide* had ironically prepared me to handle loss in a healthier way. Lisa and I lived through that together. We labored together to write *No Place* (she was up every morning with me, read every draft, heard every thought, and nudged and pushed and prodded me along the way until it was done) and stood together on the far shore of the intense personal journey the writing of that book took us on. And when the worst event of our lives happened, our hands stayed clasped together.

I realized that most parents who lose a child—really anyone who goes through tremendous loss or trial, including my brain tumor or trauma patients—have had no such prior immersion in "the furnace of suffering,"[49] as the prophet Isaiah wrote, and thus their initial experience of such pain can seem insurmountable.

By his grace God had prepared my hands for war when he equipped me to survive the otherwise nonsurvivable pain of Mitch's death, my family's experience of entering the furnace. In medicine we are trained to learn new things via the paradigm of *see one, do one, teach one.* I had seen great suffering and been scarred by its horror in Iraq. Now I had encountered it myself, with my own flesh and blood. It was time to teach one. To help others who may not have been so well equipped or prepared when their time in the furnace came.

My focus as a surgeon has always been on helping to heal disease, eliminate pain, and improve quality of life. And the jungle through which I was hacking as a writer was one of sickness, pain, limitation, and loss, all brought on by life.

My job then—first for myself and then for anyone who might be trying to follow whatever narrow trail I could carve out—was clear: people need brain surgery. Not the literal kind I perform in the operating room but a kind of self-performed brain surgery to help us prepare our minds to handle the harsh realities of life and be able to find joy in the process. Life is hard, but we need to be able to survive it with our faith intact, find peace, and experience happiness anyway. To do that, we have to change our thinking about pain and suffering.

I had found my message: you can't change your life until you change your mind.

Because every morning at three o'clock, armed with my coffee and my worship music, that's what I was trying to do for W. Lee Warren, MD.

I read countless blogs and articles from motivational speakers and self-help experts. Their sayings and advice blurred together, but two ideas stood out: "Motion creates emotion"[50] and "If you want to feel better, do better."

I knew intuitively that this was also true of faith. Or as our pastor once said, "Faith leads and feelings follow."

And although most of the time I didn't *feel* faith filled, wasn't sure if or what I believed, I *knew* in my head and in my heart that God was there and that it's best for people to trust and not give up when things are hard, no matter what. I'd seen so many patients, like Joey, who *healed* even as they were dying. And so many others who, even if they survived their illness, were rotting away from the cancer of hopelessness, doubt, and fear.

The best way to change your mind about difficult circumstances is somehow to find solid ground for your feet even when life sweeps the foundation from underneath you.

And I assure you, having witnessed many people searching for it, that no such hope may be found in science, in chemotherapy, in radiation, in surgery. Today's cures will inevitably find themselves in the same historical bucket as phrenology, leeching, bloodletting, and countless other treatments people have devised against human frailty and disease.

Harvey Cushing approached GBM with the same cynicism and despair as the first-year resident neurosurgeon does now, except that modern doctors have more expensive and impressive technologies to throw at it. Yet, outside of a few trials here and there and anecdotal reports of the occasional long survivor like Eli, the survival rates are about the same as those in Cushing's pre–World War II career. Thus, if your ability to be happy and believe in a good God depends on your diagnosis being benign or your treatment being successful, you aren't likely to achieve it over the long haul.

I had discovered a profound truth in my journey through treating cancer patients and trauma victims, through becoming a traumatized war veteran, and through losing my son: my happiness cannot depend on my life being pain-free. I had changed my mind. I knew that others could too, but it would require some help, some brain surgery.

After all, the same Jesus Christ who said he had come to earth to give people a joyful life[51] was also described as a "man of sorrows."[52] Even the Son of God experienced life as a Hobson's choice of pain *and* happiness or nothing at all, and he set an example for all of us by embracing it, facing the trials head on, and keeping up his faith even though the outcome wasn't painless or perfect for his human body.

My book released. Over the next few months, we worked to promote it: *Guide-posts, The 700 Club, CBS Evening News,* countless radio and podcast interviews and articles. But the whole experience, as interesting and fun as it was, was another moment in which all my family came together and realized how sad it was that Mitch wasn't there to be a part of it.

At work I tried to take the self-help gurus' advice: I started *doing* better. I began praying with my patients again. Even on days when I didn't feel it or neces-sarily believe it, I told God I knew that he was keeping his promises, that someday I would see Mitch again, that he was going to get us through this. And I saw in my work the results I expected: patients are better off embracing hope than accepting defeat.

I read a book by John Ortberg called *Know Doubt,* which includes a line that became my mantra for a while: "Hope is faith waiting for tomorrow."[53]

A little over a year after my son's death, we walked into the lobby of our church and ran right into Artie McBride. He was holding a baby and smiling softly. "Hi, Doc, it's good to see you," he said.

"You too. How are you, Artie? How's Teresa?"

He shook his head. "She passed away a few weeks ago. They threw every treat-ment they had at her after the baby came, but it was too late."

He held up the beautiful little girl, and Lisa and I looked into her blue eyes.

"This is our daughter. She was born a few weeks early, but she's healthy and cancer-free. Teresa died two months after she was born. And she never once re-gretted her decision. Her strength"—he stopped for a moment and swallowed—"made me believe again. No one could have that much love, that much ability to give themselves up for someone else, without God's help. That's why we named her Grace."

33

Believing Is Better Than Knowing

The life of man, solitary, poor, nasty, brutish, and short.

—THOMAS HOBBES, *Leviathan*

It was the calm of the observer, the uninvolved observer, separated from the events, knowing of them but not essentially involved.

—ROBERT LUDLUM, *The Bourne Identity*

Gordon Livingston was a psychiatrist from Baltimore who lost two sons in a thirteen-month span, one to suicide and one to leukemia. When I read his book *Too Soon Old, Too Late Smart,* I was moved by his honesty about how such grief affected him. While most people move from faith to doubt when hard things happen, Gordon realized the hopelessness offered by his professed agnosticism and his profound need to believe he would someday see his sons again.

He articulated the conundrum—and the experience—better than anyone else I'd read:

Thirteen years later, my sons, though frozen in time, remain a living presence for me. . . . I have reconciled myself to growing old without them. . . . I have forsaken any belief in an orderly universe and a just

God. But I have not relinquished my love for them nor my longing that, against all reason, I will see them again.

This is what passes for hope.[54]

When I read those words, I could not avoid another comparison with the man who approached Jesus in the gospel of Mark (I mentioned this man in chapter 5). The man's son was demon possessed and epileptic, and his life was in danger. Rather than a tidy story of the man's great faith moving Jesus to act, we read of a man like Gordon Livingston. The man asked Jesus to heal the boy "if you can."

Jesus almost laughed. " 'If you can'?" he said before adding, "Everything is possible for one who believes."

Jesus's promise that everything is possible moved the man to say, "I do believe; help me overcome my unbelief!"[55]

The more I worked around people who were sick and dying, injured beyond repair, or struggling with the hard things life brings, the more I realized something critical in Mark's story and in Gordon Livingston's words: one of the secrets to surviving the difficulties of life is to be honest with yourself about their effect on you.

For Gordon, a trained psychiatrist who understood the psychological damage incongruity can cause, it was important to acknowledge that even though losing his sons made him abandon "any belief in an orderly universe and a just God," it was even more important to hold on to the belief that such a God would somehow orchestrate the reunion with Gordon's sons on which he had hung his hope. For the man in Mark's gospel, his doubts that anything could drive away the demon, stop the seizures, and save his boy's life had to be professed in the same breath as his hope in the only possible solution: divine intervention.

Over time I came to see my patients as travelers on the same path I was on, following a road in the dark and encountering obstacles and difficulties but somehow still knowing that the only way out is to keep walking.

⸻

One morning at our monthly cancer conference, my pathologist friend Grossman presented a case of brain cancer in a patient I had not treated, someone who arrived in the ED basically dead and whose family did not want any treatment. Grossman showed the autopsy results since the patient's cancer was a rare type and thus an interesting case.

While I watched the slides go by and heard Grossman's description of the problem, something clicked for me.

The tumor was malignant, invasive, and deadly. But zoomed out, the cancer was only a small part of the larger picture. Normal, beautiful brain cells surrounded the cancer on all sides. A few millimeters in any direction, and you moved from diseased, dying brain to very healthy tissue with no signs of trouble. And even though the cancer claimed the life of the patient, taken as a whole the brain was mostly perfect.

Not having a relationship with the patient, I was able to see something I'd failed to notice in any of the cases I'd treated: all of us are more than one story.

—————

With the detached calm of the observer, I gained perspective while Grossman spoke. I remembered a day in Iraq. I'd lost a nineteen-year-old soldier who'd been shot in the back of the head, and in trying to save him, I removed a piece of broken skull that had been holding pressure on a huge hole in the largest vein in his brain. It was a catch-22: I couldn't stop the steady bleeding that would kill him over the next few minutes without removing the broken piece of skull because it was blocking the vein I needed to repair. But when I removed the bone fragment, the soldier's blood loss went from steady to torrential. I worked with another surgeon, and we did everything we could. But the damage to the vein was too great, the blood loss too rapid, the hospital too depleted of resources to give him enough blood because it was coming out faster than we could replace it. I left the operating room that day literally covered in his blood from head to toe. I had blood in my socks, and it had soaked through my scrubs into my undershirt.

Later that day, walking down the sidewalk toward my trailer, I was in a sort of shock, deep in despair and seeing nothing in every direction but brown sand and brown trucks and brown uniforms. Red and brown had become my world, and I was railing against God for this awful war and the exsanguinating soldier and the absolute lack of hope in that country and in my heart, which at that moment felt as forsaken by God as Iraq did to me.

And then I saw it: a tiny, verdant, perfect little plant with a white flower that somehow found enough soil in a crack in the sidewalk to take root and grow. Two or three inches tall, it stood straight and perfect, beautifully filling its allotted space in the world. True, the war still raged, the privates still bled out, the dirt still blew into my eyes, and my heart still ached for all of it, but the little plant reminded me that as long as there's a little crack in the sidewalk, life can still happen.

———

I snapped back to the conference just as Grossman wrapped up his presentation. The slide on the screen showed the dead patient's tumor, an island of death in his brain, suspended in an otherwise perfectly normal nervous system. As the other conference attendees cleared the room, I sat and looked at the screen as the tumblers in my brain clicked into place and unlocked something I'd been trying for years to understand.

"You okay, Warren?" Grossman said on his way to the door. "You're kind of zoned out."

I looked at him and nodded. "Yeah, just thinking about something. I'll see you later."

He left, and I stayed behind. The darkened conference room became a sort of chapel for me as I teased out the lesson I was learning from the pathology slide.

Every life ends. Everybody encounters disease or damage sufficient to cause death at some point. We have arbitrary ideas about how long someone deserves to live and about what manner of death is fair. When a person suffers a fate we feel to be too early or in some way unjust, we often question the only person we can find to blame: God. Even those who claim not to believe in a creator will almost always have similar things to say in such cases: "Where is your just God when something like this happens? That's why I don't believe."

I understand (and partake in) such blaming of God when life does not go my way. But do I then possess the integrity to praise him when life *does* meet my expectations? More commonly I take the good and consider it normal and deserved. And in truth, when I get out of my own head and detach as I did that day at the conference, I realize that most of my life here in the United States *does* play out the way I think it should, according to my sense of justice. I wonder how I'd feel if I lived in Syria or Iraq.

Grossman's slide and the little plant in Iraq are two extremes. A small tumor in the midst of an otherwise perfect brain can surely kill you as well as a bullet, but a little blade of green hope can just as certainly save your life in the midst of a war.

Thomas Hobbes wrote that life is "nasty, brutish, and short," but Jesus Christ said that although we would have trouble here, he wanted us to have peace and joy anyway.[56]

Over the next few weeks, I began to write in my blog and weekly newsletter about how life's events can affect our faith and how our faith can affect our interpretation of and reactions to those events. I called my work *You Start Today* because that had become a slogan in our family: you don't know what's going to happen tomorrow, so whatever you need to do to change your life and be happier, you'd better start today. I started a podcast and began to seek interviews with people who had experienced or accomplished remarkable things. One of the people I wanted to speak with was Dr. Gordon Livingston.

It took a while, but I eventually reached him. He agreed to meet via Skype, and we talked for over an hour. His eyes were heavy, sad, and red, and they filled with tears multiple times as we spoke. The pain of losing two sons—I couldn't imagine having to bear more grief than losing one of my sons—showed in his face and in his voice. He was a lovely man, honest about his wounds but not broken.

Gordon told a story about how he had gotten lost one day when he was in the army. He told a sergeant that he was sure he'd followed the map and that the map said there should be a hill nearby, but he couldn't see it. The sergeant said, "Sir, if the map don't agree with the ground, then the map is wrong." Gordon said he knew immediately that he'd heard a profound truth. In his career as a psychiatrist, he'd learned that one of the hardest things in life is when people's expectations are crushed as life proves to them that their "maps," their ideas about how their lives would go, were not accurate. He said his job was to help them adjust to the reality on the ground.

It was an honor to meet Gordon, to hear his wisdom culled from a career working among struggling people, and to see his strength displayed in surviving the loss of not one son but two. I knew intuitively that losing two children would not simply double your grief—that kind of pain had to be exponential. Yet he had managed to use it as a force for good, a way to harness the pain and help others. He had become a shoot of green life in some very dark places.

But as much as I respected him and his work, something about the map-versus-ground story didn't sit right with me.

Over time my *You Start Today* newsletters and podcasts spread around the world, and I began to receive emails from people in multiple countries, sharing their stories and asking questions about how we managed to carry on despite losing a child.

I began to realize that something had shifted in my work as a doctor and a writer: my sixth-sense magnet seemed to draw dead people, those whose lives had taken something from them they didn't know how to get back. My only qualification for trying to help them was that I was a little further removed from the trauma than they were, but still they asked.

And eventually I came to the most important decision I ever had to make in my life, other than to believe in Jesus and to marry Lisa: I had to settle the map-versus-ground question.

I was writing more than ever: self-therapy in the mornings as I continued to write to my kids every day, new podcast episodes, and weekly newsletters. I wrote two terrible novels that went nowhere.

But I was not yet writing this book.

My agent, Kathy Helmers, gently nudged me via email to start thinking about my next nonfiction project. I told her about my history with Philip Yancey and our many email conversations about my conundrum: How do I counsel people to hang in through hard times when I believe in my heart I already know the outcome? I'd even had Philip on my podcast, and we had a wonderful conversation about faith through trials.

But I told Kathy my problem. *No Place to Hide* was a memoir, and it was thus much easier for me to write. I had gone through something, struggled with it, and used writing to tell the story and begin to heal. This book would be different: the problem I had trying to write credibly about faith was that on so many days I didn't have any.

Kathy said, "You might yell at God sometimes when you're hurting, but at least you're still talking to him. That's a good place to start."

Yet this book—this conversation I'd been having with Philip Yancey about how to be intellectually honest with my patients and myself when we are going through impossible situations—was certainly not going to be the same story I would have written before I lost a child and entered my own furnace of suffering.

I wasn't going to write a memoir about how strong my faith was and how I used it to get myself through this hard time, because it wasn't and I hadn't. If anything, this would be a book trying to explain to myself something I didn't yet understand.

But I promised Kathy I would try to have a draft by July.

By October I had written exactly zero words of this book.

Every time I tried to write, I felt a huge pang of irrelevancy and incongruity; I was not the man to write about faith.

I received an email from Philip Yancey. He was coming on a book tour to our town. Could we meet for lunch?

Lisa and I stepped excitedly into the restaurant that day. Kathy Helmers and Philip and Janet Yancey stood, and I looked into the eyes of one of my spiritual heroes. Philip's books, emails, and kindness to me had meant so much that I almost cried when we shook hands and embraced.

We had a great conversation, and Philip invited me to breakfast the next day as well. We prayed together and talked for two hours about how life was indeed hard; his life was no exception. He shared some of the things he'd been through and how some of his family members and he had different reactions to them, some away from and he toward faith.

And then he asked me how I was holding up after losing Mitch. I was honest: "Not very well."

"Keep writing," he said. "You're helping people all over the world by just saying out loud some of the things they're thinking."

So I did.

I kept writing, kept operating, kept going, all in an effort to feel better by doing better. To prove the pastor's words that faith leads and feelings follow.

And over time I found my answer to why Gordon Livingston's map-versus-ground wisdom hadn't sat well with me.

Here it is, and I wish I were wise enough to have seen it without having to make you read all these words to get to it: there has to be something that is always right, always true, even when life—the ground—seems to say otherwise.

In other words, the ground is always going to present problems, wrong turns, potholes, and opportunities to get lost. We need something better to reference, something that will actually *guide* us when the ground is difficult and confusing.

We need a map that is always right, no matter what the ground seems to say.

The map that's always right is faith in a God who loves us, in the good news that someone loved us enough to die for us although we didn't deserve it, in the truth that this God is present in our lives even when circumstances make us doubt it, and in the knowledge that all his promises hold, all the time.

My old professor said, *"Believing is not the same as knowing. Seeing is knowing."*

But so many things in life can plunge us into such darkness that seeing is impossible. And my answer to how to survive those times—the tumors, the traumas, the terminal nature of life—is to somehow see anyway.

We must be able to reach a place where, when the ground doesn't agree with the map, we believe—we *know*—that the map is still right.

When we see the cluster of tumor with its malignancy and certain death, faith gives us the eyes to see that the map will lead us through it, that somewhere down the path we'll find the little blade of green hope springing up from the crack in the sidewalk. I'm not downplaying the devastation and pain these things bring us. I'm still living with the crushing weight of losing Mitch and the frequent nightmares from the war. But I am saying that the map will lead us to a place of shelter where those things cannot destroy us.

Faith, my friend, is being able to look for hope even when it seems impossible to find.

Faith is hope waiting for tomorrow.

I've been waiting for it since the night I received the worst news of my life.

I've been trying to show it to my patients, even moments after I've given them their worst news ever.

I've been writing about it every week for several years now.

Sometimes it's right there and it's everything.

Sometimes it's so far away that all I can hold on to is the memory of the map, God's promises, the touch of Lisa's hand.

And to slightly refine my professor's bit of wisdom, I must believe in the map so deeply that I can *know* even when I cannot see. Because there is an important difference between faith and knowledge: if you have to lay eyes on everything to believe it or put your fingers in the holes of it like doubting Thomas, you won't know what to believe when it's too far away to see or touch. That's why Jesus said those folks who believe even when they can't see are more blessed: because we humans spend a good bit of our lives in places where it's too dark for knowledge and only the candle of faith can light our way.

One evening recently my cell phone dinged. I looked down at the screen and saw it was a text from Jack Phillips, the first time I'd heard from him in over a year.

It was a picture of his son's grave and these words:

You might still believe God cares about you, but my son is in
this hole, and I still don't.

There are days still when I could write such words.

But here is what I've learned, and to quote Gordon Livingston again, "this is what passes for hope":

I believe in and have faith in Jesus Christ and all his promises. Thus, I can hold on to hope that my son is not in a hole but rather alive and well and that I will someday embrace him again. He will smell like himself again, and he'll be safe and whole.

I doubt I will ever reach a place where I can say I believe those words I just typed all the time. On some days the ground's disagreement with the map is too strong, and for a time I lean toward agreeing with the ground.

I think I know a lot about disease, about brain tumors, about medicine.

But yesterday I saw another report on Eli Bailey. He just hit five years since diagnosis, and he's still disease-free. According to his Facebook page, he's getting married next month.

So what do I really know?

I thought I'd seen the end of Eli Bailey, but I'd seen only the beginning.

I've seen tumors and trauma and terminality produce powerful personal growth and triumph, but I've also seen them destroy lives. What I've learned is that the things we think we know are just that. In every situation life brings, there are opportunities to learn, to change, to blossom, and to fail. To live well involves somehow managing to walk through these times and discovering that faith is enough of a footbridge. Doubt is not a flaw; it's a necessity. "I do believe; help me overcome my unbelief!"

In the end we have to keep taking steps, no matter how twisted and dark the path becomes. Believing there will be a light, even just a crack in the door, is how we keep moving. And in so doing, we somehow make it through.

That's what I know. I'd rather be the little plant bringing beauty to my allotted space in the world than the cluster of darkness threatening to drain the faith and life from those around me. If I am, as my Iraq War colleague Aaron said, just "a skin sack of nerves and bones and electrical impulses," then at least I can try to use the sum of those impulses to help other people become healthier, feel better, and be happier. But I do not believe my life is simply a matter of electricity and biology, because I have faith.

I realize my so recently solidified faith is like Eli's clean margins: it's true, and it's real, but it's probably temporary. Just as I was certain Eli's cancer would return because it always does, I'm sure my faith will be challenged again and there will be another time in which I find myself asking those old questions, doubting, wondering, and then repenting in dust and ashes like Job.[57]

The loss of a child plunged me into utter darkness, where there is weeping and gnashing of teeth. And somehow I've been placed in the lives of other bereaved and hurting people, and I have realized that in those darkest hours, the knife edge of survival or ultimate loss might be traversable only if one can see, no matter how dim, the light from a torch held by someone a little farther down the same path.

Life is a series of beautiful moments interspersed by great trials. The trick to being happy is to learn to have beautiful moments *during* the trials. Faith isn't a belief that God will spare you from problems; it is a belief that he's still God and will carry you through those problems.

In the battle between faith, doubt, and the things we think we know, I've learned to doubt the latter and trust the former. Doubt is not optional if you are an honest person, because as soon as you think you've banished doubt forever, you'll stumble into another problem that will plunge you right back into it.

But take heart: I've learned over time that faith is stronger than doubt.
This morning I received another text from Jack:

I feel a little better today.

A little green plant pushing its way up through a crack in the sidewalk of pain that Jack's been walking.
On that day in Iraq, the little plant was enough to get me through.
There's always something.
You just have to keep looking for it.
That's what I know.

Epilogue

Both Worse

He who learns must suffer. And even in our sleep, pain
that cannot forget falls drop by drop upon the heart, and
in our own despair, against our will, comes wisdom to us
by the awful grace of God.

—AESCHYLUS, *Agamemnon*

Chris, my optometrist, was having a hard time. "Which is better?" he said. "One or two?" He kept flipping lenses inside his fancy machine, trying to dial in a new prescription to help me see more clearly. "A or B?" *Click.*

"I can't read the letters," I said.

"Three or four?" *Click.*

"Still blurry," I said.

"C or D?" *Click.*

I sighed. "Are you tricking me? It's still totally unreadable."

"Five or six?"

I shook my head. "It's never been this hard before to get a new prescription. Are you sure the machine is working?"

I felt like *Duck Dynasty*'s Uncle Si when he went to the eye doctor and every time the doctor clicked his machine, it seemed to make Si's vision even blurrier. Frustrated when the doctor gave him yet another choice, Si said, "They're both worse."[58] (Confession: since Joey introduced me to *Duck Dynasty*, I may have watched a few episodes.)

Finally Chris figured out that I needed a prism in one lens. Apparently, instead of inheriting my father's six-one height, I got from my parents a family trait that makes one of my eyes slightly lower on my skull than the other. As I've aged, Chris said, the muscles in my eyes have lost some of their agility and are not compensating as well for the subtle discrepancy. This has made it a little harder for my brain to clarify what I'm seeing, and my glasses weren't quite as helpful as they once were.

A prism, Chris said, would bend the light a little and align it so my brain could see the letters more easily.

With a few more clicks, Chris added the prism to my left eye. Suddenly everything was crystal clear to me again.

My vision with the new lenses was correctable past twenty-twenty.

I could see the letters perfectly, and even the smallest line was now easy for me to read.

Then, as suddenly as my vision had cleared, I realized something: my inability to see the letters had not changed reality—the letters had been there the whole time.

———

I started this book by revealing a truth about my practice, something I'm not terribly proud of as a person of faith: I used to think I *knew* certain things about glioblastoma and head injuries and other health-care problems. But that was before I, in my despair and against my will, learned so much through suffering (my own and observation of others'). And the awful grace of God by which he teaches us has lifted from me the burden of thinking I can see so far down life's path.

Now, should you walk into my office with your headache or your neurologic complaint and I pull up your scan, see the menacing tumor, and recognize GBM in your parietal lobe, something very different happens in my head and in my heart.

Before, I would have thought, *I've seen the end of you.*

Now I know there is more to the story.

Maybe I've seen just the beginning.

And though I used to "know" how the disease would play out, now I profess to know only one thing: the illness (substitute *injury, bankruptcy, divorce, tribula-*

tion) you're about to face will provide a greater opportunity for gain or loss than anything else you will experience in your lifetime.

I have seen people face the worst diseases known to humanity who stood up to the test and became the best version of themselves they could possibly be, despite their bodies losing to their illness.

And I have witnessed people miraculously survive incurable cancers, people who were nevertheless rotted and malignant humans by the time they were "cured."

In pondering the twenty-plus years I've walked among the sick and broken and the several years I've been the father of a lost son, I've come to realize the difference between survivors (even those who perish) and the dying (even those who live): the survivors have a prism—faith—that allows them to see through the pain and hardship to the hope and purpose and beauty in their lives.

Two common responses to life's troubles are (1) a belief that we're alone in the cold and random universe and (2) a belief that God is real but either is against us or doesn't care. But these two responses, like Uncle Si's eye exam, are both worse.

The problem with the first response—the belief that we are alone in the universe and no one is out there to help us in our troubles, that there is no afterlife, nothing beyond the life we're living—is this: when you hear me say "glioblastoma" or "terminal" or "We did everything we could for her," you have no rational basis for hope.

The second response—the belief that God doesn't care or that he is actually against us, mad at us, or punishing us—produces feelings on a spectrum from shame and regret on one end to anger and hostility on the other. In this paradigm you hear me give you a diagnosis with a poor prognosis, and you respond by blaming yourself or God, withdrawing into yourself and becoming an empty person, or lashing out and becoming a grade IV cancer in the world regardless of your ultimate physical outcome.

Both worse.

The third response requires bending the light of our current circumstances in such a way that we can see God's presence in the moment, despite the outcome.

Faith does not magically change our circumstances and make everything happy; it merely bends the light to show us what's really there. It's the prism we need to see hope when all seems lost, to survive the furnace of suffering, to grow despite the pain.

Facing the end of your life too early, losing a child, watching your wife acciden-
tally hit her head and become a shell of a human who will never speak again, finding out that your brother has blown his brains out or your cousin has overdosed—
these are events that, if we don't have the prescription of faith to bend the light,
seem impossibly unclear to our eyes and hearts.

Some people come to these difficult parts of life prepared, armed with faith like
Samuel or Mrs. Knopf or Rupert. They slip into the stream of mortality and some-
how can see it for what it is, a part of some plan or a precursor to something better.
They can see clearly, at least far enough ahead to know that the next step is safe.

As the old hymn "Lead, Kindly Light" says,

Lead, kindly light, amid the encircling gloom. . . .
Keep thou my feet; I do not ask to see
The distant scene; one step enough for me.[59]

And for those armed with the prism, the kindly light illuminates the next step,
and it's enough.

For others, like Joey, the hard parts come first. During the storm of Joey's life,
his grandma and Pastor Jon came along and, as my optometrist did with my eyes,
offered him a different set of lenses through which to see the world. Finally, with
the lens of faith in place, the suffering allows for learning through that awful
grace—and that is the only thing that enables someone like Joey to come alive for
the first time while he's dying.

———

If your life has been relatively pain-free up to this point, you are very blessed, and
this book may seem somewhat abstract to you.

But make no mistake: trouble is coming.

The question is, What happens then?

As I've said, although some will stubbornly disagree, all of us have faith in
something. So I don't think a lack of faith is the problem for most of us. Just as our
eyes may need some correction, our faith is often simply suffering from the wrong
prescription.

If you place your faith in a benevolent universe, the stalwart physician, your indefatigable spirit, or the strength and resolve of your spouse, then randomness or fatigue or weakness or age will eventually reveal the transience and mutability of such trust.

We need something permanent, something with a consistent track record of reliability in seeing people through difficulties and making life survivable even when all seems lost.

We do not choose our belief systems because of the benefits they offer us, of course. We choose them because we believe them to be true. But faith in God has a way of proving itself over time, showing itself able to improve and steady us no matter what happens.

A word of caution: some Christians teach that if we behave a certain way, God will protect us from harm, give us good things, and make us happy.

So what happens, if we believe in that God, when life turns out not to be so painless?

If you believe that faith in God will protect you from glioblastoma or falling off a ladder or your son dying, then when those things occur, you risk falling into the most dangerous state of all, that of having lost the certainty of something you thought you knew.

Of the three things that affect how we view the world—faith, doubt, and the things we think we know—doubt would seem to be the most harmful, at least on the surface.

But I have learned that doubt is not the enemy of faith. The enemy of faith is often the things we think we know.

I knew I would never see a glioblastoma patient survive. But every day Eli Bailey is alive and cancer-free reminds me I was wrong.

I knew my children would someday bury me. But one Friday in 2013, I attended the funeral service of my son.

If my faith were predicated on life playing out according to what I thought would happen, if I believed that God's love for me meant no bad things would occur in my life, then the loss of my son would have made me, as a rational person, admit that my faith was misplaced.

And perhaps that is the reason for doubt.

Doubt allows us to critically examine what we believe, search for places where we got it wrong, and, like a good scientist, reform our hypothesis and reframe our beliefs.

But without the prism of faith, we see only the blurred lines of pain, disease, disappointment.

Faith aligns what you think you're seeing with reality. It shifts your focus from the problem to the promise.

Faith allows us to see that it's okay to have doubt, but we doubt the doubt more than the promise of the One who never breaks his word. It allows us to hold on and even grow into better people during and despite the troubles of this life.

Faith doesn't keep us from having problems. It just gives a clearer view of how God is responding to them.

Doubt is not fatal if we recognize it for what it is: a smudge on the lens. When we realize that, wipe it clear, and put the glasses back on, we'll be okay.

The things we think we know are more like cataracts. They can obscure and blind us to the truth of God's work around us that is plain to see when our eyes are healthy.

And after all I've been through and witnessed, I can make you this promise: if you don't have the prism in place, if you don't have faith, then when the storm hits your life, it could be the end of you.

Chris smiled that day when the prism fixed my vision.

I think God smiles too when we finally stop saying "Both worse" and instead read the last line on the chart and say "That's better."

Acknowledgments

This is a book about faith, doubt, knowledge, and the gray zones in between. So I must start by thanking God, who has, as the psalmist David wrote, taken note of my life (Psalm 56:8). In a life full of reasons to wonder, God's promise-keeping character has proven time and again to be the deciding factor for me between faith and doubt. He has been close when I was brokenhearted (34:18) and strong when I was weak (Philippians 4:13). He has given me shelter from the storms of life (Psalm 32:7), armed me for the battles I would face (144:1), and given me, against all odds, the most important resource for a successful and happy life: hope (Jeremiah 29:11).

My wife, Lisa, whom qualifiers like *peerless, brilliant, beautiful,* and *amazing* fail miserably to describe, has been the hands and feet of Christ's grace and love for me in this life. When we found each other, I was in the depths of "the valley of the shadow of death" (Psalm 23:4, ESV), a twitchy, traumatized, broken man. But her strength, light, and life made tangible for me the anchor that God's love promised to steady my restless soul (Hebrews 6:19).

And when the bottom fell out of our lives, when the worst thing that can happen to a parent actually happened, Lisa was unwavering in her strength. Her hand in mine, her steadiness in that storm, gave me the ability to make it through. When you can't see far enough through the darkness to see God's loving presence, it is a great blessing when he provides another person to be there in the darkness with you.

This book would not exist without Lisa's incessant belief in and support of its importance—and her encouragement (read that as "insistence") on all the days I said, "I don't have enough faith to be writing a book about faith." She steadfastly encouraged me to put down in words how our walk among the sick and broken and our crawl through grief and loss has affected our faith. All the patients described in this book were hers as well as mine, and working together through all those difficult situations and human tragedies and triumphs has deeply shaped our faith.

I could write a whole book to tell you how much I love you, Lisa (maybe I will someday). But even at the end of that long volume, I would still be searching for the perfect adjective to describe all that you are. So I'll leave it at *superlative*.

Philip Yancey saw a story he believed in, in my self-published and unpublishable first attempt to write. His kindness, grace, and belief in me created the reality of my second career as a writer. But even before that, his direction to a wandering and wondering doctor to "write about it, and you'll figure it out" gave me the notion for the first time that I could use writing as therapy. That habit ultimately helped me heal from the trauma of war, survive the loss of a son, and write this book.

Kathy Helmers is an accomplished agent and a major reason this book is in your hands, but her kindness and friendship when we were in our darkest hour changed a business relationship into a lifelong bond.

Dave Lambert takes the helpless, flailing infant first drafts I send him and coaches, encourages, and sometimes disciplines me into making them grow up into real books. Thank you, Dave. This book is so much better because of your help.

To the incredible people at WaterBrook and Penguin Random House—Susan Tjaden, Chris Sigfrids, Bev Rykerd, Campbell Wharton, Kathy Mosier, and many more—thank you.

To my children, Josh, Caity, Kimber, and Kalyn, and my sons-in-law, Nate and Bryce. Each of you has shown incredible strength in the worst of times, and your faith and love are amazing to me. I'm so blessed and thankful to be your dad, even as it is still crushing to write four names instead of five. When we all lost Mitch, you rallied together to make it through, and even in your pain you never forgot that your parents grieve too. You are all my heroes. Your brother lives on, in your smiles and your strength, and we will all be together again someday.

My parents showed me that the answers are in the Word of God. Even when I couldn't articulate the question, Wayne and Sue Warren showed me where to look. I am eternally grateful to have been armed with such a powerful weapon and defense against whatever life brings.

And Dennis and Patty McDonald, my in-laws, have been as close as parents and as dear as best friends. Dennis's wisdom and friendship have been instrumental in my ability to know what real faith is. If you ever meet him, he will remind you a lot of Pastor Jon. Patty, I miss you every day.

Notes

1. There are a few long-term survivors of GBM. These patients serve as motivation for surgeons and oncologists to keep trying and for desperate people to spend their money traveling to Duke or Hopkins or wherever the current "miracle doctor" is practicing. But these cases are so rare they don't change the statistics.

2. 1 Thessalonians 5:17, ESV.

3. James 5:15, ESV.

4. Alfred, Lord Tennyson, "The Charge of the Light Brigade," in *Selected Poems,* ed. Christopher Ricks (London: Penguin, 2007), 215.

5. Psalm 139:16.

6. Jeremiah 29:11.

7. Mark 9:20–23.

8. Matthew 17:20.

9. Mark 9:24.

10. Genesis 2:17; 3:6–7.

11. Matthew 17:20.

12. C. S. Lewis, *Mere Christianity* (New York: HarperOne, 2001), 192.

13. Matthew 5:45.

14. This is not the real name of the device, but the patient did wear one similar to this description, and it is still commercially available.

15. The Center for Cancer Cures, anti-glioplastins, and Dr. Karpowski are not real names. They are fictitious representatives of a very real industry that sells "cures" to people grasping for anything. These companies fall outside FDA regulations and operate on a cash basis.

16. Anna Taran et al., "Cardiopulmonary Resuscitation Inpatient Outcomes in Cancer Patients in a Large Community Hospital," *Delaware Medical Journal* 84, no. 4 (April 2012): 117–21, www.ncbi.nlm.nih.gov/pubmed/22856102.

17. Horatio G. Spafford, "It Is Well with My Soul," 1873, public domain.

18. Matthew 26:39.

19. Matthew 26:20–30.

20. Jeremiah 12:1.

21. *Austin Powers: International Man of Mystery*, directed by Jay Roach (Los Angeles: New Line Cinema, 1997).

22. *National Lampoon's Christmas Vacation*, directed by Jeremiah S. Chechik (Burbank, CA: Warner Bros., 1989).

23. John 16:33.

24. Matthew 26:39, 42, KJV.

25. Oswald Chambers, *The Pilgrim's Song Book,* in *The Complete Works of Oswald Chambers* (Grand Rapids, MI: Discovery House, 2000), 537.

26. John Donne, "Meditation XVII," in *Devotions upon Emergent Occasions,* 1624, 31–32, http://triggs.djvu.org/djvu-editions.com/DONNE /DEVOTIONS/Download.pdf.

27. Donne, "Meditation XVII," 31.

28. Psalm 103:3.

29. Matt Redman, "Blessed Be Your Name," by Beth Redman and Matt Redman, *Where Angels Fear to Tread,* 2002, Survivor Records.

30. Lewis Carroll, *Through the Looking-Glass, and What Alice Found There,* in *Alice's Adventures in Wonderland, and Through the Looking-Glass* (New York: Macmillan, 1897), 100.

31. Hebrews 11:27, NCV.

32. John 20:24–29.

33. John 20:29, Voice.

34. Genesis 15:1–6.

35. Romans 4:18.

36. *Saving Private Ryan,* directed by Steven Spielberg (Universal City, CA: Amblin Entertainment, 1998).

37. Mark 9:24.

38. Diogenes Laërtius, *The Lives and Opinions of Eminent Philosophers,* trans. C. D. Yonge (London: Henry G. Bohn, 1853), 19.

39. Psalm 34:18, Voice.

40. *The Sixth Sense,* directed by M. Night Shyamalan (Burbank, CA: Hollywood Pictures, 1999).

41. Psalm 144:1, Voice.

42. Psalm 34:18, Voice.

43. Romans 8:28.

44. 1 Corinthians 15:19.

45. Marx's full quote is "Religion is the sigh of the oppressed creature, the heart of a heartless world, and the soul of soulless conditions. It is the opium of the people." Karl Marx, *Critique of Hegel's "Philosophy of Right,"* ed. Joseph O'Malley, trans. Annette Jolin and Joseph O'Malley (Cambridge: Cambridge University Press, 1970), 131.

46. Thomas Hobson was a stable owner in England who gave customers the choice of renting the horse in the stall closest to the door or renting none at all. From Hobson's business model came the phrase "take it or leave it." See *Merriam-Webster,* s.v. "Hobson's choice," www.merriam-webster.com /dictionary/Hobson's%20choice.

47. Matthew 27:45, 50–51.

48. Philip Yancey, *Reaching for the Invisible God: What Can We Expect to Find?* (Grand Rapids, MI: Zondervan, 2000), 18.

49. Isaiah 48:10, Voice.

50. Tony Robbins, "Are You Stuck? 3 Reasons You're Not Making Progress— and How to Break the Plateau," *Tony Robbins Blog,* www.tonyrobbins .com/mind-meaning/are-you-stuck.

51. John 10:10, Voice.

52. Isaiah 53:3, ESV.

53. John Ortberg, *Know Doubt* (Grand Rapids, MI: Zondervan, 2008), 85.

54. Gordon Livingston, *Too Soon Old, Too Late Smart: Thirty True Things You Need to Know Now* (Boston: Da Capo, 2008), 117.

55. Mark 9:22–24.

56. John 16:33.

57. Job 42:6.

58. *Duck Dynasty,* season 2, episode 7, "Spring Pong Cleaning," aired November 7, 2012, on A&E.

59. John Henry Newman, "Lead, Kindly Light," 1833, public domain.